Shadrach A. Ambanasom

PERSPECTIVES ON WRITTEN CAMEROON LITERATURE IN ENGLISH

Kansas City (MO)

Perspectives on Written Cameroon Literature in English
by Shadrach Ambanasom

First published 2012

Miraclaire Academic Publications (MAP)
8400 East 92nd Terrace, Kansas City, MO 64138, USA

Copyright © 2012 by Miraclaire Academic Publications

All rights for this book reserved.
No part of this book may be reproduced, stored in a retrieval system, or transmitted, in any form or by any means, electronic, mechanical, photocopying, recording or otherwise, without the prior permission of the copyright owner.

ISBN (10): 0615762360/ **ISBN (13):** 978-0615762364

Printed in the United States of America

MAP is an imprint of Miraclaire Publishing LLC
www.miraclairepublishing.com

Dedication

To

**Creators and Critics of
Cameroon Anglophone Literature**

Preface

In 2009, Anglophone Cameroon literature celebrated its fifty years of existence. Now at the mature age of fifty plus this literature has a great deal to write home about even if it still has a lot to do in its pursuit of excellence. Part of its maturity resides in the fact that although the scale of literary creativity and literary criticism is skewed in favour of the former, Anglophone Cameroon literary criticism is gradually waking up from slumber in an attempt to catch up with the rapidly expanding creativity. As indicated in the conclusion of this book, a few more critical works have been published in recent years by Anglophone Cameroonian literary critics to the joy of many of us.

    A growing interest in Anglophone Cameroon critical writing has led many young people, especially those who have read my works, to confront me with several questions: What else are you working on? Which is your next critical work? And when is it coming out? Some even asked me questions about articles I had earlier published but which were not easily accessible because they are scattered in publications within and without Cameroon. Sometimes, where possible, I referred them to the Internet or to individuals with copies of the volumes in which the articles were published. In a few instances I even went as far as photocopying some of the articles to give them!

    But then it soon dawned on me that I could save myself unnecessary trouble if I assembled all the articles I had published in a single volume; it occurred to me that a compilation of my published essays would make them easily accessible and referable. This was the major motivation for putting together the various critical essays in this book.

    When I looked back, as I went about assembling these essays, their sheer number was not much of a surprise to one who, long ago, as a young university undergraduate, had made a commitment, had taken a definite stand with reference to Anglophone Cameroon literature. In matters of literary creativity and criticism, for my part, I have had a clear vision and mission with regard to the future development of Cameroon literature in English as explained below in the introduction to this book.

But the way the essays are arranged in the book does not follow the order of chronology of their publication. I have simply followed my intuition and common sense in grouping them into three broad categories: General Essays, Specific Literary Studies and then Book Reviews. The first essay in the volume is even the most recent, and chronologically speaking, should have been the last. I think the prominence given it is justified on the grounds of its comprehensiveness in its treatment of the overall subject matter of the book. It puts the readers at ease before they begin to explore more specific areas later.

If there is a justification for the title of this book it is in this that the essays have commented practically on some aspects of all the genres of written literature that the Anglophone Cameroon creative writers have produced so far: the novel, drama, poetry, the short story, the essay and children's literature. The exception, in this regard, is essay number 10, dealing with Mongo Beti, a Francophone Cameroonian writer. However, his two novels appraised in the essay are treated as translations from French into English. As a pedagogue with a specific mission of carrying out literary criticism with reference to Anglophone Cameroon literature, I believe these essays are an illustration of my own how-to-do-it method in matters of practical criticism. Herein lies the book's pedagogic relevance.

Shadrach A. Ambanasom
Professor of Literature
The University of Bamenda

Acknowledgements

I would like to thank here the editors and publishers of the various journals, collective volumes and newspapers wherein these essays first appeared. They are all found in the "Sources" section of this work. I remain grateful to Ms Masha Edith Mungwa of GBHS Bamessing, Ndop, who proofread the final draft of the work and detected many elusive errors. I owe a special debt to Mr N. Patrick Tata of PATAMAE EDITING CONSULTANCY Bamenda, for doing a good editorial job on the work, and reducing to a minimum what would have been a plethora of editorial gremlins. In addition, I am grateful to him because the present title of the book: *Perspectives on Written Cameroon Literature in English* was his proposal. Ultimately, however, I am solely responsible for any errors that the book may possibly contain.

    A critique sourced from personal experience here would not be out of place: PATAMAE EDITING CONSULTANCY is arguably the most serious editorial authority and a great partner in the development of Anglophone Cameroon literature today. It is now left for serious writers, critics and even publishers to avail themselves of its services or consider soliciting its professional expertise. I believe that in crucial editorial matters, cost ought not to be a deterrent. True, education is expensive, but ignorance is even more expensive. We cannot attain greatness in literature and art without working hard and paying for it in hard currency.

Contents

Dedication i
Preface iii
Acknowledgements v

PART ONE:
GENERAL ESSAYS

INTRODUCTION 1

1- HALF A CENTURY OF WRITTEN ANGLOPHONE CAMEROON LITERATURE 5

2- CRITICAL APPROACHES IN THE CRITICISM OF CAMEROON LITERATURE OF ENGLISH EXPRESSION[1] 30

3- CAMEROONIAN CREATIVE WRITERS AND THE LANGUAGE PROBLEM 45

4- THE AFRICAN WRITER AND THE PRESERVATION OF CULTURAL VALUES 58

5- THE CAMEROONIAN NOVEL OF ENGLISH EXPRESSION 66

PART TWO:
SPECIFIC LITERARY STUDIES

6- IDEOLOGY IN THREE DRAMATIC WORKS: VICTOR EPIE NGOME'S WHAT GOD HAS PUT ASUNDER, AND BATE BESONG'S BEASTS OF NO NATION AND REQUIEM FOR THE LAST KAISER. 83

7- THE EDUCATIONAL SIGNIFICANCE OF THE CAMEROON NOVEL OF ENGLISH EXPRESSION: FOCUS ON FOUR TEXTS 116

8- DECONSTRUCTING GENDER HIERARCHY: A STUDY OF MARGARET AFUH'S BORN BEFORE HER TIME 130

9- THE ANTI- HEROES OF L.T. ASONG'S FICTION: FOCUS ON FIVE NOVELS. 143

10- TWO OPPOSING TRENDS IN MONGO BETI'S FICTION: A STUDY OF REMEMBER RUBEN AND PERPETUA 160

11- PEDAGOGY OF THE DEPRIVED 173

12- ANATOMY OF A SHORT STORY: AN ANALYSIS OF BOLE BUTAKE'S "THE WAY OF THE CITY" 187

13- THE ORALITY OF THE WORKS OF FOUR ANGLOPHONE WRITERS: LINUS ASONG, BOLE BUTAKE, BONGASU KISHANI, FALE WACHE 191

14- THE MODERNIST CHARACTER OF BATE BESONG'S POETRY 206

15- THE QUINTESSENCE OF BERNARD FONLON 215

PART THREE:
BOOK REVIEWS

16- BOLE BUTAKE, LAKE GOD AND OTHER PLAYS, Yaoundé: Editions CLE, 1999, 199pp. 229

17- LINUS T. ASONG, THE AKROMA FILE, Bamenda: Patron publishing House, 1997, 150pp 233

18- ALOBWED'EPIE, THE DEATH CERTIFICATE, Yaounde: Editions CLE, 2004, 308pp 238

19- JOHN N. NKENGASONG ACROSS THE MONGOLO, Ibadan: Spectrum Books Limited, 2004, 200pp. 242

20- ALOBWED'EPIE THE LADY WITH A BEARD, Yaoundé: Editions CLE, 2005, 118 pp 245

21- JOHN N. NKENGASONG, THE WIDOW'S MIGHT, Yaounde, Editions CLE 2006, 152pp 249

22- JOHN NGONG KUM NGONG, WALLS OF AGONY, Yaounde, Editions CLE 2006, 60pp. 252

23- JOHN NGONG KUM NGONG, BATTLE FOR SURVIVAL, Yaoundé: Editions CLE 2006, 87pp 255

24- INTRODUCING L. T. ASONG: "THE MAJOR TALENT OF CAMEROON FICTION IN ENGLISH" 258

25- FRANCIS B. NYAMNJOH, A NOSE FOR MONEY, East African Educational Publishers Ltd, 2006, 202pp. 262

CONCLUSION 267

APENDIX: SOURCES 272

**PART ONE:
GENERAL ESSAYS**

INTRODUCTION

The name Patrick Sam-Kubam will remain for long implanted in the minds of many Anglophone Cameroonian creative writers, literary critics and historians for his seminal article: "The Paucity of Literary Creativity in Anglophone Cameroon." That critical essay, published in the now defunct *ABBIA* in 1978, sparked off, for several years, a lively debate in English newspapers in Cameroon. Opinions were varied as contributors to the discussion came up with hypotheses and rationalizations to defend their positions. But when the dust had settled on the issue, it became clear that there was actually no lack of literary creativity on the part of the Anglophone Cameroonians. There was evidence of abundant creative writing in private drawers. The problem with Anglophone imaginative writing was rather that of the lack of publishing houses and the dissemination agencies to make available to readers what was being written.

This therefore meant that Anglophone Cameroonians had been doing creative writing before that provocative article was penned. But after its publication, Anglophone Cameroonian imaginative writers and budding critics became more conscious of their role in the development of the Anglophone Cameroon literature within the bilingual, bicultural context of Cameroon where the Anglophones are numerically inferior to the Francophones with whom, to assert their identity, they are sometimes engaged in a subtle psychological and ideological warfare.

At the time of the literary controversy, I was reading English literature as an external undergraduate student of the University of London. But prior to enrolling in this university, I had read uplifting information from Gerald Moore's book, *Seven African Writers,* (1962): that Cameroon was in the forefront of African literature or something to that effect. But when I read further I discovered that Moore was talking only of Francophone Cameroonian authors like Mongo Beti and Ferdinand Oyono. Not a single Anglophone Cameroonian writer was mentioned. I told myself then that there was a daunting task ahead for Anglophones in Cameroon to carry out in order to affirm their cultural identity. To prepare myself for that onerous duty I decided to go in for further studies, hence my registration in the above university.I had a vision of better days for

Anglophone Cameroon literature; and within that vision I was fairly aware of my specific mission: that of a critic. And although I was then almost at the end of writing my novel, *Son of the Native Soil*, in addition to completing a collection of poems, I had discovered, that early, that my greater mission in the future development of the emerging Anglophone Cameroon literature would be that of a literary critic. My extensive reading in English and African literatures had groomed me for this modest project of joining the other Anglophone Cameroonian critics in guiding and shaping literary taste in matters of valuation. This therefore accounts for the genesis of the literary, critical essays in this volume, some of which span more than twenty years.

Encompassing the genres of drama, the novel, poetry, the short story, and the essay, these essays, on the whole, are a testimony of the fact that we have gone beyond the apparent drought of Anglophone Cameroon literary paucity to the actual fruitful period of Anglophone Cameroon abundance of literary creativity. In this new World Englishes Literature, the Anglophone Cameroonians have appropriated an imperial language, English, to serve the Cameroonian vision. Their various literary texts are containers of representations that are essentially cultural and ideological constructs. That is, these works are initially anchored on Cameroonian/African experiences to take on social significance. As they are grounded on moving human experiences, they necessarily make references to their immediate Cameroonian environment before taking on universal human significance.

Postcolonial critics have pilloried proponents of Euro-centric universalism with regard to literary relevance. The former now firmly believe that universal relevance of literature is no longer the exclusive attribute of established European/Western literatures. It is now a truth universally acknowledged that universality of literary relevance belongs to all literatures. All literatures of the world can attain universal significance only after substantially drawing from their local milieu, their roots.

In this regard the late Cameroonian poet and politician, François Sengat Kuo, stated it very beautifully thus:

"…l'arbre ne s'élance à la conquête du soleil qu'en s'agrippant ferme à la terre nourricière, les pieds mouillés au lac des tombeaux,"[1] literally rendered as "The tree goes out for the conquest of the sun only by holding firmly onto mother-earth, its roots soaked in the lake of graves." There is only one sun in the planetary system known to us. Once you ascend to the level of the sun, you shine on the whole world, you shine on the universe. In the context of literary creativity it means that for a writer to attain universal relevance, for a writer to produce a work that resonates with meaning, a work of thickness and maximum interest and one capable of attracting many more readers beyond its immediate community, such a writer must necessarily draw inspiration from his roots, his culture. No literary work of art worth its salt is conceived and textualized in an ideological or cultural vacuum.

The critical perspective that will be seen to emerge from these essays is what I initially christened, poetically, as Matter and Manner. I fully developed it later on to be called the Socio-Artistic Approach, as expatiated, particularly in my critical work *The Cameroonian Novel of English Expression* (2009/2007). I started off with 'Matter and Manner' because it is my firm conviction that in matters of valuation in literary criticism, the literary critic who intends to carry out a profound analysis of a work of literature, must be doubly concerned with the examination of the work's subject matter, themes, cultural, moral and ideological issues, on the one hand (Matter); and, with the analysis of the language, style, or the totality of the author's expressive devices, on the other, (Manner). For me criticism is not literary criticism which dwells solely on themes and meaning to the exclusion of technique, to the exclusion of the author's use of the totality of expressive devices. Both matter and manner must count in the meaningful literary analysis. As I see it, Matter is good; Manner is better, but the best is Matter and Manner combined.

It emerges from some of these essays that there is unevenness with regard to the degree of total achievement of the present corpus of Anglophone imaginative writing. This is not surprising, though, as one would normally expect from people experimenting with new art forms and employing a foreign, European medium of expression. Even so there is reason to be optimistic, for there are some Anglophone writers already exhibiting a sureness in technical execution and linguistic mastery. Some genres, in this connexion, can even boast of their own worthy Anglophone Cameroonian representatives who can stand their ground anywhere. The hard truth, however, is that from the point of view of technique and medium of imaginative expression, there is still a great deal to be done to take our creative and critical writing to higher heights.

Out of the selected twenty-five articles and book reviews reproduced here twenty-one have been published in international scientific journals, conference proceedings, and newspapers. Apart from a few corrections and updates here and there, I have reproduced the essays essentially in their original form. And I should like to thank here the various editors and publishers of these journals and other publications.

One essay that has not been published before but which has ironically enjoyed a wider readership because it has been posted on some websites is the very first essay in this volume: "Half a Century of Written Anglophone Cameroon Literature." A few Cameroonians who have accessed my phone number have contacted me to appreciate it, and some of my levels 400 and 500 students have proudly shown me their copies downloaded from the "net." For this exposure I remain grateful to Dr Joyce Ashuntantang, the Director of EduArt Inc. and Dr Emma Dawson, General Editor of World Englishes Literature (Fiction).

Going through these essays, many readers will definitely come across an occasional repetitiveness on my part, an emphatic attitude likely to put off some. This stylistic quirk is the more evident because the essays are now grouped in a single volume. When I wrote them long ago and published them separately in many different journals, this flaw was less evident, and little did I know that I would come to assemble them in one book. In addition, readers familiar with my other critical works will find in some of the present essays seminal material that has been fully developed in those texts. I can only appeal to the readers' indulgence that wherever they feel a sense of déjà vu, they should skip such portions and move on to other essays. I hope there is enough material in the volume to interest them.

End Note
1. Sengat Kuo. "Collier de Cauris." Edition *Présence Africaine* 21.

1
HALF A CENTURY OF WRITTEN ANGLOPHONE CAMEROON LITERATURE

The year Sankie Maimo's play, *I Am Vindicated,* was published by Ibadan University Press, 1959 marked the birth of Anglophone Cameroon literature. But six years earlier, in 1953, still in Nigeria, another Cameroonian, Bernard Fonlon, had written but not yet published, a major essay 'As I See It', a treatise on the future and welfare of Cameroon and the role of the clergy in the building of the nation, intended to memorialize his approaching ordination as a Catholic priest. Now, from 1959 to 2008 is close to 50 years, or half a century. Fifty years in the life of many individuals, couples, institutions or organizations is a time for reflection, a time for stocktaking, a period for counting their blessings or celebrating their achievements. In our literary situation the inevitable question that comes to mind is: on the eve of this mature age of 50, does Anglophone Cameroon literature have anything positive to show for its existence so far? And the general answer is yes. The thesis defended in this keynote address is that at 50 Anglophone Cameroon literature has achieved a great deal, that it is alive and doing very well; however, its creators and critics face challenges that have to be overcome if its quality and scope must be improved upon.

A glance at the latest bibliography on Anglophone Cameroon literature, published in *African Literature Association Bulletin* early in 2004 by Joyce Ashuntantang (112 – 123) is enough to convince any doubting Thomas of the wide range of Anglophone Cameroon literary productivity. All of this creative output did not come by chance but partly by design. It is the result of a number of stimulating literary activities: debates in classrooms or clubs, discussions in some of our newspapers and the radio, workshops, seminars, conferences and book launches within the Anglophone literary community before 1982, and especially thereafter.

In this regard we should single out for recognition a few individuals and groups that have done a great deal to promote creative writing in Anglophone Cameroon. We must mention here the significant editorial role played by Professor Bernard Fonlon in *ABBIA, Cameroon Cultural Review,* which was partly a forum for fostering many creative writers, his Creative Writing Class of 1972 in the Federal University of Cameroon, Yaoundé, and his literary contests in short fiction writing; we must acknowledge here Professor Charles Alobwed'Epie whose University Poetry Club has done a lot to awaken consciousness in poetry writing and poetry appreciation among many writers of English expression; we must applaud here the laudable endeavours of Professor Bole Butake who, while still a student in the Yaoundé University, edited *The Mould* and *Thunder On the Mountain,* journals of creative writing where many aspiring writers cut their teeth on the art of imaginative writing; and finally we must recognize here the crucial efforts of Professor John Nkemngong Nkengasong, current President of Anglophone Creative Writers' Association during whose tenure many Anglophone creative works have been published with the help of subvention from the Ministry of Culture. Now he has launched a poetry contest.

Three publishing houses, Buma Kor in Yaoundé, Patron Publishing House in Bamenda, and Editions CLE in Yaoundé, have helped to publish some Anglophone Cameroon literary works, while two theatre troupes stand head and shoulders above the rest. On the one hand there is the Musinga Drama Group, founded in 1974 by Victor Elame Musinga which helped to perform many of his own plays in several Anglophone towns. On the other there is the University of Yaoundé Theatre and the Flame Players who worked in close collaboration with Bole Butake to take the latter's plays to jammed theatre halls in some major towns of the Anglophone provinces in Cameroon. Prior to 1999 the Flame Players had even staged Butake's *Shoes and Four Men* in *Arms* in three German cities.

The history of Anglophone Cameroon creative writing will be incomplete without, at least, a paragraph on *Balafon: An Anthology of Cameroon Literature in English* (1986) edited by G. De La Taille, K. Werner and V. Tarkang. The uniqueness of this text lies in being the first of its kind as far as Anglophone Cameroon is concerned. It consists of the works of 15 Anglophone Cameroon imaginative writers, grouped under five sections according to the following genres: the novel, the short story, poetry, drama, and the essay. Each of the genres is represented by three authors, an arbitrary number decided upon, one would imagine, more to reduce this seminal work to a manageable size than to delimit the scope of literary production by the Anglophones.

There remain other contributing factors to the growth of Anglophone Cameroon imaginative writing. To highlight just a few we should mention here the Workshop on Anglophone Writing in Cameroon, the first of its kind held at the Goethe Institute, Yaoundé in 1993, and whose proceedings were published that very year by Bayreuth African Studies 30 (WEKA NO 1). This was followed in 1994 by a conference on Cameroon literature, hosted by the University of Buea, and whose proceedings were published in a special edition of *EPASA MOTO* by the University of Buea in 1996. In 1999 came the 3L Conference (Language, Literature and Liberty) that took place at the University of Yaoundé I. Then there was the Anglophone Creative Writers' Association (ACWA) Second Annual Conference, held in Buea on November 11, 2004. Prior to that ACWA had in 2003 organized two enriching workshops in Yaoundé and Limbe, and its First Annual Conference in Bamenda.

In many of these forums papers on various aspects of Anglophone Cameroon literature were presented and discussed, with literary critics clarifying or modifying their critical positions. While some creative writers were receptive to what was said about their work, a few took issue with the critics on their critical pronouncements, so that, in some cases, we witnessed literary battles that were fiercely fought between some creators and critics in the columns of some of our popular newspapers; in a rare instance a booklet, reminiscent of Alexander Pope's acrimonious attacks on his literary foes, was published by Sankie Maimo as a 'reply to a critic'.

While a good number of Cameroonian creative writers have published with established international publishers like Heinemann, Longman, Macmillan, Kola Press and Edition CLE, etc, most have published with local printing houses. On their part Anglophone Cameroonian literary critics, especially those teaching in the universities, have accessed professional/scientific journals in Cameroon, Nigeria, Britain, France, Germany and the U.S. Two of Anglophone Cameroonian outstanding dramatists, Bole Butake and Bate Besong, have attained literary immortality and put Anglophone Cameroon on the map of high intellectualism by featuring in the *Encyclopaedia of African Literature* (2003)[1]. In 1992 Bate Besong had won the ANA Award for Literature for his play *Requiem for the Last Kaiser* (1988), and this in a country as creatively and intellectually competitive as Nigeria. Bate Besong had also been arrested and detained a year earlier (1991) in Yaoundé when his fiery play, *Beasts of No Nation*, directed by Bole Butake, was premiered in that city. Babila Mutia's short story has featured in an international publication on 20th century short stories, while Mathew Takwi has won some international awards for his poetry.

There is a literary project, initiated by the English Department of the University of Buea, edited by Roselyne Jua, Hilarious Ambe, and Bate Besong, and aimed at assembling critical perspectives on Anglophone Cameroon Drama[2]. This project has elicited lively responses from scholars all over the world and promises to be really impressive when finally accomplished. If things go according to the wishes of the initiators, the book should be coming out soon. On his part Professor Edward O. Ako is editing a different but related project, Critical Perspectives on Cameroon Literature in English, Vol. 1, (Fiction and Drama) which should be out by now. Dr Emmanuel Fru Doh in the USA is also working on a critical text on both the oral and written Anglophone Cameroon literature.

At the level of consumption some Anglophone Cameroon literary works are school texts at the primary, secondary and university levels. With regard to the General Certificate of Education Examination, three Anglophone authors have featured in the section for African Literature. They are Kenjo Jumbam with his *The White Man of God,* L.T. Asong with his *Crown of Thorns* and *No Way to Die,* and Shadrach A. Ambanasom with his *Son of the Native Soil.* Dr. Joyce Ashuntantang has taught *The Crown of Thorns* several times at the University of Connecticut at Storrs / Hartford (Tande 10).

On the whole, the Anglophone Cameroon creative writers have adopted the English language and the various art forms to serve the Cameroonian vision. They are variously exploring, dramatizing and exposing the social ills that plague the Cameroonian society, entertaining, interpreting and educating the very society. But, although there seems to be no taboo subject beyond their imaginative gaze, these writers do not write with the same degree of commitment.

Notable Anglophone Cameroonian Playwrights include Sankie Maimo, Victor Elame Musinga, Bole Butake, Bate Besong, Victor Epie Ngome, John Nkemngong Nkengasong, John Ngongkum, Ndumbe Eyoh, Anne Tanyi Tang, Tangyie Suh Nfor, Emelda Samba, Nsahlai Christopher, Francis B. Nyamnjoh, Julius Ndofor, Babila

Mutia, George Nyamndi, Jetimen (John Menget), and Tah Protus. They have experimented with traditional and modern dramatic forms. To the extent that these playwrights are critical of social ills and mores, to the degree that they satirize human foibles with the sole moral purpose of changing peoples' social behaviour for the better, virtually all of these writers are committed dramatists. But from their midst emerge radical visionaries, revolutionary writers committed to bigger and more serious socio-political change. The latter group includes people like Victor Epie Ngome, Bole Butake, Bate Besong and John N. Nkengasong.

In Victor Epie Ngome's play, *What God Has Put Asunder,* the purported marriage between Weka and Miche Garba is a metaphor for the political union between the people of the former Southern Cameroons, on the one hand, and those of La République du Cameroun, on the other; that is, the Anglophones and the Francophones in present day Cameroon. This metaphor, an ingenious theatrical device, allows for two levels of meaning, the literal and the symbolic, with the latter being the more significant. When in the court Weka says "Ours, was a relationship too fraught with deceit and irregularities to be considered marriage', she is making an important pronouncement and a grave accusation against her husband Garba. Beyond the domestic level this indictment represents, on the political plain, the myriad of collective grievances held by Anglophones against their Francophone brothers, a composite of complaints that has come to be known in Cameroon today as the 'Anglophone Problem'. Victor Epie Ngome imaginatively sees the relationship between Weka and Garba as one characterized by irreconcilable differences – hence the very suggestive title of his play: *What God Has Put Asunder.*

With regard to the plays of Bole Butake, whether drawing from a mythic imagination or from the contemporary social scene, Butake succeeds in making his dramas scathing commentaries on contemporary social life in Cameroon, in particular, and Africa in general, especially where there is irresponsible political leadership, unconscionable dictatorial rule, corruption, immorality and the misuse of power. This malpractice by power-wielding elite provokes the anger of the oppressed masses who advocate a change of the status quo, a protest in which women play a primordial role. For in most of

Butake's dramas women have moved from their traditional backseat role of passive players to the foreground as a powerful force.

While Ngome, and Bole Butake and many of the other playwrights belong to the traditional, realistic drama, Bate Besong and John N. Nkengasong have been influenced by the practitioners of the Theatre of the Absurd. Their plays are characterised by the basic elements found in modern drama: lack of well-told stories, or lack of chronological plots or fully developed characters; there are disjointed dialogues; there is the use of stream of consciousness technique; characters are deformed people or dregs of humanity; the playwrights occasionally resort to the use of surrealism, trance or hallucination, etc.

However, thematically speaking, Besong and Nkengasong still use their unconventional plays to explore socio-political issues relevant to both Cameroon and Africa. On the whole, the plays of these modernist dramatists constitute a study in political dictatorship, the consummate quest for power, brutality and economic mismanagement. But also featuring in their works is the issue of the Anglophone Problem. The plays raise issues that prick the conscience of the average Cameroonian. But neither in their works nor in that of Epie Ngome is the accent on secession given as a solution to the problem. By and large, most Anglophones within the larger social context of the plays would prefer a moderate approach to the solution of the problems that pit them against their Francophone brothers.

Some of the important Anglophone Cameroon poets are Bate Besong, Emmanuel Fru Doh, Mbella Sonne Dipoko, John N. Nkengasong, Kitts Mbeboh, Afuh Margaret, Fale Wache, John Ngongkum, Nol Alembong, Giftus Nkam, Mesack Takere, Mathew Takwi, Tennu Mbuh, Jacob A. Ndifon, Bernard Fonlon, Babila Mutia, Peter Abety, Julius Abiedu, Sankie Maimo, Tikum Mbah Azonga, Shadrach A. Ambanasom, Lloney Monono, Patrick Mbunwi, Bongasu Tanla Kishani, N. Patrick Tata, Tameh Valentine, Gahlia Gwangwa'a, Bumu Martin, Buma Kor etc. Among these poets we have, on the one hand, those one can term liberal humanists, people who write poetry, generally expressing a whole range of different emotions on all types of topics that catch their fancy. In the process they articulate, memorably and through the medium of beautiful images, some eternal verities of life. We believe that their poetry deserves to be valued and appreciated for its sincerity, sensitivity, and maturity of thought and feeling as well as for its clarity and beauty of expression. On the other hand, there are firebrands who exploit their overall Cameroonian subject matter with the intention of ideologically transforming their society for the better.

The Anglophone Cameroonian poets have experimented with different poetic forms, encompassing traditional and modernist/post modernist attitudes. Generally, most of the poets write free verse in accessible language; but a few produce difficult poetry less accessible to the common man. Top on the list of the latter category is Bate Besong who has cultivated obscurantism and seems to glory in postmodernist apparent disorderliness.

Written in a combative spirit, Bate Besong's poetry is out to denounce political and economic malpractice in society. But to articulate these and other themes, Besong employs a modernist/postmodernist mode of discourse that renders his poetry, in places, dauntingly difficult, accessible only to those ready to roll up their sleeves and read his work with determination. Some of the modernist characteristics that make his poetry obscure and difficult are: the poet's penchant for rare words, his tendency to use ellipses and fragments of sentences, the disorderly movement of his poetry, its high allusive nature, and Besong's propensity to bring his recondite learning to bear on his writing. However, guided by the sentiment of anger that runs through much of his poetry, the mature conscientious readers can reasonably penetrate many of Besong's poems and reap more from them. Only an immodest literary student would claim to have mastered all of Bate Besong's poetry. The best a sober critic should do is to offer to the literary community the benefit of his insight into aspects of the complex work of this avant-garde poet, Cameroon's enfant terrible, in the hope that other scholars will pick up the gauntlet and, with time, Bate Besong's poetry will be put in proper perspective. Only then will it cease to puzzle.

According to Professor Tala Kashim (187) the short story is 'one of the few literary forms' wherein the Anglophones seem to be ahead of the Francophones in Cameroon, an advantage, in his view, largely attributable to the efforts of the late Professor Fonlon in encouraging the writing of short stories and also in sponsoring short-story contests. Out of Fonlon's Creative Writing Class emerged talents like Peter Abety, Bole Butake, Peter Atabong and Nol Alembong. But there are writers who probably had no direct contact with Fonlon. They include Stephen Ndeley Mokoso, Tikum Mbah Azonga, Eunice Ngongkum, Ayugho Edward, Chop Samuel, and Babila Mutia.

All of these writers have produced charming short stories embodying key elements of good short stories: plot, conflict, suspense, surprise, and concentration on a single character. Like the other literary genres in Anglophone Cameroon, the short story has as its basic subject matter the postcolonial Cameroonian society with all its social ills, intrigues, problems and contradictions. Because of limitations of space, we can briefly comment here only on the short fiction of a single writer: Eunice Ngongkum's *Manna of a Life Time and Other Short Stories*.

To the present writer, these readable, suspenseful and moving stories constitute an artistic statement, a scathing critique of a society whose citizens increasingly feel alienated from it and have to seek solace and livelihoods abroad. Here are tales of hard times, economically hard times, times that push men, women and especially young people into desperate deeds even at the supreme price of death. The stories are about crooks, devils, and determined desperadoes; but they are also about decent and well meaning people victimized and transformed by the vicissitudes of life, confirming the bleak view that life is full of more sadness than joy. In her short fiction, Eunice Ngongkum employs an ingenious technique to transmute bare facts and commonplace events into intriguing works of art-literature. Beautifully crafted with a tough muscular touch, these short stories bear the imprint of a fine and talented artist full of promise.

In their seminal article, 'Cameroon Literature in English,' in the now defunct *ABBIA* (1982), Nalova Lyonga and Bole Butake stated unequivocally that the Anglophone Cameroonian novel, with only three published titles then, was the least developed genre in Cameroon. However, it is comforting to note that, twenty-six years after that pronouncement, at least 30 more titles have since appeared to the credit of the Cameroon novel in English. Some of our novelists include L.T. Asong, Margaret Afuh, Mbella Sonne Dipoko, Peter Nsanda Eba, Kenjo Jumbam, Langha Kizito, Alobwed'Epie, John N. Nkengasong, Eugene Kongnyuy, Azanwi Nchami, J. Neba Ngwa, Talla Ngarka, Margaret S. Ngwa, Jacob A. Ndifon, Zaccheus Ntumngia, Francis Nyamnjo, Ngoran C.T. and Shadrach A. Ambanasom. In handling their subject matter and subtly revealing their moral indignation, virtually all these novelists are serious in their ultimate artistic intention. Making use of satire, the novelists explore, expose and critique the social ills that plague their society and subtly urge readers to view life from their (the novelists') ideological or moral positions.

Some make their creative debut by espousing cultural nationalism or anti-colonial nationalism; some focus their fictional gaze on the sordid underbelly of their society, while others articulate burning issues of patriarchy versus feminism. But, above all, there are highly conscientised novelists with a heightened sense of ideological development who explore their basic subject matter, the Cameroonian society for a better future. Visionaries, they endeavour to reinvent a Cameroon with an alternative dispensation.

From the point of view of artistry and handling of language, the Anglophone writers have handled the novelistic form and the English language with varying degrees of success or failure. Some have manipulated plot, characterisation, structure, point of view, and language fairly well, while others have been less successful. With the exception of novels published by Heinemann and some iconic publishing houses of international standing, nearly all of those printed locally can be faulted for editorial shoddiness, and as such stand in urgent need of editorial and technical improvement. However, viewed globally, the creative output by Anglophone Cameroonian novelists is a positive contribution to the development of Anglophone Cameroon literature. Technically speaking, with particular reference to the fiction of Alobwed'Epie, Margaret Afuh, L.T. Asong, Tah Asongwed, Mbella Sonne Dipoko, Kenjo Jumbam, Azanwi Nchami, John Nkemngong Nkengasong, and Francis B. Nyamnjo, the Anglophone Cameroonian novel has contributed significantly to the extension of the frontiers of the novel as an art form. (Ambanasom *Cameroonian Novel* 280)

The critical analysis of the essay as a literary genre is a comparatively more recent phenomenon; and this is because, in contrast to fiction, poetry, and drama that are imaginative representations of reality, the essay is essentially concerned with factuality. In the essay it is explicit facts and ideas that are in ascendancy; it is the desire to instruct and persuade through arguments that is uppermost in the mind of the essayist. Generally, less central in the essayist's scheme of values is the intention to delight and move the reader. And, as Di Yanni has said, it is this pre-eminence and explicitness of facts and ideas in the essay that, for long, has rendered uncertain its status as literature (1523).

Nevertheless, while the goal of the essayists is to persuade readers to buy their ideas, many essayists are equally out to please and move the readers. Indeed, readers would miss much of the pleasure that some essays offer if the latter were to be read solely for their facts and ideas. Because of their style and language some essays can indeed, be poetic, dramatic and imaginative; for it is the comparative figures they use, and the linguistic strategies and formal patterns they employ that elevate the work of many essayists to the status of literature. Deprived of their figurative dimensions and the creativity of their linguistic patterns, many essays would be stripped of their literary pleasures and become less fascinating as literature. Therefore, to qualify as literature are those essays that embody validity of ideas, depth of imagination, and beauty and richness of linguistic expression, essays in which there is a refreshing blend of matter and manner. As I have always said, while matter is good, manner is even better; but the best is matter and manner combined.

In Anglophone Cameroon the essayists who best represent this nice balance between valid ideas and an engaging manner of linguistic expression are pre-eminently Bernard Fonlon and Godfrey Tangwa. There are other impressive essayists who came into the lime light within the Anglophone Cameroon sub-system in the 1990s with the advent of multiparty democracy and the liberalization of the press. Many of them were columnists in papers like *Cameroon Post, Le Messager, Cameroon Life, Post Watch, Time and Life, The Herald The Sketch, Weekly Post,* and *Cameroon Today* (Tangwa 'Other Side' 171). Professor Tangwa's list of these essayists includes Francis Wache, Martin Jumbam, Ntemfac Ofege, George Ngwane, Sam Nuvala Fonkem, Charlie Ndi Chia, Tande Dibussi, Bate Besong, Rotcod Gobata, Jing Thomas Ayeah, Hilary Fokum, etc. The list is far from exhaustive. One can add a few more names to it like Saul Tan, N. Patrick Tata, Victor Epie Ngome, Azore Opio, Tennu M. Mbuh, and Peterkins Manyong.

From the above list one essayist that many Anglophone Cameroonian readers will probably remember for long because of the incisiveness of his analysis of the Cameroonian socio-political scene, and the elegance of his linguistic expression is Francis Wache. It would be a treat for the reader if all of Francis Wache's essays were assembled in a single volume as many of Fonlon's and Tangwa's are. The essays of Tangwa and Fonlon have become philosophical and literary landmarks.

Godfrey B. Tangwa's collections of essays include *Democracy and Meritocracy, Road Companion to Democracy and Meritocracy, The Past Tense of Shit,* and *I Spit on their Graves.* Tangwa generally writes on a wide range of political and philosophical topics; but specifically he is more concerned with the welfare of his country, with democratic change in Cameroon. Many of his essays first appeared under the pen name Gobata in the early 1990s in a column in *Cameroon Post* titled 'No Trifling Matter'. But in his own words, 'I was not writing simply to entertain ... I was simply trying to wake up Cameroonians from decades of dogmatic slumber. I was simply shouting to deeply sleeping and drowsy members of the household that there were armed robbers in the house.' (*I Spit* viii)

Tangwa's subject is therefore serious and weighty, but he treats it in a manner different from Fonlon's without being less engaging. Tangwa's style is classical. At times it is informal, but generally incisive, witty, humorous, satirical and light-hearted. With a strong philosophical background he is very analytical and philosophical but writes in a language more accessible to the general reading public.

His essays are readable and engaging; they please while they teach. When they first appeared in *Cameroon Post*, they immediately won for the author a faithful readership that felt disappointed each time the ace writer announced his imminent retirement from the column. At the time the present writer, a devotee of Gobata, always looked forward to buying his copy of *Cameroon Post* and relished reading, in the comfort of his room, 'NO TRIFLING MATTER.'

It is surely with a sense of nostalgia that some of Gobata's readers look back to the early 1990s in Cameroon. For those who have read them, many of Gabata's essays are memorable works of art. But particularly unforgettable to the present writer, for the courage, conviction, cogency and, above all, the clarity and beauty of Gobata's declarations are, to cite but these few, 'A Day at the French Embassy,' 'Force of Argument Versus Argument of Force,' 'Our

Mungo Bridges,' 'Is there Really an Anglophone Problem in Cameroon?' and 'Kleptocracy and Mendacity...'

With Bernard Fonlon we are in the company of a different kind of personality in matters of language and style even if both Tangwa and Fonlon exhibit analogous scientific and philosophical attitudes in their analysis of socio-political issues. Some of Fonlon's works include *As I See It, Will We Make or Mar?, The Task of Today, The Genuine Intellectual, Ten Years After, An Open Letter to the Bishops of Buea and Bamenda, The Idea of Cultural Integration,* etc.

Even this short list of only some of his essays indicates the wide range of his topics. But whether he is writing on urgent issues that confront Cameroon, whether he is writing on economic, political, cultural, religious, or philosophical topics which he announced in his very first major essay, 'As I See It,' way back in 1953, Fonlon exploits to the fullest the possibilities of his creative medium; he manipulates to the maximum the effects that words and phrases can produce (Ambanasom 87). In his own words, 'I always made sure my writing had a literary dimension (Balafon 159).

The latter is accentuated by a distinctive style that is dignified, elegant, formal, allusive, elevated, and solemn. Generally, Fonlon's prose is rhythmical; that is, it is poetic prose, marked, at times, by the use of periodic sentences and parallelism. The periodic sentence is the kind of sentence wherein Fonlon's ideas hang in the air until all the insertions and interconnections are clinched by the main verb, the key word, or the central phrase. The periodic sentence often carries a three-tier parallel construction, piled one on top of the other, not out of a vain display of his mastery of the English language but rather for a rhetorical purpose: to put forth a point forcefully, to persuade the reader, an effect which adds to the formality and solemnity of his style:

> And finally, with our indigenous way of life restored and enriched by the absorption of a healthy foreign contribution, with the emergence of a new culture, unified, productive, dynamic and dignified in the eyes of the world, with communal divisions eliminated and communal unity recovered, the healing of the Negro's wounded psyche, and soul will follow as a natural consequence. (qtd in Ambanasom *Matter and Manner* 76).

The literary quality of Fonlon's essays can be best illustrated by the following significant case of plagiarism of his work. In 1999 a Cameroonian had boldly lifted, verbatim, from Fonlon's later foreword to his 1953 essay, 'As I See It,' portions of pages 7 and 8 and sent to BBC FOCUS ON AFRICA COMPETITION for the STAR LETTER of the month. And for his easy effort the fellow won the coveted first prize. Readers who may be inclined to take this information with a grain of salt should turn to the publication where the intellectual theft is well documented: BBC FOCUS ON AFRICA April – June 1999, page 60. The portion in question reads as follows:

> Today most of Africa is free at last, to some degree. And today, in Congo, we have before us the horrid spectacle of a seething fratricidal bloodbath in which many African countries have immersed themselves. The seeds and causes of the disaster are present almost everywhere, ready to sprout and explode. And from what does all this stem? From the fact that the law of the jungle holds sway in our 'renascent' Africa. What have we not seen in these decades of African independence? Mad ambition, runaway greed, insatiable lust, general absence of a sense of public service, treachery, betrayal, assassination, massacre. Lord! What have we not seen? Indeed we have seen so much that we are now inclined to take it all with a shrug of the shoulders, as though it was rather in the nature of things. But on the contrary we should pause with shock and ponder and wonder and ask with dread: whither Africa? The augury is disquieting. (Fonlon *See It* 7 – 8)

So far, the genres of Anglophone imaginative writing we have reviewed, i.e. drama, poetry, the novel, the short story, and the essay, have been literary forms implicitly produced for the general adult readers. But there is an age bracket, that constitutes the bulk of our general population, but whose reading habits and interests have not yet been considered; for, without a sound reading foundation built around children and their related interests, without a good imaginative literature, deliberately constructed and tailored to suit the tastes of children, we would be labouring in vain to produce successful adult readers. Such a foundational genre is what we call children's literature. It consists of simplified but readable novels, plays, poems, and stories written on topics and issues of interest to children and young adolescents. This genre is the motivational reading material, par excellence, that will form the solid base for general and specific reading in other subject areas, projecting children and young adolescents into the reading orbit, a crucial factor for general success in life which today depends, to a great extent, on literacy.

There are Anglophone Cameroonian creative writers already producing this kind of literature. And our major prose writers of children's literature are Comfort Ashu, Tah Protus, George Che Atanga, Nsanda Eba, Kenjo Jumbam, Sankie Maimo, J. Neba Ngwa, and Joseph A. Ngongwikwo. The playwrights include Hansel Ndumbe Eyoh, Tah Protus, and Anne Tanyi Tang, while the poets are Mesack Takere, Jacob A. Ndifon, and Lucia Bekaku Bitame. All of these writers have as a general goal to instill long lasting reading habits in children, educating them as well as inculcating cultural values into them. Some of these values are respect for tradition, the young and the elderly; love for the community and the fatherland; courage and bravery; care for the environment, particularly for water, trees, and the vegetation as a whole; indeed, care for our flora and fauna.

Were this brief survey to end here, one might conclude that the picture thus painted of the development of the Anglophone Cameroon literature is a rosy one, indeed, that our achievements at the levels of creative and critical productivity are flattering. While it is reasonable to see in what has been sketched so far, much that has been done, there is still a great deal to do to lift our achievements higher. If one takes a cold, critical eye at the site of imaginative and critical writing within our community, one must perforce concede that there are challenges at various levels.

In this regard, there is a need for Anglophone writers to remind themselves that they are all using someone else's language and that we ought to show respect towards it; 'that the linguistic furniture belongs to somebody else, and therefore shouldn't be moved around without permission' (Barry 194). Therefore, we should first master our medium of expression, the English language. Though it can never be pure in our hands, given our post-coloniality, we should diligently assimilate its grammar and internalize the rules that govern its function so that when, in the exercise of our poetic license, we violate these rules, let this grammatical transgression be committed from a position of linguistic competence and not from syntactic ignorance and naiveté. I believe that, as creators and critics using English as a working tool, this is one of our major challenges: the mastery of our medium of imaginative expression.

In this connection, perceptive Cameroonians are already facing the challenge. I am thinking of the PATAMAE Editing Consultancy that is already salvaging manuscripts from the weaknesses of expression and structure. This is a praiseworthy attempt to fill up the gap of both individual and publishing house lapses. It is perhaps left to the writers to make use of this rescue consultancy. It is also perhaps worthwhile mentioning that even the best of us are third rate editors of our own works and that while friends and non-professionals may offer some help, a functional editing house is professionally best suited for independent service in this direction, and that is the value of PATAMAE Editing Consultancy whose seat is in Bamenda.

Another challenge is making our publications available to as many readers as possible; for unless our readership can access our works, we may publish and still remain unknown. Sometimes one hears that a book launch has taken place in Bamenda, Buea or Yaoundé. But when one makes an effort to procure a copy of such a book, one is told that the book is sold out.

Occasionally, some authors are said to complain that their works are ignored by intellectuals even at the university level. Sometimes this may be true, sometimes not. University lecturers may be forgiven for not including in their courses Anglophone Cameroon literary works they cannot easily lay hands on. Would anyone seriously take to task a lecturer for not teaching a rich work like L. T. Asong's *Stranger in His Homeland*, for example? Some twelve years after it was published, a copy cannot be found in any bookshop in Bamenda town where it was produced and, maybe, not even with the author/publisher himself. Yes, the situation can be that depressing. The challenge here is that of the sustainability of our publications, inevitably tied to the eternal pecuniary question at the root of many of our social problems.

Even when the non-availability of texts is not an issue, we are still faced with a different kind of challenge: that of overcoming the fear of the unknown, linked to the calculated avoidance of some of our imaginative works even at the iconic university level, of all places. Is it not something of an irony that while Bole Butake, Bate Besong, Victor Epie Ngome and John Nkengasong are famous beyond Cameroon as imaginative dramatists with a revolutionary vision, there seems to be an unacknowledged embargo on their works even among us critics?

Such an evasive attitude is bound to produce from our midst a species of indifferent critics, like dealers in foreign merchandise who stand at our coasts and gaze wistfully westwards as they hunger and thirst after Western products, while at the same time they turn their backs on our fertile hinterland of cultural expression. I am not against foreign texts; indeed, I consume them. We all need them for the enlargement of our sympathies and humanity. But they should not be our sole literary diet to the exclusion of our own rich imaginative products.

It is the venerable Professor Fonlon who tells us that a characteristic of the genuine intellectual is 'his obligation to tell the truth as it is, his non-conformism, his role as critic of society, as Keeper of the Public Conscience' (Fonlon *Genuine Intellectual* 141). Cameroonian intellectuals should borrow a leaf from the politicians and the sixteen candidates in the presidential elections that took place in Cameroon as recently as 2004. From my own perspective, an obvious lesson emerging from their frantic nation-wide campaigns, brought into our bedrooms, thanks to the hi-tech magic of the TV and the Radio, is that there seems to be no taboo subject in Cameroon any more; that under the permissive New Deal Regime of President Paul Biya, Cameroonians can now discuss freely, openly, responsibly and even 'elegantly' any topic that catches their fancy.

Come to think of it, why would we, mere critics and interpreters, dealers in a secondary discourse, entertain more fears than the visionaries of the primary discourse? Why would anyone choose to cry louder than the bereaved?

Therefore, fellow creators and critics, cast aside your garment of fear, and put on your armour of objectivity and discuss the content of our literature objectively and fearlessly. For, beyond the critical character of their significant work, our most sensitive imaginative minds mean well for our country. Beyond their figurative discourse, beyond the metaphors, allegories and symbols in which their work is couched, the fundamental aim of their creative endeavour is this one moral imperative: to transcend entertainment and get to the level of instruction, to construct a better, fairer and more prosperous Cameroonian society.

These committed dramatists and their counterparts in poetry, the novel, the essay, and the short story are real sons and daughters of Cameroon who have given the word 'patriotism' a new meaning. They rightly deserve our accolades instead of the cold, indifferent shrug of our shoulders.

Some of the critics of Anglophone Cameroon literature are Bole Butake, Nalova Lyonga, John N. Nkengasong, Tennu M. Mbuh, Nol Alembong, Eunice Ngongkum, Fai Donatus, Linus T. Asong, Bate Besong, Henry K. Jick, Kashim Ibrahim Tala, Edward O. Ako, Alfred A. Ndi, Roselyne Jua, Hilarious Ambe, Joyce Ashuntantang, George Nyamndi, John N. Ndongmanji, N. Patrick Tata, Edward Ayugho, Peter Abety, Tangyie Suh Nfor, Shadrach A. Ambanasom, Godfrey Tangwa, Kenneth Usongo, Tata H. Mbuy, Francis Wache, Azore Opio, Peterkins Manyong, Tande Dibussi, Ndofor Julius, Emmanuel Yenshu, Charles A. Nama, Asheri Kilo, Emmanuel Fru Doh, Buma Kor, Tah Protus, and Hansel Ndumbe Eyo etc. These critics have produced articles, commentaries, critiques and reviews on various aspects of Anglophone Cameroon literature. Some have either written on an author or a combination of authors. Apart from the current projects on critical perspectives mentioned above, very few substantial, book-length studies exist on Anglophone Cameroon literature. The two published books, on the subject by the present writer are: *Education of the Deprived: A Study of Four Cameroonian Playwrights* (2003), and *The Cameroonian Novel of English Expression: An Introduction* (2007). Dr Oscar C. Labang has published the most recent study on John N. Nkengasong's work entitled *Riot in the Mind* (2008), and this focus on a single writer's work may well be the trend in the future.

Dr Oscar Labang happens to be a publisher too. His publishing house, Miraclaire Publishing, Yaoundé, has an international connection with Charleston, SC, USA. It is amazing that in just under five years of existence, Miraclaire Publishing has many titles of Anglophone Cameroonian creative and critical works already, with a good number of them by the publisher himself. While this is not yet the time for me to comment substantially on Dr Labang's literary works, I would just like to add here, in passing, that his *The Trial of*

Bate Besong, a humorous, provocative play, written in the tradition of drama of ideas as propagated by George Bernard Shaw, is, I dare say, guaranteed to spark off spirited discussions relating to the role of the creative writer vis-à-vis the socio-political issues of the day, and the function of literature in society.

From the look of things, given his tireless involvement in multifarious literary activities, Dr Labang may just be an unstoppable literary phenomenon in Anglophone Cameroon. And this can only be good news for the health Anglophone Cameroon literature. Let us hold up the green light to this young man who is poised to do wonderful things for our burgeoning literature.

An important challenge is for creators to be receptive to criticism, and for critics to be objective and honest in delivering their critical judgment. A balanced and constructive approach to the works we criticize would help the authors to develop into better artists, while a biased approach would not be helpful to their professional growth at all. A critic worth his salt must be intellectually honest. If he is moved emotionally or intellectually by a work, he should say so, despite any ideological differences between him and the creative writer. As critics we should all avoid the fault of which D. H. Lawrence accuses Macaulay, a brilliant scholar:

> A man like Macaulay, brilliant as he is, is unsatisfactory, because he is not honest. He is emotionally very alive, but he juggles his feelings...A critic must be emotionally alive in every fibre, intellectually capable and skillful in essential logic, and then morally very honest. (qtd in Coombes 8)

A good critic should feel free to quarrel with the infelicity or clumsiness of an expression, with the inconclusive or illogical conclusion, with the lop-sided treatment of a conflict, with the absence of symmetry or balance and proportion, but he should abstain from insulting the author at a personal level. But where he finds, in a work of the imagination, felicity of expression, balance and proportion, where there is artistic truthfulness, he should say so without mincing words; he should say so honestly and generously. True critics, in this regard, should be unstinting in their praise.

> Give to Afuh what is Afuh's, and to Ashu
> what is Ashu's. Let Tanyi Tang have her
> share.

> Give to Alembong what is Alembong's,
> and to Nchami what is Nchami's. Let
> Tangyie Suh Nfor have his praise.

Of course, I am well aware that these essentially Structuralist notions of balance, proportion and symmetry are now suspect; for it is the aim of Post-Structuralism to subvert them, to de-hegemonise them, as Jacques Derrida (1994) insists, showing that imbalance, asymmetry and lack of proportion in a work of art are not automatically synonymous with artistic weakness. On the contrary, they may be positive values, emblematic of alternative systems within a 'decentred planet'. Post-structuralism and Deconstruction are out to dismantle totalizing notions. Ultimately, then, it depends on the critic's school of thought, his genuine critical conviction and the perceived intention of the artist. At the centre of the issue is artistic and theoretical competence, which brings us to our next challenge, keeping abreast with theory.

As creators and critics, if we must maintain our intellectual tone, there is a need for us to keep abreast with what is happening in the domain of literary creativity and criticism in matters of theory. We are living in a globalized world and cannot afford to be theoretically innocent. But far from a simple notion, literary theory today is a collection of complex critical approaches whose literature has reached such a frightening and intimidating level that only the most determined can keep pace with it. But somehow we must manage to come to terms with theory or aspects of theory; we must try to grapple with it if our literature and criticism must evolve in a meaningful way.

We are post-colonial subjects producing our literature mainly in an imperial language. But the intimate and immediate circumstances of our lives that make up the subject matter of our works are Cameroonian (African), a reality that betrays our hybridity. We are hybrid subjects emerging from a situation of a superimposition of a conflicting European language and culture upon ours. We are children of two worlds: the one by virtue of our colonial educational upbringing, the other by our close attachment to our traditions. Our imaginative works, therefore, celebrate diversity, difference and hybridity. Indeed, as creators and critics, we are empire writing back, to echo the title of a pioneering work in post-colonial criticism (Ashcroft *et al* 1989). We are writing our way back 'into a history others have written' (Culler 131), but more critically, we are appropriating that history for our own ends.

We are living in the second phase of Post-colonial criticism, an approach that emerged as a distinct category in the early 1990s; and the post-colonialist project is one that privileges cross-cultural experiences, cultural polyvalency, and hybridity in literary texts. It regards conditions of marginality, plurality and perceived 'Otherness' not as weaknesses but as 'sources of energy and potential change' (Barry 198).

As a result it is not difficult to see why post-colonial writers and critics, hybrid subjects like us, should be interested in Post-structuralism, another critical approach; for, according to Peter Barry,

> Post-structuralism is centrally concerned to show the fluid and unstable nature of personal and gender identity, the shifting, 'polyvalent' contradictory current of signification within texts, and the way that literature itself is a site on which ideological struggles are acted out. This mind-set is admirably suited to expressing the numerous contradictions and multiple allegiances of which the Post-colonial writer and critic is constantly aware. (195)

Therefore, if we must be viable creators and critics, we are bound to be conversant with both Post-Structuralism and the Post-colonialist project. The latter has acquired a vocabulary of its own, its own jargon, like many contemporary theoretical formulations, a syncretism, an accretion emerging from a dialectical relationship with allied conceptualizations. It is characterized by richly compounded and inflected words and expressions, often rhythmical utterances like commodification, objectification, orientalising, transgressivism, textuality, inter-textuality, self-reflexity, etc. We must master these terms to be able to produce or discuss our literature meaningfully in the context of contemporary discourses.

Some may object that the Post-colonial approach, containing other sub-categories like feminism, Marxism, gay and lesbian criticism, etc., is itself only an addition to many critical discourses, which the critic is supposed to master; that it is only another sophisticated weapon in the arsenal of a literary critic. Isn't this an unreasonable request? Some may ask. How many of the approaches at his disposal should a critic apply when confronted with a literary text? One, two, three or four? Or should he, in the interest of a democratic display of theoretical competence, evenly spread them across the text? Well, I do not think so. I would go along with Peter Barry who says, 'for most readers one of these issues tends to eclipse all the rest... These perspectives cannot be put on and off like a suit – they have to emerge and declare themselves with some urgency' (Barry 197- 198). It is the creative work that calls forth a critical approach. If I may be permitted the use of my favourite hunting analogy in this regard:

> The critic's tools are his weapons at different times; and ... a weapon presupposes a hunter on the one hand, and the game to be killed, on the other. The weapon may range from a broomstick to an automatic rifle, and the game from a fly to an elephant. Now when a fly presents itself, the hunter uses a broomstick to bring it down; when a rat shows up, he uses a stick; when a bird comes his way, a catapult is enough. In the same way, a gun is appropriate for an antelope, and an automatic rifle for an elephant. Let the weapon match the animal. It makes no sense to face the elephant with a broomstick, nor with a rifle to bring down a fly. (Ambanasom *Education* 17)

Before we round off this discourse, we can say that, like all literary artists, the Anglophone Cameroon imaginative writers play all kinds of language games with the infinitely flexible syntax of their creative medium of expression. Working within their chosen literary forms, they creatively use English to achieve their various artistic intentions. With a world view of their own, these writers have fantasies, dreams, and aspirations they would like to translate into reality (Nyamnjoh 350); for, working on their basic subject matter, some would like to reinvent a Cameroon of their dream as opposed to the present Cameroon which, like many other African countries, is an imperfect society, with its own share of socio-economic and socio-political challenges.

But, coming from different ideological schools of thought, these writers do not agree on the type of approach to bring about an ideal society. On the one hand, you have moderately committed writers who feel that, imperfect as the actual Cameroon is, it is still a reasonably good society which needs only socio-political reforms here and there to be the best of possible worlds. In their view, the latter can come about through criticism, of the malpractices of the society, through the exposure to ridicule of these voices of its citizens. On the other hand, there are revolutionary writers who feel that socio-political salvation can come only through a total overhauling of the political machinery. Each of the five major genres more or less has writers from both ideological tendencies though not in equal distribution. But it is safe to affirm that the moderately committed writers are in the majority.

While it is possible for critics to proffer ideas about what creators could be exploring, it is certainly not their place to prescribe what creative artists should write on, nor how they should do so. That would be unrealistic; for heterodoxy, and not orthodoxy, is the normal way of life. As individuals with our differing natural endowments, and different intimate circumstances in life, we cannot all be comfortable in a monolithic mould.

Of course I am well aware of the need for writers to deliver a 'political punch,' the criterion fashionable these days in some Anglophone quarters for the conferment of the seal of relevance to literature. My humble opinion in this regard is that important and central as politics is in our corporate existence, it should not be the one and only subject matter of our literature. In any case, it is not given to just any writer to produce genuinely good political literature. May those capable of pursuing more vigorous committed writing do so; may our radical visionaries bloom. But let there be room for liberal humanists too. To prescribe only politics and proscribe any other subject matter would be to kill our creative spirit, to stultify our imaginative efforts and to truncate our literature.

Although we are a people with a problem, a fact that calls for the accentuation of our condition of marginality, and although when our creative works are examined globally many of us can qualify as committed writers, we do differ in our degree of commitment. Some, because of their heightened level of ideological development, are more engaged, more radical than others. But the dynamism, the vibrancy of Anglophone Cameroon literature cannot be fostered by a spirit that encourages a straitjacket mentality. Neither monolithism nor orthodoxy can be a viable way of life in a world as diverse and complex as ours today.

Perspectives on Written Cameroon Literature in English

Just as we meet among the motley crowd in the street the Manichean binarism of the tall and the short, the young and the old, the beautiful and the ugly, the calm and the violent, the radical and the moderate, so do we expect our literature to signalize this diversity in its various forms. Pierre Fandio captures this spirit of our imaginative writing very well when, in an interview with Bate Besong, he affirms that Anglophone Cameroon literature is 'at the same time piercing, incisive, tender, soothing and controversial.' And that is how it should be.

Indeed, as it exists today, our literature reveals a reality we cannot escape from, but one that literary critics should rather begin to appreciate: a growth in various directions, a diversity in themes, styles and attitudes, encompassing a wider spectrum of human emotion that objective literary critics must now begin to address. (Ambanasom Preface *Homage*)

We must know that even though a vector of ideology, a site on which antagonistic ideological hegemonies are often dramatized, literature 'is less purely ideological' than political and economic theory (Engels as quoted in Eagleton 16). Good literature is not the plain advocacy of overt populism. It achieves its effects by indirection: through the use of artistic, linguistic and para-linguistic devices. It is the effective mediation of socio-historical forces through the agency of form.

My final word to young Anglophone Cameroonian writers is this: write according to your God-given talent. Many roads lead to Rome. The Anglophone Cameroonian story can be told in diverse ways. In the words of Mao Tse Tung, 'Let a hundred flowers blossom, a hundred schools of thought contend' (qtd in Fonlon *Genuine Intellectual* 147). The quantity and quality of Anglophone creative writing is on the rise, and there is the need on the part of Anglophone critics of these works to school themselves and hone their tools for the task that is inevitably theirs. The Anglophone creators and critics owe an obligation to posterity to set the pace today for what tomorrow will be the great Anglophone Cameroon literary and critical heritage. We are the ones to tell the Anglophone Cameroonian story now. If not us, who? If not now, when? If not here, where?

Thank you very much.

End Notes
1. Edited by Simon Gikandi and published by Routledge, London.
2. It is a tragic fact of Anglophone Cameroon literary history that Bate Besong, Hilarious Ambe, Gwangwa, including their driver, were all killed in a ghastly road accident at Edea on their way to Yaoundé in the early hours of March 8, 2007. The passing away of these three, university lecturers and dramatic icons, has left a huge void on the Anglophone Cameroon literary scene.

Works Cited

Ambanasom, Shadrach A. 'Cameroon Literature in English: An Opinion on Balafon.' *Matter and Manner: Essays On African Literature.* Unpublished, Bamenda: 1990. 51 – 80.

— — —.'The Quintessence of Fonlon.' *Matter and Manner: Essays On African Literature.* Unpublished, Bamenda: 1990. 81 – 92.

— — —. *Education of the Deprived* (A Study of four Cameroonian Playwrights). Yaoundé: Presses Universitaires de Yaoundé, 2003.

— — —. *Homage and Courtship (Romantic Stirrings of a Young Man).* Bamenda: Agwecam Printers, 2007.

— — —. *The Cameroonian Novel of English Expression*: *An Introduction.* Bamenda: Agwecam Printers, 2007.

Ashcroft, Bill, Gareth Griffiths and Helen Tiffin (eds). *The Empire Wrties Back: Theory and Practice in Postcolonial Literatures.* London/New York: Routledge, 1989.

Ashuntantang, Joyce A. Anglophone Cameroon Literature: A Comprehensive Bibliography of Primary Texts and Selected Criticism.' *ALA Bulletin* Vol. 29 Fall 2003/Winter 2004 3:112 – 123.

Barry, Peter. *Beginning Theory: An Introduction to Literary and Cultural Theory.* Manchester and New York: Manchester University Press, 1995.

Coombes, H. *Literature and Criticism.* Harmondsworth Middlesex: Chatto & Windus, 1953.

Culler, Jonathan. *Literary Theory.* Oxford New York: Oxford University Press, 1997.

De la Taille, G; K. Werner, and V. Tarkang (eds). *Balafon: An Anthology of Cameroon Literature in English.* Essex: Longman Group Limited, 1986.

Derrida, Jacques. *Specters of Marx.* (Eng. Trans.) New York Routledge, 1994.

Di Yanni, Robert. *Reading Fiction, Poetry, Drama, and the Essay* 2nd ed. New York: McGrawHill, Inc., 1990.

Eagleton, Terry. *Marxism and Literary Criticism.* Berkeley and Los Angeles: University of California Press, 1976.

Fandio, Pierre. 'Anglophone Cameroon Literature at the Cross Roads: An Interview With Dr. Bate Besong'. n.p., 2004.

Fonlon, Bernard. *As I See It.* Buea: Catholic Press, 1971.

__ __ __. *The Genuine Intellectual* Yaounde: Buma Kor Publishing House, 1978.

__ __ __. Interview. *Balafon: An Anthology of Cameroon Literature in English.* Eds. De la Taille, G.K . Werner, and V. Tarkang. Essex: Longman Group Limited, 1986. 156 - 174.

Gikandi, Simon (ed.) *Encyclopaedia of African Literature.* London: Routledge, 2003.

Gobata, Rotcod. *I Spit on their Grave* (Book Two of *The Past Tense*) Bellingham: Kola Tree Press, 1996.

Lyonga, Nalova and Bole Butake. 'Cameroon Literature in English: Appraisal.' *ABBIA: Cameroon Cultural Review,* 38-39-40, (1982) 123-174.

Lyonga, N. E. Breitinger and B. Butake (eds). *Anglophone Cameroon Writing.* Bayreuth: Bayreuth University, 1993.

Maimo, 'Sankie. *'Sankie's Literary Bravura (A reply to a critic). Yaoundé: SOPECAM,* 1984.

Nyamnjoh Francis B. 'Protest Journalism as a Literary Genre: The Case of Anglophone Cameroon Journalism Today.' *Epasa Noto.* Special Edition (1996): 350 – 357.

Tala, Kashim Ibrahim. 'The Development of Cameroon Literature.' *Balafon: An Anthology of Cameroon Literature in English.* Eds. De la Taille, G.K. Werner, and V. Tarkang. Essex: LongmanGroup Limited, 1986. 175 - 189.

Tande, Dibussi.'Meet Joyce Ashuntantang: A woman on the Go!' *Summit.* (February – April 2008): 9-11.

Tangwa, Godfrey B. 'The Other Side of Anglophone Writing.' *Anglophone Cameroon Writing.* Eds. Nalova Lyonga, Eckhard Breitinger, Bole Butake. Bayreuth: Bayreuth University, 1993. 166 – 171.

2
CRITICAL APPROACHES IN THE CRITICISM OF CAMEROON LITERATURE OF ENGLISH EXPRESSION[1]

Literary criticism is the examination, description, analysis and evaluation of works of literature through the aid of formulated approaches and aesthetic principles. Because it deals with values that are subjective rather than scientific, literary criticism is a controversial discipline. Its speculative nature attracts many views, but the opinions that count are those governed, first, by literary principles before ideological ones. The position defended in this article is that critics of Cameroonian creative works of English expression are free to use whatever critical approaches they find useful in elucidating these imaginative works; however, while doing so, they should endeavour to make their own unique theoretical contribution to the critical debate.

The word 'criticism' in the expression 'literary criticism' should not be taken to mean only a negative attack as in its popular usage; it rather connotes something like a general appreciation involving the positive and negative aspects of a work of literature. All readers of literary works are potential critics. But the real critics are those readers who, after putting aside the book, begin to reflect on, explain and evaluate their experience with it, especially if they commit such a reasoned response onto paper to be shared with other readers and critics.[2] The central role of the critic resides in the fact that his insights, perceptions and judgment on a work of literature can serve as useful feedback to the artist, and invaluable aid for the common reader's fuller enjoyment and understanding of it.

Within the literary critical enterprise, primordial to the efforts of critics is the examination, for their overall technical coherence, of the central elements found in prose fiction, drama and poetry. For fiction we have plot, theme, characterization, setting, point of view, style and tone; for drama we have all of the above plus conflict, and dialogue minus point of view; and for poetry we have sense and sound, feeling, imagery, rhythm and other poetic devices. Therefore any meaningful appreciation of the novel, play or poem must take into account these respective formal elements.

In addition, for an effective evaluation of a work of literature, the critic should bear in mind the purpose or function of literature. This function, for Horace, a critic of old, is twofold. Horace puts it in this way that poets or literary artists are out 'to say things that are simultaneously pleasing and applied to life,'[3] which pronouncement has come to be variously rendered as literature entertains while it instructs, or it pleases while it teaches. We consider both the pleasing and teaching functions of equal importance.

In literary criticism, the pleasing, the entertaining aspect reveals artistry or technique; and the instructional, teaching dimension is embodied in the content or the subject matter. I have summed up these two key aspects of literature in a different work entitled 'Matter and Manner.'[4] As I see it, as far as a valid analysis of any piece of literature is concerned, I simply call its subject matter and themes, matter; and its language and technique or artistry, manner. In my view criticism is not literary criticism which dwells solely on themes and meaning to the exclusion of technique and language, or vice versa. It is my firm conviction that a serious literary analysis must involve both matter and manner, the key ideas that animate my own approach to any imaginative work that I have analysed.[5]

Students of literature would agree with the view that in attempting to appreciate literature many critics have devised what may be dubbed new-fangled theories and approaches to account for literary phenomena. In doing so some have remained essentially in the literary domain, but others have found their way to literary appreciation through related disciplines like linguistics, sociology, psychoanalysis, anthropology and Marxism. Some have gone all out to develop pseudo-scientific and even more complicated theories to explain, in some cases, something less complicated.

From the point of view of methodology many of these academic critics are disappointed with literary criticism as a discipline; for it possesses neither accepted aims nor a standard methodology. That is why, for the sake of a rigorous methodology, some of the critics pass through ancillary disciplines to get to literary criticism. This absence of agreed aims or lack of unity in methodology makes Terry Eagleton call literary criticism a non-subject:

> Any attempt to define literary theory in terms of a distinctive method is doomed to failure. Literary theory is supposed to reflect on the nature of literature and literary criticism. But just think of how many methods are involved in literary criticism. You can discuss the poet's asthmatic childhood, or examine her peculiar use of syntax; you can detect the rustling of silk in the hissing of the s's, explore the phenomenology of reading, relate the literary work to the state of the class-struggle or find out how many copies it sold. These methods have nothing whatsoever of significance in common. In fact they have more in common with other 'disciplines'-linguistics, history, sociology and so on – than they have with each other. Methodologically speaking, literary criticism is a non-subject. If literary theory is a kind of 'metacriticism', a critical reflection on criticism, then it follows that it too is a non-subject (197).

By virtue of their university education and intellectual training at home or abroad, Anglophone Cameroon literary critics have had acquaintance with some of the numerous approaches in literary criticism. So when they apply them to the criticism of works of the imagination by Anglophone Cameroon writers, it is but normal. In the special edition of *Epasa Moto* Vol. 1 N° 3 of October 1996, we have three instances of the application of critical approaches to the criticism of Anglophone Cameroon literary works.

There is Emmanuel Yenshu's sociological approach: 'Towards a Sociology of Cameroon Anglophone Writing,' (105-109). In the sociology of literature more emphasis is placed on the social content of literary works, the social context of the author and the impact of the literary work on its society of origin, and less attention on aspects of style and form. The major question Yenshu's paper sets out to answer is: In what way is Anglophone Cameroon literature a reflection of its society? Or how has this literature been a projection of the problems and pre-occupation of Anglophone Cameroonians?

After a brief review of Anglophone Cameroon literature, Yenshu reckons that in general it has failed to project indigenous Anglophone cultural values even though it has succeeded in reflecting Anglophone concerns. If the literature shows the conflict of cultures, if it pits traditional values against new Christian ones, it nevertheless 'fails to champion traditional values' (107). Yenshu feels that the writers run the 'risk of eclipsing indigenous values in the blind attempt to uphold imperial European values' (*Ibid*). He then concludes that for Anglophone writing to survive it must be ready to re-examine the values it must champion and draw inspiration from the values of its setting.

One has the impression that Yenshu seems to believe that values are fixed, static things that writers can draw on at anytime. But in reality a colonial society, for instance, is one whose values are in a state of flux; the writer who depicts such a society, if he is true to his art and faithful to his material, cannot but show that society to be in a crisis of values. For a society in transition is one with unstable values. Any literature that depicts this instability of values is a true reflection of the existing values of that society. Does not Yenshu's call almost amount to an uncritical embrace of our romantic past that has nothing to do with the hard realities of the present? In this regard a book likely to win Yenshu's approval exists already: it is Ngwa J. Neba's ethnographic novel *The Golden Arrow* (2000), set in an idyllic Bafut community.

As our societies are increasingly becoming urbanized with the inhabitants sloughing off much of their cultural coloration, as cross-cultural experiences become the order of the day, it will be difficult, at least in the future, to produce literature inspired by purely 'indigenous values,' reflecting traditional societies. For now, however, this can still be partially possible, but the future of globalised mankind is not really in favour of virginal humanity.

Then there is Emmanuel Chia's and Charles A. Nama's sociolinguistic appreciation of L. T. Asong's *The Crown of Thorns* (167-176). Drawing on insights by such linguists as Saussure, Barthes, Stubbs and Trudgill, Chia and Nama are able to read *The Crown of Thorns* as a semiological system with a system of structures. That is, from a structural point of view the language systems or levels of discourse in *The Crown of Thorns* divide the novel into a system of structures each with its subtle meaning reflecting the world-views of their authors. The critics then proceed to examine the language systems of the various principal characters of the novel, namely, Ngobefuo, the D.O. and Chief Nchindia.

Ngobefuo's level of discourse is rebellious, diplomatic, reconciliatory, aggressive and confrontational, while the D.O.'s language system is political, manipulative and authoritarian. Chief

Nchindia's level of discourse is one of personal rebellion for his own freedom, and also of guilt (see letter to his brother). In the critics' opinion it is the grouping together of the various language systems used by the major characters of the novel that accounts for the work's artistic and ideological success.

The third approach is Charles A. Nama's 'A Psychoanalytical Reading of Asong's *No Way To Die*' (201 – 210), a psychological novel par excellence, given that much of what is depicted in it takes place in the minds of the major characters. Drawing inspiration from psychoanalytical theorists and using a few psychoanalytical concepts, Nama is able to give a psychoanalytical interpretation of *No Way To Die*. At the center of his analysis is Dennis Nunqam, a severe neurotic suffering from schizophrenia, a mental affliction marked by lack of connection between thoughts, feelings and action, and leading to a split between the self and the body. Consequently, says Nama, such a character possesses two personalities, i.e. the Imaginary self and the Real self.

The causes of Dennis's schizoid condition are poverty, the collapse of his family and his failure to go abroad and study art. The net effect of these on the protagonist is his mental withdrawal from society. This psychotic condition is made worse when his former school mate, Max Essemo, arrogantly arrives on the scene and offers to transform Dennis from 'Nothing' to 'Something', a proposal that deeply wounds Dennis's self-pride, making him even more reclusive. Thanks to his psychoanalytical reading of the novel, Nama is able to account for Dennis's strange behaviour. Had this insight been available to Max, Dennis's benefactor, the latter might have improved relations with his friend, saving himself some money and time.

On his part John N. Nkengasong has published a full-length book on an aspect of literary criticism: *A Stylistic Approach to Literary Appreciation* (1999). Style is the choice and distinctive use of language by a writer in such a way that his individuality is brought out. Stylistics, on the other hand, is the analysis of literary discourse from a linguistic perspective. The stylistic critic concerns himself with the careful analysis of the characteristics of language used in a literary text. He highlights the prominence of certain features and deviant forms present, as well as intuiting their literary relevance.

The stylistic approach means that the study of literature must involve the study of style and its communicative effects. To fully understand the meaning of a poem or prose passage, evaluate the style, and pass judgment on the whole work, the student has to examine and interpret the writer's use of language very carefully. This approach presupposes a mastery of linguistic categories (lexical features, grammatical features, figurative features and phonological features), which a traditional literary critic must also master. Both the traditional critic and the stylistic critic handle more or less the same critical ideas (levels of appreciation). However, the difference is that the stylistic critic has a heightened sensitivity to the characteristics of language. In addition, with the stylistic critic one occasionally hears echoes of the language of a professional linguist: 'semantic significance,' 'collocation', 'decoding', 'deviant forms', and 'linguistic repertoire.'

As with the traditional approach to criticism, the stylistic approach also takes into consideration issues of subject matter, theme and meaning. But in stylistic criticism these issues are arrived at only after style and the communicative effects of the text (47) have been examined, and not like in the traditional approach where one begins first with comprehension then style, and evaluation. Sometimes it is not quite safe to be categorical about these things. The style of a literary discourse is sometimes better apprehended when one has grasped the latter's sense. Occasionally, one works back and forth: from style to meaning and then to style again, or vice versa. However, when Nkengasong comes to practice exercises on the stylistic approach (Part Five) his levels of appreciation, as revealed by his set of questions, follow, in some instances, the pattern of the traditional approach to criticism: subject matter, style and evaluation, his examination of the linguistic characteristics of the text having taken place in pre-task activities mentally only. The justification for this could be that his book is targeted at people still trained for the traditional-approach examination, notably the 'A' Level G.C.E. Examination.

With regard to methodology in oral literature, Alfred Ndi in his article 'Critical Perspectives in African Oral Literature: A Case Study of Nso Elegy' (2000) has proposed an encompassing approach which crosses boundaries of analysis, emphasising the link between sociological, imagistic, paralinguistic and kinesic features. It stresses the creative relationship between social setting, a participating audience, an inspired artist and tonal resources. Using the Nso' Elegy as a case study, the author demonstrates that no single critical approach can viably bring out the way an elegy is fully realized. Any approach that falls short of this requirement, says Ndi, should be considered as a mere dissecting study concerned with a fossilized version of the literature; it surely cannot be seen as a comprehensive investigation into the unedited and living form of the literature in its natural environment.

From these few examples we can say then that critics within the Anglophone Cameroon literary establishment are generally aware of the existence of critical approaches. But, by and large, from evidence contained in published literary journals in Cameroon, many are apparently operating without theoretical awareness, preferring to work, as Terry Eagleton would say, 'by glimmers and hunches, intuitions, and sudden perceptions' (198).

From the lack of sufficient published evidence to show that there is a proliferation of critical approaches in the criticism of Anglophone Cameroon literary works, one can safely conclude that the model of criticism mostly practised within this country is still that of Practical Criticism, popularized in Cameroon through the use of H.L.B. Moody's famous book *Literary Appreciation* (1984) which demands that University or High School students 'pit themselves unaided against anonymous passages of verse and prose' (7). Moody's book, still used in some Anglophone Cameroon High Schools, is itself a descendant of I.A. Richards' work *Practical Criticism* (1929), the book that had a revolutionary effect on English studies throughout the world.

In that book Richards carried out a literary experiment with his undergraduate literature students in which they were presented with anonymous poems (protocols) for appreciation, a practice that until then was totally new. And the results were interesting and revealing, for many of the students missed even the basic meaning of the poems, obliging Richards to make this observation:

> I would like to repeat, with emphasis, that there is no reason to suppose that a higher capacity for reading poetry will be manifested by any similar group anywhere in the world. Sons and daughters of other universities who are tempted to think otherwise may be invited to bring experimental evidence collected under the same conditions (92).

At this point an important question needs to be addressed: Does the fact that there exists, in the world of English studies, a multiplicity of critical approaches, some with very sophisticated formulations,[6] mean that the last word in the critical debate has been said? Does it mean that we in Africa and in Cameroon have nothing to add to the already frightening literature on literary criticism and critical approaches? Do we fold our arms and look for solutions to our critical issues only from the mountain of material already accumulated?

My modest response is no; we should make our own unique contribution to the literary debate. We need to formulate our own critical approaches in the light of the African cultural frame of reference against which our imaginative works are written. According to Abiola Irele, the fact that critical issues have produced so much literature on the subject already 'need not deter us from re-opening these issues for ourselves, for we must come to them with a sharp awareness of our specific context and situation' (102-103). As for Richard Dutton, the discovery by the student of literature that a great deal has been written on the subject down the ages should have, instead, a 'liberating effect' on him/her. 'It should lead us to appreciate that there is always a place for a fresh and honest response to any text or question – however limited in range and inarticulate that response may initially be' (14). Examples of such fresh responses on the African literary scene include Emmanuel Ngara's *Stylistic Criticism and the African Novel* (1982), and *Art and Ideology in the African Novel* (1985); Sunday O. Anozie's *Christopher Okigbo: Creative Rhetoric* (1972); and *Toward the Decolonization of African Literature* (1983) by Chinweizu, Onwuchekwa Jemie and Ihechukwu Madubuike.

If a Zimbabwean, if Nigerians or other African academics can formulate approaches to criticism, why not Cameroonians? It is in this context that we can situate the significance of John N. Nkengasong's *A Stylistic Approach to Literary Appreciation* (1999). This very question has pre-occupied me for a long time; indeed as long ago as 1991, when I came up with a reasoned response to a number of African prose fictional works through the aid of my own formulated Socio-Artistic Approach. I continue to work and improve on this work which has been existing only in a monographic form.

Though first conceived with only the novel in view, this approach can also be applied to the criticism of drama and, to some extent, poetry. I present here only a synopsis of it. The Socio-Artistic Criticism is an eclectic approach which, as its name implies, combines the salient features of the sociological and artistic approaches. It holds that both approaches are needed for a full appreciation and understanding of the African novel, thus placing equal emphasis on the aesthetic and thematic aspects of a work of art.

The sociological aspect of the approach encompasses subject matter, themes, ideological issues raised in the work, relevant cultural and social references that may throw more light on the literary work, and the social significance of the work itself. The artistic dimension concerns the aesthetic qualities of the work in question. This embodies the critical consideration of the novelistic, dramatic or poetic features as well as the devices or technique, and linguistic choices the writer has made use of to achieve technical coherence.

To assess the artistic success as well as the social relevance of a novel, the approach makes use of four evaluation criteria: Effectiveness of Technique, Artistic Truthfulness, Readability, and Social Significance. The monograph consists of two parts, the theoretical and the practical. Part one, the theoretical section, deals with the definition, discussion of key concepts and the elaboration of the theory of criticism. Part two is the practical application of the theory to eight selected novels by five African novelists, with a chapter devoted to each novelist. The novelists are: Ayi Kwei Armah of Ghana; Chinua Achebe, and Elechi Amadi of Nigeria; L.T. Asong of Cameroon, and Ngugi wa Thiong'o of Kenya.

After everything, what one would like to suggest to fellow critics of Anglophone Cameroon creative works, and other aspirants to the critical enterprise is that they are welcome to devise whatever critical approaches they feel are suitable for the apprehension of these works. But they should endeavour to define and simplify the terms of their approaches, remembering that, as critics, their role is to shed some light on aspects of literary art that might have eluded other readers; their effort is to elucidate, rather than complicate, literary phenomenon. They should not devise an alchemical equation which, instead of turning base metal into gold, transforms gold into wood ash. They have no right to put off readers from a good book because of their tedious, obscure jargon.

The criticism of a work of literature should include description, analysis, interpretation and evaluation. An approach with any claim to adequacy must include these basic elements. Now, with regard to evaluation, the point is worth making that critics should state clearly their evaluation criteria, the yardstick for judging the work they want to evaluate.

No single critical approach is valid for all works. No matter its claims and supposed validity one should not carry a single approach blindly to a work of art; it is rather the work that calls forth the type of approach suitable for its apprehension, depending on the particular character of its social environment as well as its 'authorial and aesthetic ideology' (Ngara: 108). For example, an approach that best suits L.T. Asong's *A Legend of the Dead* or *Stranger in His Homeland* may need some modification when applied to *No Way To Die* or vice-versa; and even a more serious adjustment before being applied to Bate Besong's *The Most Cruel Death of the Talkative Zombie, Beasts of No Nation,* and *Requiem For the Last Kaiser,* or John N. Nkengasong's *Black Caps and Red Feathers*. Any approach to the works of Bate Besong and Nkengasong would have to first recognize and accommodate the fact that these are playwrights influenced by a unique literary convention and stylistic stances (modernism). Therefore, to make sense of their plays, the standards used in evaluating them should not be criteria pertinent to the traditional plays of Epie Ngome or Bole Butake, for example, but rather those belonging to the Theatre of the Absurd.

When all has been said and done, an imaginative work, in its unique composition and structure of its verbal expressions, will dictate, to some extent, the nature of the critical tools or aspects of critical approaches appropriate for its apprehension.

The critic's tools are his weapons at different times; and in hunting imagery, a weapon presupposes a hunter on the one hand, and the game to be killed on the other. The weapon may range from a broomstick to an automatic riffle, and the game from a fly to an elephant.

Now, when a fly presents itself, the hunter uses a broomstick to bring it down; when a rat shows up, he uses a stick; when a bird comes his way, a catapult is enough. In the same way, a gun is appropriate for an antelope and an automatic rifle for an elephant. Let the weapon match the animal. It makes no sense to face the elephant with a broomstick, nor with a rifle to bring down a fly.

Before we conclude this paper, a word or two regarding the type of critical attitude appropriate for us Cameroon Anglophone critics is in order. Critics should master the works they set out to criticize. Deep learning ought to foster more humility without which a critic might be more immodest and recklessly presumptuous, in which case he may well be rushing in where angels fear to tread and, in the process, becoming the only fool. For imaginative creators are often jealous of their works. We should remember that as we go about criticising and, sometimes, destroying their works, in the eyes of some, many of us critics are failed creative writers who, to paraphrase Alexander Pope, having failed to woo the mistress, have settled for the inferior maid, in the same way as inferior chemists arrogate to themselves the prerogatives of medical doctors.[7]

In his critical effort, the critic should stick to the central literary analysis without ignoring whatever ideological implications there may be in the work, support or buttress his opinions with evidence from the text, and avoid impressionistic generalizations. When in doubt, leave it out; when a critic is tempted to make an observation he cannot justify from the text, he should leave it out.

A critic must be intellectually honest; if he is moved emotionally or intellectually by a work, he should say so despite ideological differences that may lie between him and the creative writer. As critics, we should all avoid the fault of which D. H. Lawrence accuses Macaulay, an otherwise brilliant scholar:

> A man like Macaulay, brilliant as he is, is unsatisfactory, because he is not honest. He is emotionally very alive, but he juggles his feelings... A critic must be emotionally alive in every fibre, intellectually capable and skillful in essential logic, and then morally very honest[8].

A good critic should feel free to quarrel with the infelicity or the clumsiness of an expression, with the inconclusive or illogical conclusion, with unequally matched forces in a conflict,[9] with the lack of artistic truthfulness, with the absence of symmetry or sense of balance and proportion, but he should not insult the author. If the critic abandons the work for the author, he will be creating extra-artistic controversies beyond the realm of artistic criticism. Some creative writers are jealous of their works and sensitive of critical comments they may perceive as innuendoes on their person.

Once Alexander Pope got so offended by the severe criticism of his *Shakespeare* (1725) by Lewis Theobald that, in revenge, he crowned Theobald the king of dunces in an earlier version of his poetic work *The Dunciad (*1728).[10] About a decade ago, in our own country, a comment by Mejame Njikang on Bate Besong's poetry so upset the poet that the critic became the subject of the poet's scathing articles in one of our popular newspapers.[11] When he felt insulted, Sankie Maimo, the playwright, devoted a whole 31-page booklet to the vitriolic attack of a critic, Nkemngong Nkengasong, for his unkind observations on Maimo's *Succession in Sarkov* (1986).[12]

By citing these examples we are not in any way endorsing the writers' defence of their works. A poorly executed work is a bad work of art; no amount of authorial defence can make it better. A solid work of art is its own best defence and needs no authorial armoury. As I see it, self-defence by authors would be unnecessary, or much less so, if critics would endeavour to be as honest, fair, decent and objective as possible. A critic should point out artistic flaws in a work of art without resorting to nastiness at the personal level. But, above all, he should first try to pick out what he finds to be the author's forte. It is rare to find a writer who would take the pains to publish a work worth criticising without possessing a single good thing to be said about his work or style, no matter how many bad ones there are.

Therefore, where there is felicity of expression, balance and proportion in the artistic composition, where there is artistic truthfulness, where, indeed, there are these and many more positive aspects, he should say so without mincing words; he should say so honestly and generously. Genuine critics, in this regard, should be unstinting in their praise.

A good critic should take no offence at insignificant details or faults, nor should he judge a work, as Pope says, by the part but by the whole.[13] Judge a work by the total impact it makes on you, incidental flaws notwithstanding. There is no perfect work of art; there has never been any, nor, one can be sure, will there ever be one. There is no work that has inspired universal consensus for the simple reason that critics and scholars will always disagree on one thing or the other, given their peculiar cultural or ideological scheme of reference.

There are, however, works which, despite incidental lapses, possess more positive and enduring aspects that have helped to move readers and critics emotionally and intellectually; there are artistic creations that, from the point of view of execution, are full, complete and beautiful, works that contain noble ideas as well as beauty of expression. So, when a critic finds a literary work that is full, complete and beautiful, one containing a fine balance between matter and manner, he should count it a successful work of art, in spite of minor weaknesses.

The quantity and quality of Anglophone Cameroon creative writing is on the rise, and there is the need on the part of Anglophone critics of these works to school themselves and hone their tools for the task that is inevitably theirs. And this role is not merely limited to an interpretation of the imaginative works, but one that must be seen to include a collaboration 'with the writer in the social dialogue which every work initiates'; in that way literary criticism 'gives articulated resonance to the writer's intuitions so that these acquire the force of public communication.'[14] Some have asserted that the future of Cameroon literature is Anglophone, a hypothesis yet to be confirmed or disconfirmed. In any case, the time has come for us to make and not to mar that literature; the moment has come for us, critics and creators, to set the pace for what tomorrow may well be the great Anglophone Cameroon literary tradition.

End Notes
1. This paper was first presented at a language and literature seminar organized by the English Department of the University of Buea in January 2001.
2. James H. Pickering and Jeffrey D. Hoeper, *Literature* 3.
3. Horace, *The Art of Poetry*, verse translation by Burton Raffel. New York: State U. of New York, 1974, 57
4. Shadrach A. Ambanasom, 'Matter and Manner' (Monograph). Bamenda: Unique Printers, 1990.
5. See my book *The Radical Romantics: An Introduction,* published by Presses Universitaires de Yaoundé, 2001 and *Socio-Artistic Criticism of the African Novel*: Bamenda : Unique Printers, 1991.
6. See, for example, Terry Eagleton's brilliant review of some of the approaches in his book *Literary Theory: An Introduction*. Minnesota: University of Minnesota Press, 1984.

7. Alexander Pope, *An Essay on Criticism* in M. H. Abrams (Gen. Ed.) *The Norton Anthology of English Literature* Vol. 1, 2197.
8. As quoted in H. Coombes *Literature and Criticism* 8.
9. See Bernard Fonlon's *The Genuine Intellectual* 91-92.
10. See *Pope: Poetry and Prose* (Introduced by H.V.D. Dyson) xi-xii
11. See *Cameroon Post* N° 59 of February 27, 1991, 8.
12. Sankie Maimo, *Sankie's Literary Bravura* (A Reply to a Critic) Yaounde : Sopecam, 1984.
13. In M. H. Abrams 2200
14. Abiola Irele, 'Literary Criticism in the Nigerian Context,' in Yemi Ogunbiyi (ed.) *Perspectives on Nigerian Literature 1700 to the Present* Volume One 1988 105.

Works Cited

Ambanasom, Shadrach A. *Matter and Manner: Essays on African Literature* (Monograph) Bamenda: Unique Printers, 1990.

_____. *Socio-Artistic Criticism of the African Novel*. (Monograph) Bamenda: Unique Printers, 1991.

_____. *The Radical Romantics: An Introduction*. Yaoundé: Presses Universitaires de Yaoundé, 2001.

Besong, Bate. 'Mejame Njikang Who? Query To An Ostentatious Iguana'. *Cameroon Post* No 59, 1991 8.

Chia, Emmanuel and Charles Atangana Nama. 'A Sociolinguistic Appreciation of Asong's *The Crown of Thorns*' *EPASA MOTO* Volume I Number 3, 1996 167-176.

Coombes, H. *Literature and Criticism*. Harmondsworth Middlesex: Chatto & Windus, 1953.

Dutton, Richard. *An Introduction To Literary Criticism*. Essex: Longman York Press, 1984.

Dyson, H.V.D. (ed.) *Pope: Poetry and Prose*. London: Oxford University Press, 1971.

Eagleton, Terry. *Literary Theory: An Introduction*. Minnesota: University of Minnesota Press, Minneapolis, 1984.

Fonlon, Bernard. *The Genuine Intellectual*. Yaoundé: Buma Kor, 1978.

Horace. *The Art of Poetry*. Verse trans. Burton Raffel. New York: State University of New York, 1975.

Irele, Abiola. 'Literary Criticism in the Nigerian Context' in Yemi Ogunbiyi (ed.). *Perspectives on Nigerian Literature 1700 to* the Present. Volume One pp. 93-105 Lagos: Guardian Books of Nigeria Limited, 1988.

Maimo, Sankie. *'Sankie's Literary Bravura.* Yaoundé: SOPECAM, 1984.

Moody, H.L.B. *Literary Appreciation.* Essex: Longman, 1984.

Nama, Charles Atangana. 'A Psychoanalytical Reading of Linus Asong's *No Way To Die*'. *EPASA MOTO* Volume I Number 3, 1996 201-210.

Ndi, Alfred Akongnyuy. 'Critical Perspectives in African Oral Literature: A Case Study of Nso, Elegy,' *Voices: The Wisconsin Review of African Literatures,* 2000 69-67.

Neba, Ngwa J. *The Golden Arrow Yaoundé:* The Bookhouse Publication, 2000.

Ngara, Emmanuel. *Art and Ideology in the African Novel.* London: Heinemann, 1985.

Nkengasong, N. John. *A Stylistic Approach to Literary Appreciation.* Bamenda: Patron Publishing House, 1999.

Pickering, J. H. and Hoeper, J. D. *Literature.* New York, N.Y.: Macmillan Publishing Co., 1986.

Pope, Alexander. 'An Essay on Criticism' in M.H. Abrams (Gen. ed.) *The Norton Anthology of English Literature.* Fifth Edition. Volume I, pp. 2214-2232. New York/London: Norton, 1986.

Richards, I. A. *Practical Criticism.* San Diego, New York, London: Harcourt Brace, 1929.

Yenshu, Emmanuel. 'Literature in Anglophone Cameroon and the African Context: Towards A Sociology of Cameroon Anglophone Writing'. *EPASA MOTO* Volume I number 3, 1996 105-109.

3
CAMEROONIAN CREATIVE WRITERS AND THE LANGUAGE PROBLEM

Summary

For over three decades now the issue of writing African Literature in non-African languages has been a controversial one. Cameroonian creative writers of international standing are writing exclusively in either English or French. Unlike some critics who feel that there ought to be no creative African writing in non- African (non-Cameroonian) languages, the author of this article holds the view that critics should not be too hard and too swift in passing judgment on creative writers competent only in a European medium of expression.

These writers, brought up within a colonial or neo-colonial educational set-up, had mastery of only a colonial language, English or French, their only mother of invention. During this time no Cameroonian language had been fully developed to be a credible tool for sustained imaginative writing. Consequently, the author feels that the present Cameroonian creative writers should continue to write in English or French, but that they should strive to write well and effectively, placing the European medium of expression at the service of the Cameroonian vision.

For this to be effectively done, these imaginative writers must study and master the techniques of narrative and poetic eloquence found in our oral tradition so as to incorporate them into their creative works to give them a Cameroonian flavour, coloration and identity as some Anglophone Cameroonian writers are already doing. The most proper thing is, of course, for true Cameroonian literature to be elaborated in Cameroonian national languages, a reality that can only be achieved through a vigorous and well-guided language policy by the government of the Republic of Cameroon, a policy that, in the long term, will be aimed at gradually replacing English and French as mediums of instruction across the curriculum, with well chosen Cameroonian languages.

Everything being equal, creative writing will then be done in Cameroonian languages. In this way the literatures of the various nationalities within Cameroon will reveal the country's diverse national identities. When grouped under the national literary umbrella, these literatures will constitute the truly Cameroonian literature because it draws sustenance from our authentic oral tradition, and is elaborated in our truly national languages. Only then can we really relate to it with both our heart and soul, because it derives, in a fundamental sense, from our very roots, our soil.

Introduction

The Republic of Cameroon, like many other African countries, is made up of many ethnic groups, including the Bamilikes, Betis, Bassas, Bakweris, Bayangis, Widikums, Ngembas, Tikaris and Fulanis. Each of these groups has a language or languages, a literature, even if the latter exists only at the oral level, and a culture sufficiently different from one another to make for its unique identity. Together with their different languages the various groups represent the diverse colourful, national identities of Cameroon. But superimposed upon the many Cameroonian home or local languages (henceforth to be referred to as national languages) are English and French, both of them languages of the erstwhile colonial masters. This then is the complex linguistic context within which the Cameroonian creative writers operate.

In what language or languages are these writers writing? What is the implication of elaborating their imaginative, cultural experiences, ostensibly for local consumption, in an alien medium of expression? Faced with the European languages, what is the fate of the national languages and the literatures they are capable of sustaining? Or what does it mean for these languages to develop in the shadow of European languages? Finally, what does it mean, for the sensibilities and identity of Cameroonians, to have their national languages develop their full capacities as well as the written literature that they are able to carry?

The aim of this paper is to attempt to shed some light on these and other questions linked to literary production and, the issue of language and national identities within the Cameroonian context. Let us, however, first briefly look at how language, literature and culture are related.

The human language is a system of communication between one man and another through the medium of the spoken or written word. Literature, on the other hand, is imaginative language, spoken or written, that calls attention to itself owing to its peculiar beauty. Literary production takes place within language, or language causes literature to be what it is. In other words language is the basic formal material out of which literature is made. Literature is unthinkable without language, and language used in a special way may become literature.

Linguistic categories - nouns, verbs, adjectives, adverbs, prepositions, pronouns, articles, conjunctions, etc., — are the basic formal material at the disposal of the literary artist. In the process of creation the creative writer avails himself of units of linguistic structures like words, phrases, clauses and sentences to explore and develop his subject matter; to express beautifully the ideas, thoughts, feelings and emotions of his fictional characters. Common to both language and literature is the act of communication; but while the former communicates objective knowledge, the latter communicates experiential knowledge.

As I see it, nouns, verbs, adverbs, adjectives, pronouns, etc., - the basic linguistic material out of which literature is made - when carefully chosen, ordered and arranged in a special way confer a particular character to a literary piece in the same way that iron rods, stones, marble, sand, cement and wood, etc, — the basic material out of which a mansion is erected - when well selected, chiselled, chipped, arranged and put together, give an edifice a unique architectural aspect.

Now we look at the relationships between language and culture, and then literature and culture. Culture is the totality of behaviour patterns, arts, beliefs, institutions, and products of human effort and thought that distinguish one community of people from another (West, 1975:171). These characteristics are transmitted from one generation to another through the crucial medium of language.

Generally, where there is a culture you have a language, and where there is a language, you have a culture. Both are thus inextricably linked to each other. And, except in situations of minimal foreign language communication to maintain basic trade contact, where the culture behind the trade language is less obvious, language cannot exist without culture.

Any language possesses a dual character in the sense that it is both a means of communication and a carrier of culture (Ngugi, 1986:13). Ngugi further affirms that language as communication and as culture are products of each other in that communication creates culture, and culture is a means of communication (Ngugi, 15-16). So when we talk of communication creating culture and culture as a means of communication we are talking of, language and literature creating culture, and of culture being the means of spreading language and literature. For, as we have established above, the act of communication is common to both language and literature, differing only in degree.

'Language carries culture and culture carries, particularly through orature and literature, the entire body of values by which we come to perceive ourselves and our place in the world' (Ngugi, 16). Thus a whole value system is kept alive, and transmitted from one generation to another through oral and written literature. In other words oral and written literatures are transmitters of cultural values. Literature is, therefore, a carrier of culture, and culture, a means of spreading literature.

In a non-colonial or non-neo-colonial society where no foreign language has been imposed on local ones, where there is a single language spoken by the community from the family through the immediate environment to the school, there is total linguistic harmony from oral to written literature. In such an ideal linguistic situation the language the child speaks in the family, the language he speaks at recreation time, and the language he speaks and writes in at school are one and the same language. In short his home language and his language of conceptualization are one and the same language.

He learns and performs oral literature at home, and studies written literature at school in one and the same language. The written literature is constantly enriched and revitalized by the oral; there is thus a constant flow from the one into the other. Tradition and continuity are consequently ensured, thanks to the one continuous 'stream of imaginative expression' (Irele, 1981:46).

Now, because the written literature is elaborated in images and symbols familiar to the child, because it draws on a rich oral tradition the child has already been exposed to, the child studying his written literature can afford to enter it with his body and soul, and justifiably lay claim to it because it genuinely belongs to him. Learning for him, far from a rarefied, intellectual experience, takes the dimension of an 'emotionally felt experience' (Ngugi, 17).

Had the African continent not been colonized by European powers, the above ideal linguistic situation would probably have prevailed in many African countries. Alas colonialism did disrupt the linguistic situation, leading to the fact that African languages were intentionally undervalued while the language of the colonial power was elevated to higher ground. The European language became the language the colonial subject had to master to make it within the colonial set-up. It became the language of education, thinking and conceptualization; in short, the language of success.

In most cases that language was either English or French. But in the unique historical situation of Cameroon it was both English and French, that is, English for Anglophone Cameroonians, and French for Francophone Cameroonians. For the Cameroonian colonial or post-colonial subjects, the language of success was, and continues to be, either English or French, or both.

The Cameroonian child speaks one language at home, and a different one at school. There is thus a rift between the language at home and that of conceptualization at school. At home he is exposed to his oral literature with all its rich cultural values, but at school to written literature in a European medium of expression, often with a European frame of reference. It is difficult for him to relate to the written literature in a way that is full and complete unless he is quite versed with its European literary echoes and overtones.

There does not seem to be a viable language policy in Cameroon with serious thought given to the national languages. This much is clear from Gisele Tchoungi's article (Tchoungui, 1983:114). Therefore, as far as Cameroon is concerned, and from the look of things, English and French will still hold sway for some time to come. With English and French thus on the pedestal while our national languages languish in their shadows, with the European mediums of expression bestriding the Cameroonian landscape like a colossus while our national languages peep fearfully from under their huge legs in search of dishonourable roles for themselves. It would appear Cameroon has quietly succumbed to Chinua Achebe's 'fatalistic logic of the unassailable position of English [and French] in our literature ...' (Achebe, 1975:XIV)

All Cameroonian creative writers of international standing write exclusively in either English or French, whether we are talking of Mongo Beti, Ferdinand Oyono, Calixte Beyala, Were Were Liking, or Francis Bebey, to cite but these few from the Francophone side, or of Kenjo Jumbam, L. T. Asong, Bate Besong, Bole Butake, Babila Mutia or Joseph Ngonwikwo to cite but these from the Anglophone sector. The exception is Bongasu Kishani. These Cameroonian writers do not use English or French out of choice. There has been no choice for them. Given the colonial and post-colonial linguistic situation, the present-day Francophone Cameroonian creative writer has no other language but French; and the present-day Anglophone Cameroonian creative writer no other language but English to write in. Each has simply inherited a colonial language: English or French. For them then choice has not been the question; the European medium of expression has been the only mother of invention.

From the day Obi Wali, the Nigerian critic, wrote his passionate article on the futility and sterility of writing African literature in non-African languages close to 40 years ago, discussions of the language question in African literature have often been marked by spirited debate. While most critics are unanimous that African literature should be written in African languages, there is no agreement as far as writing in non-African languages is concerned. On the one hand Obi Wali and the later Ngugi wa Thiong'o would go for total writing in African languages. On the other hand, scholars like Abiola Irele, Chinua Achebe, Chinweizu, Onwuchekwa Jemie, and Ikechukwu Madubuike, while endorsing writing in African languages by those who have mastered them, would give a chance to African writers competent only in European languages, provided they make effective use of techniques of eloquence found in African orature.

A few years ago Teddy Ako's review of *WEKA NO I* in one of our English language local newspapers drew spirited reactions from Emmanuel Doh and Bole Butake on the issue of creative writing in non-African (non-Cameroonian) languages. My advice to critics and advocates of creative writing in our national languages is this: They should not be too hard and too swift in passing judgment on literary artists employing a European medium of expression because, as we have said above, there was no alternative language available to them. Besides, during the colonial time only a few Cameroonian languages had a well-developed alphabet to sustain the translation of the Bible into them, an enterprise carried out mostly by missionaries. Since independence the Bible has been translated into more Cameroonian languages, thanks to the effort of scholars of the Summer Institute of Linguistics (SIL).

Some Cameroonian languages like Lamnso, Wimbum, Mungaka, Kom, etc., have a rudimentary written literature in the form of proverbs, tales, legends, or poems, etc., and although these and other Cameroonian languages are capable of sustaining a full-fledged literature, the truth is that the literature is yet to develop. It is still in its infancy.

We certainly admire the circumstances that worked in favour of the young Ngugi wa Thiong'o who wrote a composition in his mother tongue, Gikuyu, in Class Four in the primary school in 1952, and for which he received a standing ovation (Ngugi, 11). Many of us have not been blessed with such happy circumstances. Some of us do not even speak our own mother tongues very fluently, much less writing an excellent composition in them, for all our advanced Western degrees.

Critics should be modest in their attack on creative writers not writing in Cameroonian languages because if we take a hard, critical look at this issue, many of us would be guilty, creative writers and critics alike; for the critic does his criticism of the literary artist's choice of a European language in the very language itself. So judge not that ye be not judged, as the Bible says.

Having said this, do I appear to be advocating writing in non-Cameroonian languages and by that act condemning writing in Cameroonian language? Certainly not. I would like to be understood as suggesting that since many creative writers now do not master their national languages sufficiently enough to be able to carry out serious and sustained creative writing in them; since their upbringing, training and education have prepared them for mastery of only the European languages; since there has been no rigorous language planning policy on the part of the Cameroon government to effectively promote the teaching of our national languages in schools; since creative writers are people with a limited life span and cannot therefore go on writing indefinitely, those of them who have opted to write in either English or French should go on. But they should write well and effectively; they should place the European language at the service of the Cameroonian imagination; or they should re-appropriate the English or French language to express the Cameroonian vision.

For this to be effectively done these imaginative writers must study and master the techniques of narrative and poetic eloquence found in our oral tradition, our orature, (Chinweizu *et al*, 1983:274-285). Scholars and researchers collecting, transcribing, translating or analyzing African orature have established elements integral to it

(Ambanasom, 1993:118). Among many of the features are proverbs, invocation or prayers, parallel phrases, repetition, onomatopoeia, alliteration, songs, chants, praise names, choral responses, riddles, etc. So, the creative writers using either English or French as a medium of imaginative expression have to make a conscious effort to go for these oral features of narrative and poetic eloquence, incorporating them into their imaginative works to give them a Cameroonian flavour, coloration and identity.

Some Anglophone Cameroonian writers, drawing on the rich African heritage encompassing African thought, experience, folklore, myth, custom and religion, have given their work a flavour and coloration essentially Cameroonian. They include L.T. Asong, Kenjo Jumbam, Bole Butake, Bongasu Kishani, Fale Wache and Nol Alembong. For example, the way they live, talk, behave, and react to intrusive stimuli in their environment; the language they use, their idiom, their proverbs, images and symbols, as they communicate with one another; the manner they face opposing negative forces and expose their basic beliefs and values, Asong's characters in his trilogy, *How A People Die* (1998), reveal a unique way of life and a view of the world, as seen through the eyes of the bulwarks of tradition like Ngobefuo, Achiebefuo, Ndenwontio, Ngangabe, etc., essentially African (Cameroonian). This shows us the way traditional life in areas of Lebialem could be or used to be.

Similarly, Bongasu Kishani in *Konglanjo* (1988), and Bole Butake in *And Palm-Wine Will Flow* (1986) draw on the inexhaustible Cameroonian pool of oral tradition to enrich their imaginative work. They incorporate invocation, proverbs, apostrophe, incantation, myth and ritual. The world they depict (Nso and Noni communities, respectively) is basically traditional, one wherein the old spiritual order is still very much in place. The ancestors, the living and the unborn are part of the cyclic trinity, with the revered ancestors and deities still exerting tremendous force on the living, acting as their guardians and protectors. The living worship them and perform rituals for them; sacrifices and libations become a communication link that keeps the living, the dead and the unborn in common. The idiom of their fictional characters is replete with proverbs, images and symbols from their local flora and fauna.

Despite the obvious linguistic difficulties they have to surmount, these writers tell their stories well, an indication that our best imaginative writers, even when employing a foreign medium of expression make use of oral techniques of narrative and poetic eloquence and give us the feel that not all that is African (Cameroonian) is lost; that a great deal still comes across to us as essentially African; that a European medium of expression can still be reasonably pounded, kneaded, and moulded to take on subtle African shapes and exude subtle African flavours without losing much of its essence.

Yet the bulk of this literature in European languages is not accessible to most Cameroonians owing to the language problem. So, in spite of their relative success, the truth remains that our writers using a European language are in search of elements of poetic eloquence which are there in our national languages, readily available to those with mastery of any of these languages. In this regard the laudable examples of two East African writers, Okot p'Bitek and Ngugi wa Thiong'o, writing in both their national languages and English are worth citing. Writing initially in their home languages and using traditional modes of expression before translating their works later on into English, these two East African authors produced imaginative works that made them instantly popular.

Upon the publication of *Song of Lawino*, Okot p'Bitek became an instant celebrity. This long satirical poem, light-hearted in tone and dedicated to the defence of the African way of life, inspired spontaneous enthusiasm and continues to draw accolades for its author; this is an unusual phenomenon, indeed, for a poem because rarely do we find people becoming crazy with poetry reading as we do with those showing great interest in stories and novels. Similarly, within Kenya Ngugi wa Thiong'o's novel *Caitaani Mutharabaini* (*Devil On the Cross*), a critical and satirical examination of present day Kenya under the relentless grip of capitalistic, neo-colonial forces, was, upon publication, received with even greater enthusiasm. Written in Gikuyu, the novel was read everywhere. 'It was read in families. A family would get together every evening and one of their literate members would read it for them. Workers would also gather in groups, particularly during the lunch break, and they would get one of them to read the book. It was read in buses; it was read in taxis; it was read in public bars (Ngugi, 1986:83).

These imitable examples serve to illustrate the advantage of writing in a national language for a national audience. By so doing, the two authors have eliminated the problem of the contradiction between their medium and audience. There is total harmony between the language spoken in the family and the language of the imaginative works. In other words the language of their family, the language of their immediate environment, and the language of their creative work are one and the same language! Total linguistic harmony. Herein partly lies the secret of the popularity of these East African writers.

If we do not enjoy this linguistic harmony in Cameroon, if, between the family and the school, we suffer instead from a linguistic cleavage, this situation ought not to persist in the future. Our children's children should not grow up with the same feeling of alienation from our own national languages that colonialism or neo-colonialism openly or subtly induced in us.

The government of the Republic of Cameroon should embark on a more vigorous, and a well-guided language policy with a view to effectively integrating our national languages into the educational system. To do this, it is not necessary, nor is it even possible now, to radically root out English and French from the school system. It will not be realistic, given the tremendous role they have played in the education of the bulk of literate Cameroonians today. To begin with, both languages should be maintained, but the point of their introduction into the school system should be re-examined and redefined in relation to the initial introduction of the national languages into the educational system.

That is, if the national language is the medium of instruction in the first three years of the primary school, for example, the European language could be introduced in the fourth year or Class Four, etc. Given the multiplicity of our national languages, the formula for the selection of which national languages to teach could be based on the regional, provincial or divisional wide-spread nature or popularity of such a language, or the potential for it to reach out to more people. In this way English and French could gradually be phased out from the primary school system but maintained only at the secondary and university levels.

The same phasing-out logic will eventually liberate the secondary school system of the European medium of instruction while English and French will be studied as other academic subjects and no longer the omnipresent medium of instruction across the curriculum. In the future, for the purpose of national integration and cohesion, and based on its potential for teachability and rapid spreading, one of the national languages taught in the schools will be chosen to be the official language of administration and government business.

Everything being equal, one can foresee a situation where our orature will hold sway in the family, will be reinforced in the primary school in written form, while written literature in our national languages will be strengthened and broadened in the secondary school. At the level of the university we can envisage research to be carried out on our literature in our national languages.

With sufficient mastery of our national languages and the literatures they can sustain, a new generation of Cameroonian creative writers will produce imaginative works in these languages. Given the harmony that will be between the language of creativity and that of the immediate audience; and in view of the fact that the written literature will be constantly fed and revitalized by our rich pool of oral tradition, our new breed of creative writers will draw easily and extensively on our inexhaustible oral tradition to articulate artistically their feelings and experiences of the new Cameroon. They will be able to employ images, symbols, and sounds that make sense to us that we can understand.

These Cameroonian creative writers of the future will be imbued with confidence in themselves. Far from being apologetic when confronted with foreign languages and literatures, they will be proud in that they are, first of all, masters of theirs. They will therefore approach foreign languages and literatures from a position of strength. And when they explore them it will be to benefit from the scope of their humanistic values. The ideal Cameroonian writers of the future will not bring to the study of foreign languages and literatures the usual baggage of inferiority complex and sense of guilt that is the daily lot of many of us today.

Eventually the Cameroonian tradition of English/French bilingualism will occasionally produce creative writers capable of writing in both a national language, and an international one as Okot p'Bitek and Ngugi wa Thiongo'o have done in their national languages and English. These future bilingual creative writers will be the people with a genuine choice of language to write in: either a national or an international one. And in the case where a writer chooses to write in English or French, he will, to quote Abiola Irele, 'bring to his expression in that language the vitality of an imaginative consciousness nurtured within the climate of his original culture and the language which is its natural vehicle' (Irele, 1981:61).

Hopefully, the present tradition of translation already implanted in the country thanks to English/French bilingualism, will go beyond these two languages to include translation of national languages. Some of the creative works will then be translated from one national language into another for a wider national audience, and then into English, French, or both, for a wider international audience.

In this way the literatures of the various nationalities within Cameroon will reveal the country's diverse national identities. When grouped under the national literary umbrella, these literatures will constitute what will be truly called Cameroonian literature. Only then can we lay intimate claim to it; it is only then that we can really relate to it with both our heart and soul because it derives, in a fundamental sense, from our very roots, our soil. Such a literature truly becomes ours because it draws sustenance from our authentic oral tradition, and is elaborated in our truly national languages.

Some critics may view what I have outlined here as too visionary, but in my view it is not impossible. We ought to exercise the right to dream great dreams: to produce our authentic literature in our national languages. If we dream, we may fail; but if we do not dream, we will surely fail. So, let us exercise the right to dream great dreams.

Works Cited

Achebe, Chinua. *Morning Yet On Creation Day*. London: Heinemann, 1975.

Ambanasom, S. A. 'The Orality of the works of Four Anglophone Writers: Linus Asong, Bole Butake, Bangasu Kishani, Fale Wache' in Nalova Lyonga, Eckhard Breitinger, Bole Butake (eds. 1993) *Anglophone Cameroon Writing* Bayreuth: Bayreuth University, 1993.

Chinweizu; Jemie, O; Madubuike, I. *Toward The Decolonization of African Literature*. Washington D.C: Howard University Press, 1983.

Irele, Abiola. *The African Experience in Literature and Ideology*. London: Heinemann, 1981.

Ngugi Wa Thiong'o. *Decolonising The Mind: The Politics of Language in Africa Literature.* London: James Curry Ltd, 1986.

Tchoungui, Gisele. 'Focus On Cameroon: Its Relationship to Education' in Edna L. Koenig, Emmanuel Chia, John Povey (eds. 1983) *A Sociolinguistic Profile Of Urban Centres in Cameroon* Los Angeles: Crossroads Press, 1983.

West, Fred. *The Way of Language: An Introduction.* New York: Harcourt Brace, 1975.

4
THE AFRICAN WRITER AND THE PRESERVATION OF CULTURAL VALUES

What are cultural values and why should they be preserved? By the way, what type of African writer are we talking about and how should he go about preserving cultural values? In brief, dear readers, these are some of the questions I will attempt to discuss in this article. And without any delay, I would like to first define the word "Culture." You can take my word for it that I do not wish to take you through many and, at times, reductive definitions of the word Culture.

At the risk of oversimplification, I will just cut asunder the Gordian knot by saying that culture relates to that quality that distinguishes a whole way of life of a particular group of people from that of another group of people; that is, culture, in relation to a unique group of people, embodies the distinctive way they think, feel, behave, dress and view the world. Out of these people's way of life certain principles, certain qualities, certain things emerge which they cherish, they hold dear, they value. Now, these things, these qualities, these principles that they value, cherish, and hold dear are indubitably what we call cultural values, qualities that are intrinsically valuable and desirable.

These values may be aesthetic, humane, moral or religious. We all love a well-told story or a beautiful tale; we all appreciate an enlightening proverb, an intriguing riddle, an inspiring legend; everybody is excited at soul-elevating drumbeats, well-blended musical sounds or full-throated harmonious voices. These are the things we cherish because they give us mental and emotional pleasure, intellectual and emotional stimulation. Some include respect for the elders, the young and the infirm; others embody decency towards strangers, family members, and neighbours; some include decorum towards traditional as well as religious authorities; others embody concern and thoughtfulness for one another; yes, they comprise the spirit of solidarity, the spirit of sharing, indeed the communal spirit.

These are the things we cherish for the dignity and respectability they give man in his day to day relationship with his fellowmen. These values must be preserved because of the basic sanity of human behaviour that they make possible; they must be safeguarded because without them boundless brutality, ruthlessness, darkness or, indeed, chaos would be unleashed onto the world; they must be perpetuated so that we can bequeath to our children and their children's children a spiritual habitation in a world that is increasingly becoming impersonal. Ours is a world that is progressively producing soulless individuals, too much occupied with getting and spending, a world wherein humane values are counting for little and for less. In short, these values must be preserved to ensure our basic African cultural continuity.

As I see it, writers with an interest in preserving cultural values fall into two broad categories. The one deals with conceptual and informative knowledge; the other is concerned with experiential and creative knowledge. Their methods are radically different in that the former handles ideas and concepts in an obvious, straight-forward manner; the latter handles ideas and concepts in a subtle, artistic fashion. The first category may include anthropologists, sociologists, and formal essayists; the second generally includes novelists, playwrights and poets. But I do not intend to examine both groups of writers in detail. I will limit myself to the creative writers.

To the extent that our creative writers are writing in foreign languages instead of in our home languages, the real mediums of a genuine transmission of our cultural values, it can be said that these writers cannot be completely successful in the task of preserving our cultural values. For a language that a people speaks is the best vector of its culture. And only that language can best reveal the cultural nuances, realities and subtleties of its speakers.

Now any attempt to expose these realities and subtleties in a language other than that native to the cultural context, that which is the authentic embodiment of the thought and feeling of its users, would at best produce only partial results: results that would be mere approximations, results that would be only the closest things to the real things, still falling short of the authentic things themselves. That is, some of the original sense and beauty will be lost in the attempt to translate concepts, idioms, proverbs, riddles, and other expressions from the home languages into European ones.

Despite this linguistic problem, however, our best writers, even when employing foreign languages, can, and do, make us feel that not all that is African is lost; a great deal still comes across to us as essentially African. Thus a foreign language in the hands of our competent, imaginative writers can still be reasonably pounded, moulded and kneaded to take on African shapes and flavours without losing much of its essence.

Well, granted that we have cultural values that we hold dear for reasons outlined above, how does a creative writer – a novelist, a playwright, a poet, etc. knowing very well the peculiarity of his method, go about incarnating these values? Two options are available to him. The first is the romantic option in which he may choose to look at his culture and everything connected with it through romantic spectacles: he may choose to praise and glamorize everything he sees. This approach, essentially the one adopted by the first wave of Black Francophone intellectuals of the Negritude school, justifiable to some extent in their circumstances, is now, in our changed circumstances, largely untenable, unrealistic.

The negritudists, many of them thousands of miles away from home, on an alien soil, were disillusioned, disoriented and deracinated in a real and immediate sense that you and I can hardly imagine. They were not only writing in the colonial period but they were also writing against the backdrop of 19th century European ideas about Africa. And Africa, in the average European consciousness, in the common European imagination, was a land of brutes, of people a little more than animals but less than men; Africa then was a land of people with hardly a history and no culture at all; Africa then was the whiteman's burden, the Africa that justified the European "Mission civilisatrice".

With these ideas, with the benefit of hindsight, one can now appreciate with sympathy the rhetoric and eloquence in the voices of tigers that went around proclaiming their tigritude. They were forced to declare, loud and clear, to whoever had ears to listen, that they too had a culture, that they had a way of life that was dignified, that was respectable.

The second option, the one we would call critical realism, is that which while it allows the writer to expose all that is attractive in his culture, it does not make him gloss over the less desirable aspects. In this respect, the word "preservation" may not be quite adequate for the purpose of the critical artist who must look at his culture in a realistic light, without understating, without overstating anything.

The creative writer's role in this question of preservation of cultural values should be such that while helping us to appreciate the desirable elements of our culture, he should, by the same token, stir our consciousness to the existence of any less attractive ones. He should help us to examine closely to see whether our favourite pie can be our subtle poison. This is because I believe that our cultural values, in the general sense, ought not be static; they should not remain pristinely the same. If ours were unconditionally so, some parts of Cameroon would today be an embarrassing anachronism, a cultural embarrassment out of time and tune with the modern Cameroon. For instance, can we imagine an ethnic group, in today's Cameroon, that still puts a premium on drinking palm wine out of a human skull? Or can we confidently point to a modern African country where twins are considered a curse and must be dumped into an evil forest to avert the wrath of a whimsical god?

Many of such values, coming into contact with different cultural values, have since changed. Today we live in countries that are far from cultural islands. We are at the crossroads of cultural values. Our values and Western values are in a state of war; they are in a state of contention for the possession of our souls. The obvious results from this struggle are that everywhere in our modern societies there are tensions and contradictions; there is incoherence. The critical artist must be ready to capture those configurations and permutations. And where possible, he should indicate, in an artistic manner, the right set, or modified set of values that the virtual characters, emerging from this state of apparent confusion, can adopt. Similarly, the readers, the audience may then translate the vicarious experience into real life for a meaningful direction.

Now, granted that today's creative writer will face his culture with realism, given that he will not exaggerate unduly, where does he place his work within the scheme of time: in the past, in the present or in the future? Many critics would say in the present and in the future; they would assert that dwelling on the past can become a meaningless obsession, tantamount to mere escapism with little or no relevance to the present and to the future. By and large these critics have a point. The past, with its bewitching nostalgia, with its appeal to the sense of the good old days, can, indeed, be irresistible, but it can equally be irrelevant if exploration of the past is not more than undertaking a sentimental journey down memory lane for its own sake.

But my concern with the contemporary does not rule out an occasional and meaningful return to, or an initial debut with, the past. A creative writer, whatever his ideological orientation, ought to exercise his imagination the way he wants. I firmly believe that no material, no area of human experience ought to be beyond the limit of an artist; I feel that creative writers ought not to be confined by a debilitating proscription.

Having said this, I would like, however, to sound this cautionary note: that is, that a writer electing to explore a well-trodden territory, an artist choosing to rush in where angels now fear to tread, must needs write well and with considerable imagination to be able to attract and maintain his readers. He must work hard at using old and familiar material, in a fresh way. Failing this, he runs the risk of writing and not being read, of writing to sleep on the shelves. For any creative writer falling in love with simply painting static pictures of his culture, no matter how alluring and attractive such pictures may be, without making them artistically functional, without weaving them inextricably into the fabric of the propelling story, such a writer would be writing to sleep on bookstalls: he would be writing his way to oblivion. Such pure cultural exhibitionism militates against successful art; such material usually develops feet of lead in that it considerably slows down the story-element in a novel, for instance, or completely stifles it.

To avoid this pitfall the creative writer who wishes to incorporate cultural material into his work must be firm in leaving out attractive but useless material; he must be selective and discriminatory; he must use his imagination and intuition to know what to include and what to leave out, what he thinks will work and what he thinks will not work. He must strike a fine balance between paying homage to his culture and paying tribute to his art, between displaying his culture and telling his story successfully. In short, he should blend his culture and his art so that both should become one indissoluble artistic whole.

At this point, I would like to cite a few examples of creative writers who have incorporated sociological material into their work without the latter suffering seriously from such inclusion. Chinua Achebe and his compatriot Elechi Amadi in *Things Fall Apart* and *The Concubine,* respectively have maintained this fine balance between revealing their culture and telling their stories well. Both novels are, first and foremost, moving tragic stories about individuals struggling against forces beyond their control. But they are also stories about communities of people with essentially respectable ways of life, with their own culture, with their own civilization. These are people who value the art of good conversation, people who spice conversation with proverbs, that delicious palm oil with which words are eaten, particularly with reference to *Things Fall Apart.*

Nevertheless, much as he is eager to prove that his people had a culture, Achebe does not gloss over the ugly. He is realistic and subtly critical of the barbaric elements of the Ibo culture. Witness his dramatization of the confrontation between the Ibos and the Christians over the fate of outcasts and the accursed twins; witness the reservations, or the muffled objections raised by the coolheaded and respectable Obierika concerning some of the inhuman aspects of the Ibo culture.

In both novels concern for one another is shown; the spirit of solidarity, the spirit of sharing, the communal spirit is everywhere manifest; decency towards neighbours and respect for law and order are norms that are highly regarded, highly valued. But when they are violated and disregarded, behold chaos is come again.

This chaos or a similar visitation is what the people of Madoh village in Talla Ngarka's novel, *The Herbalist,* are suffering from. In this novel, Ngarka also makes judicious use of cultural material. In the tragic succession story in the Wimbum Country Ngarka shows us what it means for a people to violate law and order, to disregard the long standing tradition of the land, to bypass, so to speak, the constitution of the land and behave irresponsibly. Talla Ngarka shows us how, without due recourse to tradition, without sound justification, a group of king-makers waves aside the rightful heir to the throne, Tamfu, in favour of his less deserving younger brother, Ngeh. Consequently, they incur the wrath of the ancestors who exact the ultimate penalty of death by taking away the lives of three successive rulers.

With regard to drama, *Lake God*, by Bole Butake, reveals a conflict of values; that is, traditional African values versus Western values as evidenced in the confrontation between Father Leo and Fon Joseph on the one hand, and the rest of the villagers on the other. But these values are not simply displayed for their own sakes. The author uses them as a means to examine the states of mind of people caught up in a crisis; he employs them as a means of probing the basic motives of human behaviour. Fon Joseph, for instance, behaves as he does essentially because he has acquired new values – Western values. There are signs that he is an exploiter, a capitalist, one with little regard for the economic welfare of the local women.

Wole Soyinka in *The Swamp Dwellers* takes a realistic view of traditional values. We emerge from reading, or better still, from watching, this play with the realization that Soyinka thinks that cultural values are what they are only to those belonging to that culture that the values are precious to their upholders only because common practice has blinded them to think that they are so. But that when juxtaposed with foreign values, they can be seen in a new light. This is clearly what The Beggar makes Igwezu see in *The Swamp Dwellers* regard for the Kadiye and what he stands for. Indeed, one good custom can corrupt the world!

In Ola Rotimi's *The Gods Are not to Blame*, we see how an essentially Greek tragedy by conception has been successfully transplanted onto African soil to take on African colouring, to pulsate with African feelings. The way they speak, think and behave, the characters – Odewale, Adera Po, Ojuola, Baba Fakunle, etc.. reveal an African outlook in general, and a Yoruba world view in particular. In this play Ola Rotimi successfully invests the speech of his characters with Africanisms, particularly proverbs, in a way that can make Chinua Achebe turn green with envy.

Not long ago this play was staged in Bambili by the GHS Mbengwi Drama Club under the professional guidance of the enormously talented Peter Tangie Suh Nfor. The appropriate use of African proverbs was such an emotional and mental scintillation to the audience that at the end of the show, I actually overheard some highly thrilled, respectable members of the audience saying that they were going to document their oral literature, especially their proverbs.

I think this instance alone, if nothing else, is a clear indication of the playwright's success in the judicious selection and incorporation into his work of African cultural material. But the mere inclusion of cultural material into this play and into the two previous ones would hardly have constituted alone the basis on which to judge them as successful dramatic works of art. Rather, the strengths of the works partly reside in a nice combination of an imaginative use of the dramatic technique and an intuitive sense of selection of the appropriate sociological material.

In a thought-provoking poem entitled "You Laughed and Laughed and Laughed" a Nigerian poet, Gabriel Okara, makes an interesting case for African cultural values coming to the rescue, indeed, breathing new life into Western culture. Here the West is shown as sophisticated, polished, and technologically advanced; Africa comes through as less sophisticated, less polished, and less technologically advanced. Yet, for all its technological development and polish, the West is inhuman, cold, and, indeed, dying. It is only the life – sustaining fire in the African that can resuscitate the West, that can bring the West back to life.

Okara pays an enduring tribute to that valuable quality in African culture that all of us cherish, hold clear, and value: the warmth and generosity, the basic humanity of the African. This is what, he believes, should come to the rescue of the West.

Now, outside the context of Okara's poem, this may sound like a platitude, a truism lacking in originality: things like this have been said again and again before. So what's the big deal? Well, the big deal is Okara's style, Okara's manner of stating the matter. His diction, his imagery, his distinctive rhythm and music lend to the common place statement force, power and memorability.

It is an attractive style such as this that grabs the attention of the reader and keeps him reading and leads him to fully discover the cultural content, cultural implications and cultural values embodied in a work of art. In the success of a literary work of art both matter and manner count for more; mere enthusiasm and propagandistic intentions count for less. Therefore, creative writers with the intention of preserving African cultural values should do so through an artistic sense of proportion; they should do so not through artlessness, but through artistic competence

Works Cited
Achebe, Chinua. *Things Fall Apart.* London: Heinemann, 1958.
Amadi, Elechi. *The Concubine.* London: Heinemann, 1966.
Butake, Bole. *Lake God and Other Plays.* Yaoundé: Editions CLE, 1999.
Ngarka, Talla. *The Herbalist.* Limbe: Trans-Media Communications, 1988, 1998.
Okara, Gabriel. *The Fisherman's Invocation.* London: Heinemann, 1978.
Rotimi, Ola. *The Gods Are Not To Blame.* London: Longman, 1973.
Soyinka, Wole. *Three Short Plays.* Ibadan: University Press, 1969.

5
THE CAMEROONIAN NOVEL OF ENGLISH EXPRESSION

In the heyday of British imperialism, when the British imperial flag fluttered with awe over her colonies, the prestigious English language, following the intentional undervaluation of the local languages of the colonized subjects, became the language of education, thinking, and conceptualization, in short, the language of success. Since serious creative writing by colonial subjects could be done only in English, the former appropriated the latter to articulate their cultural experiences, preoccupations and diverse fortunes in the aftermath of their historical encounter with disruptive British colonialism, giving birth to the now numerous English literatures of post-colonial societies. It is in this broad context that we must situate the Cameroonian novel of English expression, since, following peculiar intervening historical circumstances, particularly the outcome of the First World War, the present English-speaking regions of Cameroon had become part of the British colonial empire. The opinion held in this paper is that contrary to the views of some critics, the Anglophone Cameroonian novel today is generally doing well, although, as an art form, it needs to be improved upon.

In their seminal article, "Cameroon Literature in English", in the now defunct *ABBIA* (1982), Nalova Lyonga and Bole Butake stated unequivocally that the Cameroonian novel of English expression, with only three published titles then, was the least developed genre in Cameroon. However, barely above twenty years after that pronouncement, at least twenty more titles have since appeared to the credit of the Cameroon novel in English. Because of limitations of space, this article takes but a bird's eye-view of the novels' central thematic concerns, and some aspects of their artistry.

Like their counterparts in other post-colonial societies, the Anglophone Cameroonian writers, having adopted the novelistic form and the English language, are imaginatively exploring, dramatizing and exposing the social problems that preoccupy Cameroonians. Three novels are pre-occupied with the theme of cultural conflict: between the Cameroonian way of life and the European civilization. They are Kenjo Jumbam's *The White Man of God* (1980), Joseph A. Ngongwikuo's *Taboo Love* (1980), and Azanwi Nchami's *Footprints of Destiny* (1985).

Set in Nso in the North West Province of Cameroon, *The White Man of God* dramatises the consequences of early European Christian incursion into that part of Cameroon. In the text there are two opposed camps: the Nso people with their African traditional ways, on the one hand, and the European missionaries with their Western Christian values, on the other. Much of the conflict in the novel is played out within the family of the adolescent Tansa, the first person narrator of the story. It pits Tansa's Christian parents against his grandmother, Yaya, the epitome of African tradition, a conflict manifest in the contrasting lifestyles within the family. While Tansa's Christian parents are doing their best to bring up their children in a Christian manner, Yaya is just as eager to let them follow the way of her ancestors. The ideological battle lines are drawn clearly in the manner Yaya carries out searching discussions, in turn, with her son-in-law and daughter, raising, in the process, fundamental questions about Christian theology.

The high point of the broad conflict is reached when the Rev Father (Big Father) in anger unmasks a juju to the profane view of the public only to discover, to his shock, that the man behind the mask is none other than Matiu (Matthew) his own head catechist. This shock will eventually disable Big Father, symbolising the power of African traditional ways. If, in the Christian sense, Yaya is saved by finally succumbing to Christian baptism, Big Father, in the African traditional sense, is eliminated from the scene by his audacity to confront and affront a mysterious power like the *Kibaranko,* an open clash that leaves the central ideological foes at parity.

The art that informs *The White Man of God* proceeds from a restrained spirit essentially classical. Jumbam's choice of words is simple and economical, and his sentences are often short and felicitous, revealing a painstaking technique. Jumbam is not in a hurry to develop a scene carefully, fully and realistically by choosing the appropriate words, the right expression and phrase to string out in an unambiguous sentence. The result is the evocation of human experience that rings true, that carries a compelling air of verisimilitude and inevitability. His characters are realistically portrayed.

In contrast, Joseph A. Ngongwikuo in *Taboo Love* places his cultural documentation ahead of his artistic mission. Set in the Kom country in the Northwest Region of Cameroon, *Taboo Love* is the tale of star-crossed lovers, Jam and Iyafi. Jam is a young man who has fallen in love with his childhood friend, Iyafi, now the wife of his Highness, the *Foyn* of the Mukomangoc ethnic group. Theirs is a taboo love because, according to tradition, it is a grievous crime for any man to make love to a *wintoc,* the wife of the *Foyn.* So, for having had sexual intercourse, the young lovers are condemned to death by a powerful gerontocracy. Jam is brutally and methodically amputated, and his dismembered limbs and remaining torso are shoved into a nearby grave. Iyafi escapes this macabre treatment only because she is discovered to be pregnant. However, the distraught woman cannot survive without her lover; as a result, she commits suicide. But the coming of the Roman Catholic Church and then of the German and, later, the British colonial administrators backed by their superior "gun" power, puts an end to the inhuman practices of the natives.

Much of the novel is devoted to the depiction of the customs and traditions of the Kom people, a major theme being the richness and diversity of Kom culture. From the enthusiasm that characterises the depth and scope of his cultural documentation, it is clear that one thing is dear to the author: the overriding desire to sell Kom culture abroad, to immortalise their customs and traditions. But in doing this the artist in him takes the backseat while the sociologist is foregrounded.

When we come to Azanwi Nchami's *Footprints of Destiny* (1985), we find yet another novel on the subject of Africa's sad collision with Europe, but this time, a more radical confrontation of a sort; for, in the central drama that unfolds in the text, pitting the Cameroonian nationalists against the German colonialists, we have some of the early beginnings of anti-colonial protest in African fiction. The novel is set in Africa and Europe, and historically it covers the period from the late 19th century to the end of the First World War.

In places the novelistic material is given summary treatment; potential scenes and events are simply dismissed in one-sentence paragraphs (see pages 10, 18, 27, 28, 85). The novelist does not fully explore the possibilities offered by the conflict between Cameroonians and Germans. However, this and other flaws linked to editorial lapses are minimized when compared with the novelist's artistic strengths. *Footprints of Destiny* is a readable book because of the art that informs it in general, and the strong stamp of individuality that defines Nchami's prose, one characterised by a poise, strength, precision and confidence, indicating her command of the English language.

Azanwi Nchami is the first major female Anglophone Cameroonian novelist, and the second is Margaret Afuh whose *Born Before Her Time* (2003), from an ideological point of view, must be considered an attack on patriarchy. Set in Momo Division of the North West Region in the early 1960s, this female *bildungsroman* is the story of a brave girl, Abo, betrothed to an old man, Worewum, before she was even conceived. When she is born, her marriage to Worewum becomes a fait accompli, and at the tender age of 14, she is forced into the house of a man in his early sixties.

To fight this formidable monster that is tradition, Afuh positions Abo and John, the heroine and the hero, constructing the former as her female subject while making enough room in her narrative for her central male character, John. Through the agency of these young lovers the author launches a scathing attack against patriarchal authority. The heartlessness of the latter is no where better illustrated than in the "slaughtering", so to speak, of Abo on the slab of reactionary ideology of male supremacy, as she is bound, hands and feet, by her own parents, and carried like a goat and dumped on Worewum's bed. The objectification and commodification of the woman in this context become complete. Within this particular patriarchy Afuh is saying that women have become mere objects, commodities to be carried and sold to the highest bidder, in this case, the rich old Worewum.

The dialogic tension within Afuh's text becomes evident in the conflicting discourses of modernity and tradition, inscribed respectively in the utterances of the pair of young lovers and the older generation. In matters of the heart the former fearlessly face the latter. The discourse of the young is invariably marked by rebelliousness, one that would favour deconstructing gender hierarchy while valorizing gender equality; for it regards women to be equal to men and not their slaves and thus seeks to transcend the manichean allegory of gender, looking forward to the emergence of a society wherein "women will live hand in hand with their husbands as two complementary parts and not like master and slave" (74).

With Z.F Ntumngia's *He Would Have Made Himself* (1988) we are in the early 1960s. The text is the fictional biography of a hard-working Bafut young man, Ngwasiri, sentenced to life imprisonment for manslaughter. With the aid of the flashback technique, the author delves into the colonial past of the Bafut people in the North West Region, and also takes a satirical look at what was happening in the Cameroonian society during the period of early post-independence.

The novelist, however, does not explore and develop his incidents and situations fully and adequately. But he shows more patience when depicting the traditions and customs of the Bafut people with regard to practices like offering sacrifices to their ancestors, hunting of mice, trapping of animals and trading in clay pots, involving trekking from Bafut to Ndop.

Like in Ngongwikuo's *Taboo Love* ethnographic activities take up the greater portion of Ntumngia's novel, and the impression is strong that this fictional form is merely an excuse for the novelist to dwell on, according to the publisher's blurb, "anthropo-sociological and historical material which makes interesting reading". Indeed the anthropological material in the text may well be of interest to departments of Anthropology in some universities, but not necessarily to the reader who goes to the novel to enjoy it as a work of art in which sociological material, no matter how alluring, is incidental rather than central.

As for Ngwa J. Neba's The *Golden Arrow* (2000) and *Manka'a* (2002) they can be dubbed ethical novels, that is, texts about good up-bringing or right behaviour as exemplified by the central characters. Tangi, the hero of the former, epitomizes the ideal of physical courage, bravery and youthful manliness, while Manka'a the heroine of *Manka'a* represents spiritual courage, determination and strong Christian conviction. Both are exemplary characters who work for the well-being of their immediate communities.

The Golden Arrow contains some beautiful evocation of the idyllic life of the local people, and also the depiction of arousing dramatic actions and situations. However, as a work of art, the novel, beside other artistic flaws, is too episodic; the various activities depicted do not cohere. There is no cause –effect relationship and, as a result, action is sequential rather than consequential.

Perspectives on Written Cameroon Literature in English

From the artistic point of view *Manka'a* is even much less satisfactory. It is not only episodic but its greatest weakness is its narrative thinness. Situations are not fully and adequately explored. The thin story is stretched out over a very long period of time. It begins with Manka'a as a teenager and ends when she is a great grandmother. Many years are covered within a few pages; the characters become aged without the readers being convinced of this. The text reads like an abridged story. Judged as novels for adult readers, the two texts, particularly *Manka'a,* must be considered artistically less satisfactory, even if they will ensure Neba's place in the history of the development of the Cameroon Anglophone novel.

When we come to L.T. Asong, we are in the presence of the most prolific Cameroonian novelist writing in English today, and his seven published novels within the last decade of the 20th century must be seen by the literary establishment as an impressive contribution to the Cameroonian novel in English. They are *A Legend of the Dead* (1991), *The Crown of Thorns* (1993), *No Way To Die* (1993), *The Akroma File* (1996), *Stranger in His Homeland* (1997*), Salvation Colony* (1997), and *Chopchair* (1998). With such a wide range of titles covering a broad spectrum of human experience, it is difficult to find a single theme that would neatly capture the spirit of all of Asong's imaginative works. It would be better to treat them in groups, and the most prominent category is the now –entitled *How a People Die*, comprising the three familiar texts of *Stranger in His Homeland, The Crown of Thorns* and *A Legend of the Dead.*

The trilogy tells the tragic story of the people of Small Monje, fatefully brought into confrontation with an arrogant, heavy-handed and dictatorial governmental system. The outcome is a communal catastrophe for the people. There is the desecration of their god, the destruction of their chieftaincy institution and the debasement of their traditional practice and cultural values.

But the causes of the people's physical, moral and spiritual death are varied and complex, found in the flaws inherent in human characters, in the governmental system, and in the king-makers' submission to the forceful, energetic external pressure from the District Officer to replace the rightful heir to the throne of Small Monje against the authoritative will of the late Paramount Chief.

Written in clear, crisp and classical prose, *How a People Die* is a readable novel with a wide canvas of interesting characters and numerous instances of arousing, dramatic situations to entertain all readers. Above all, the novel contains enough substance to occupy critics and scholars for a long time.

No Way To Die (1993) is the story of Dennis Nunquam the central character and anti-hero of the text. Victim of fate and unique circumstances, Dennis is misunderstood and later rejected by friends and relatives. He lives below the poverty line and ekes out his livelihood as a small office messenger in a tiny co-operative. Because he has been crushed by fate, he withdraws into himself and becomes a baffling psychological case. He takes no initiative to engage himself in any worthwhile activity outside his passion for art.

Yet, Dennis is not mad but simply a victim of a peculiar set of circumstances that cannot be fully apprehended by his acquaintances. The novel's narrative technique is that of interior monologue. With complete authorial detachment the technique consists of the individual characters telling the story from their own perspectives, as if they were speaking their thoughts aloud. The result is immediacy, casualness and freshness, producing prose different from a leisurely and discursive narrative guided by the omniscient narrator.

Asong's other novels like *The Akroma File* and *Salvation Colony* are works pre-occupied with societal crooks, the former with a swindler and the latter with a counterfeiter, both of whom are foreigners operating in Cameroon and taking advantage of some of the security loopholes in the Cameroonian security system. *The Akroma File* is a rare fictional exploration of criminology with frightening implications. Faced with debts at home and threatened by poverty, a brilliant and well-educated Ghanaian, Akroma, using unorthodox means, successfully gets into Cameroon where he is bent on making a fortune. He arrives in Cameroon virtually penniless but draws on his tremendous presence of mind to build up a fabulous fortune for himself. How this illegal alien eludes the police or bribes his way through them is a mark of L.T. Asong's genius in character conception and a telling comment on the Cameroonian security system, one that for the most part, thrives on venality.

Salvation Colony, on its part, concerns itself with an exclusive community of members of a Cameroonian religious sect, founded by an American, Rev Pastor Shrapnell. It is made up of the scum of the Cameroonian society, the dregs of humanity that society has turned its back on. Rev Shrapnell gives them spiritual fulfillment and a sense of self-worth. Inquisitive journalists expose Shrapnell for what he really is ... a rapist, a discredited medical practitioner, a counterfeiter and a bogus pastor. A hardened criminal and a devil in disguise, Shrapnell poses as a devout spiritual leader. His salvation colony is built on a sleazy foundation, on counterfeited money secretly produced by him and smuggled into a local bank.

The thesis developed in the novel is that religious sects pose a grave danger to society; for a brilliant criminal like Pastor Shrapnell, the anti-hero of the text, can assume the innocent mien of a religious leader to wreak havoc on a gullible community. Virtually deified by his devotees, Pastor Shrapnell wields unlimited control over his sheep. It is against such unconditional loyalty to influential but potentially dangerous cranks that Asong's text appears to be warning us. The horrendous example of the mass suicide of Jim Jones's faithful followers in Guyana in the late 1970s is still fresh in the minds of many readers. Twenty seven years after, on 26/3/1977 police found thirty nine bodies of identically dressed Heaven's Gate Cult suicide members of the exclusive San Diego under the leadership of the charismatic and controversial Marshall Applewhite. This was referred to as America's first mass suicide. But, to be sure, it was not perhaps the last.

With Nsanda Eba's *The Multimillionaire* (1997) we are still in the world of men of the underworld: con men and racketeers, those who live by their wits and keep alive the flame of the infamous phenomenon known as "4-1-9." Set in Yaoundé Cameroon's Capital City, *The Multimillionaire* is the story of an academically ambitious young man, Divine Fonkeng, duped out of his hard-earned money and that of his parents by crooks led by a Nigerian. The gullible Divine is bamboozled into believing that with just a little financial contribution, he can be transformed into a millionaire. But the reality is quite different. When it becomes clear beyond reasonable doubt that he has been duped, he cracks up.

Eba's text is a warning against the lure of easy money, for all that glitters is not gold. As a study of the crisis of the soul within the context of the nefarious impact of the 4-1-9 scam, the characterization of Divine is impressive, indeed. But the work betrays editorial blunders that call for serious editorial work.

Another imaginative product of the modern Cameroonian socio-cultural environment is Talla Ngarka's *The Herbalist* 1988/98, dealing with societal misdeeds, centred around the activities of a quack doctor, Tamfu, the herbalist. A charlatan who at one point seems to be a jack of all trades, Tamfu finally narrows down to one area of specialisation: stomach-related problems, with a clearly defined clientele consisting of college girls and unmarried women. In other words the branch of his expertise is abortion, and here he gets into shady deals with his clients, receiving as fee and reward, cash and sexual gratification. But when pregnant Beri, one of his clients, dies from his prescription, Tamfu becomes a fugitive from justice as he escapes into a neighbouring country.

The artistic weaknesses of this work, like those of the preceding novel, centre around editorial lapses. Therefore, as it stands, even in its revised form, *The Herbalist* still needs serious editorial attention. Its most obvious flaw is the mixing of tenses in its narrative set in the past. Recently, *The Herbalist* has been reworked and retitled.

As for Francis Nyamjoh's *Mind Searching* (1991), it is, from the perspective of technique, quite a different kind of novel on the Anglophone Cameroon literary scene, but one that, like John N. Nkengasong and Bate Besong's plays, is inspired by literary modernism as practised in Europe. It is a modernist novel whose author has thrown overboard much that is commonly considered indispensable to the novel, whether its method be dramatic or descriptive: description of places and people, explanation of environment, a plot of external action pitting two or more opposed forces, arousing dramatic scenes, climaxes and conclusion.

The social ills of the Cameroonian nation exposed through Yanda's naïve and insouciant approach to issues include bribery and corruption, perpetuation of mediocrity, prostitution, superstition, hypocrisy, governmental squandermania, and forgery. However, Yanda does not criticize the system with the intention of proposing a better moral alternative. He simply exposes it for what it is and himself benefits from its venality. Once secure with a good job, Yanda hypocritically becomes a staunch defender of the system he had previously raised questions about. Francis Nyamjoh is saying, through the rise to prominence of mediocre Yanda, that this is how the system comes by its cabinet ministers, in the main, immoral and mediocre elements.

The first Cameroonian to publish a major novel originally in English is Mbella S. Dipoko. In his *A Few Nights and Days* (1966) and *Because of Women* (1968) Dipoko has made the subject of the erotic relationship between a man and a woman inimitably his own. Indeed the novels would mean much less outside the sexual context. *A Few Nights and Days* deals with young people who fall in love in Paris. There is Doumbe, a Cameroonian, who is in love with a French girl, Thérèse, on the one hand, and on the other, Laurent, a French boy, in love with Bibi.

Doumbe and Thérèse are seriously preparing to get married, but Thérèse's bourgeois father, Mr. Vaele, is strongly opposed to the wedding, which hostility leads to the daughter committing suicide. This is the basic plot line around which Dipoko, crafts his engaging novel. A major theme emerging from the book is the racial barrier to true love, for it is hard for Mr Vaele to digest the idea that his daughter and sole child is eager to get married to a black African. This hurdle in the way of the lovers is proof, of Shakespeare's insightful statement, that the path of true love does not always run smoothly.

But there is another side to the love theme: the unfaithfulness in love. Doumbe is a kind of sexual scoundrel. He is in love with Thérèse but has no qualms sleeping with her best friend, Bibi; Laurent is in love with Bibi but also makes sexual advances at Thérèse, her intimate friend. On her part, Bibi is not at all bothered by her conscience when she dates Doumbe even as she knows she is in love with Laurent, Doumbe's friend. In this game of loose sexual behaviour the faithful Thérèse stands out as the only naïve lover and greatest victim of infidelity.

The novel is written from the first person narrative point of view, which is essentially Doumbe's, a straight forward, readable and, occasionally, lyrical account. The reader will find it difficult to put down the novel until he has reached the end.

Sexual pleasure, or the joy of love-making is the main theme of Dipoko's second novel, *Because of Women*. The story is set within the creeks somewhere between the South West and the Littoral Provinces of Cameroon. If, in the previous novel, Doumbe is obsessed with women, Ngoso, in the second, is even a greater womaniser. Sexual indulgence is a common habit of the people in this novel; and in Ewudu we have a nymphomaniac ruled by a single passion: that of making the best use of the moment, of seizing the day, the "Carpe Diem" theme so beloved of the Metaphysical poets.

Because of Women is told from the third person narrative point of view but does not possess the unrelieved narrative competence of the earlier novel. Its narrative style is a bit diffuse, however slight, so that the reader sometimes feels like skipping a portion here or there to get back to the central story. Yet for all this, *Because of Women,* in one sense, at least, is a technical advance of *A Few Nights and Days*. This is particularly so with regard to the use of effective flashbacks and even in the deployment of a variation of the forward approach, or prolepsis, by Ngoso. The novelist equally endows his characters, especially Ngoso and Ewudu, with interesting interior monologues – wherein the reader becomes absorbed in their imaginative life. The overall effect is psychological or realistic exploration of character. However impressive they may be as artistic works, Dipoko's novels must be considered, from the criterion of social significance, as ultimately lacking in moral seriousness.

The subject of women and sex is equally one handled by Langha Kizito's *Esther* (1993), the story of an attractive, innocent village school girl around whom men hover and who eventually becomes a whore. She gets into trouble in a bar when men, fighting over her, sustain injuries in a brawl that results in a lawsuit. Esther escapes a prison term only because she is pregnant.

The young man with the longest relationship with her is Victor Lenja, a naïve Form V student, also in love with a classmate of his, Edith. Physically strong and academically sound, Victor is, however, simple and immature with regard to the ways of the world. In this connection his inexperience comes to light early in the novel when he is literally "raped' by Alice, a beautiful oversexy housewife (27-28). But it is through his links with Esther, the central female subject of the text that Victor's naivete is most clearly revealed. His relationship with her leads him into some misadventures that leave their psychosomatic scars on him. If the author shows a good mastery of the English language, his narrative, nevertheless, betrays some missing links that vitiate the text's artistic truthfulness, narrative gaps within his story which do not enhance its verisimilitude.

As for Ngoran C. Tardzenyuy's *Nyusham* (2002), it focuses on the woes of Nyuysham, a man who seems cursed to bring disaster unto himself and his whole family through his irresponsible sexuality.

Nyuysham's sexual scandals lead to the break-up of his large family of 15 children. It is his peculiar ill-luck that his sexual desires result in abominable acts. His ex-wife sets up herself as a prostitute in a brothel, and, without knowing it, he secretly courts and makes love to her under darkness, and this to a woman he had earlier lost appetite in. He is cursed to commit incest (again unknown to him) with his own daughter now also a harlot. Above all, he is doubly doomed, as it were, to lure and rape his own minor (another daughter of his without knowing it still), an incestuous affair that condemns him to prison. And it is another ironic coincidence that Nyuysham is locked up in the same cell containing, among other hardened criminals, his two grown-up sons. Upon setting eyes on the felons, he collapses and dies.

These rather contrived instances of coincidence constitute a structural weakness that undermines the text's artistic coherence. Another serious technical flaw is the tendency, at times, for the novelist to be condescending vis à vis the reader, to talk down to the reader, more or less, leaving nothing to the latter's imagination. However, for these and other artistic flaws, *Nyuysham* is, relatively speaking, a better artistic work than Tardzenyuy's other text, *Victims of Circumstances* (2002), an apprentice work, by the author's disarming admission, containing many of the faults associated with texts of first impressions. But the most obvious weakness of *Victims of Circumstances* is the author's stilted style which, occasionally, makes no distinction between the language of the virtual characters and that of the omniscient narrator, betraying a lack of linguistic sensitivity.

Occasional lack of linguistic sensitivity is equally the most prominent artistic fault in Eugene J. Kongnyuy's otherwise impressive novel, *The Deadly Honey* (2002), a work which when well-edited, will be even more remarkable than some other Anglophone novels. Set in Nso in the North West Region of Cameroon, *The Deadly Honey* is the harrowing but eye-opening tale of how an ignorant but sexually active people blissfully invite death and disaster upon themselves.

The "axis of evil" involves the movement of young HIV-infected persons (mostly girls) from the city of Douala to the Nso rural community, itself immersed in sexual promiscuity. These "young fresh" things from the city are eagerly and lustfully pounced upon by unwary village lechers; thereupon a wave of sexual scandals and abominations hits the community. Soon afterwards, the libertines, one by one, become ill, manifesting various symptoms of an unknown disease; one by one they begin to die at an alarming rate. A plague of an unknown name and origin has struck the population; a curse of some sort has come upon the Nso people.

To fight the pandemic the natives turn to their tradition. They consult their *Sheys* and *Fais* and carry out acts of atonement; they perform sacrifices and rituals to their ancestors and gods; and offer gifts to alienated kindred to pacify them, all this in a bid to stem the ravages of the "slim disease." All the traditional medicine men come together to unearth a buried "evil" pot purported to have been the source of the frightful pestilence. But the net effect of these palliatives on the epidemic is nil.

In the hands of the novelist the deadly scourge becomes a device for exposing certain aspects of the Nso culture, and also for delivering a moral message to mankind, a means of revealing the best and the worst in human nature at a moment of an existential crisis. And one of the best moments in the narrative is the pleasant surprise the author reserves for the reader on the penultimate page of the novel. It is one of the rare but happy probabilities of science of great moralistic import, and it is this: the faithful, innocent and devoted Kila, the central female subject of the narrative, despite her marriage to the infected villain, Tumi, is found, upon medical examination, to be sero-negative.

However, as literature, *The Deadly Honey* is marred by many linguistic gremlins that need to be flushed out before it is fit for consumption by students, its targeted readership, else while the text sets out with the laudable didactic intention of eliminating one deadly virus, it may, paradoxically, implant a different disease in students. And this is the linguistic virus that language and literature teachers would like to discourage in students: their penchant for bombast, a tendency towards linguistic inflation and grammatical impropriety.

The novel is essentially a Western form, and the English language an imperialistic medium, both of which the Anglophone Cameroonian imaginative writers have adopted to serve the Cameroonian vision. The latter is marked by individuality of insight and uniqueness of human characters that define each novelist's work, communicating socio-cultural realities that are Cameroonian in particular, and African in general, and, constituting an interesting addition to post-colonial literatures. Within the Cameroonian socio-cultural context, there seems to be no taboo subject beyond the novelists, although they are not as ideologically radical as their counterparts in drama and poetry.

Despite the acknowledged limitations of this paper, its tenor must be translated to mean that the Anglophone novelists briefly treated here have handled the novelistic form and the English language with varying degrees of success or failure. Some have manipulated plot, characterisation, structure, point of view, and language fairly well, while others have been less successful. In addition, with the exception of novels published by Heinemann, nearly all of those published locally can be faulted for editorial shoddiness, and as such stand in urgent need of editorial improvement. However, looked at globally, and technically speaking, the creative output by Anglophone novelists is a positive contribution to the development of Cameroon literature in English.

Works Cited

Afuh, Margaret. *Born Before Her Time*. Bamenda: Patron Publishing House, 2003.

Asong, Linus T. *A Legend of the Dead.* Bamenda: Patron Publishing House, 1991.

_____. *The Crown of Thorns*. Bamenda: Patron Publishing House, 1993.

_____. *No Way To Die.* Bamenda: Patron Publishing House, 1993.

_____. *The Akroma File.* Bamenda: Patron Publishing House, 1996.

_____. *Stranger in His Homeland*. Bamenda: Patron Publishing House, 1997.

_____. *Salvation Colony*. Bamenda: Patron Publishing House, 1997.

Dipoko, Mbella Sonne. *A Few Nights and Days*. London: Heinemann, 1966.

_____. *Because of Women*. London Heinemann, 1968.

Eba, Nsanda. *The Multimillionaire*. Mankon: The Copy Printing Technology, 1998.

Hoffman Bill, and Cathy Burke. *Heaven's Gate Cult in San Diego.* New York: Harper Paperbacks, 1997.

Jumbam, Kenjo. *The White Man of God*. London: Heinemann, 1980.
Kizito, Langha. *Esther*. Bamenda: Patron Publishing House, 1993.
Kongnyuy, Eugene J. *The Deadly Honey*. Yaoundé: AMA-CENC, 2003.
Lever, Katherine. *The Novel and the Reader*. New York: Appleton Century-Crafts, Inc., n.d.
Lyonga, Nalova and Bole Butake. "Cameroon Literature in English: An Appraisal.' *ABBIA: Cameroon Cultural Review,* 38, 39-40, (1982) 123-174.
Nchami, Azanwi. *Footprints of Destiny*. n.p.: ALFRESCO, 1985.
Neba, Ngwa J. *The Golden Arrow*. Yaoundé: The Book House Publication, 2000.
_____. *Manka'a*. Limbe: ANUCAM, 2002.
Ngarka, Talla. *The Herbalist*. Limbe: Trans-Media Communication, 1988, 1998.
Ngongwikuo, Joseph Anchangnayuoh. *Taboo Love*. 2nd Edition. Yaoundé: Editions SOPECAM, 1991.
Ntumngia, Z.F. *He Would Have Made Himself*. Bamenda: Atlantic Press, 1988.
Nyamnjoh, Francis B. *Mind Searching*. Awka: Kucena Damian, 1991.
Tardzenyuy, Ngoran C. *Victims of Circumstances*. Bamenda: Patron Publishing House, 2002.
_____. *Nyuysham*. Bamenda: Patron Publishing House, 2002.

PART TWO:

SPECIFIC LITERARY STUDIES

6
IDEOLOGY IN THREE DRAMATIC WORKS: VICTOR EPIE NGOME'S *WHAT GOD HAS PUT ASUNDER*, AND BATE BESONG'S *BEASTS OF NO NATION* AND *REQUIEM FOR THE LAST KAISER*.

The well-known Marxist model of society consists of the economic base and the superstructure. The base is made up of the material means of production, distribution and exchange, while the superstructure is the 'cultural world of ideas, art, religion, law and so on' (Barry 1995: 158). According to Marxist scholars, the elements of the superstructure are not 'innocent' but invariably shaped or determined by the economic base. In the domain of Marxist criticism there is nothing like an original Marxist aesthetics for the simple reason that beyond their scattered comments on art and literature, the founders of Marxism, Karl Marx and Friedrich Engels, never evolved any sustained theory of art and literature. The narrative of Marxist aesthetics today is but an attempt by later scholars to apply Marxist ideas to art and literature, one of which is 'ideology', the key term in this article. While an orientation in Marxist aesthetics, known as 'vulgar' Marxist criticism, would privilege the exploration of works of literature solely for their ideological content and relating it to class struggle and the economy, the critical Marxist approach adopted in this article is one which seeks to explain the three Anglophone Cameroonian dramatic texts under discussion from both the ideological and aesthetic perspectives, showing how these are rooted in the social and general history of the authors' epoch.

Coined by a French man, Antoine Destutt de Tracy in 1796, the term 'idéologie' (ideology) was fated to develop fully in the hands of Marxists like Karl Marx, Lenin, Antonio Gramsci and others, hence its centrality in Marxist Criticism today. A slippery term that does not have a single accepted definition but rather rival definitions, 'ideology' is considered by David McLellan to be 'the most elusive concept in the whole of the social sciences' (Quoted in Heywood [1992] 2003:5).

The impossibility of an easy definition thus indicated, the definition chosen for the purpose of this study, which will be modified in the course of the discussion, is the one proposed by Andrew Heywood:

> Ideology is a more or less coherent set of ideas that provides the basis for organized political action whether this is intended to preserve, modify or overthrow the existing system of power. All ideologies therefore (a) offer an account of the existing order, usually in the form of a 'world-view' (b) advance a model of desired future, a vision of the 'good society,' and (c) explain how political change can and should be brought about – how to get from (a) to (b). (*Ibid*: 12).

A weapon sometimes used by people to criticize or condemn those with a rival set of ideas or beliefs, ideology possesses an emotional and affective character since it is a means of expressing people's hopes and fears as well as their aspirations and sympathies.

The objective world is out there, but the way we see or interpret it is due to our ideology; for, according to Heywood, we 'look at the world through a veil of theories, presuppositions and assumptions that shape what we see and thereby impose meaning on the world' (*Ibid*:13). And when we sometimes accuse others of being 'ideological' even when we are guilty of the very sin, adds Heywood, it is because in making us see the world through a 'veil' of assumptions, ideology is 'effectively invisible'.

Radical critics with unpopular "social priorities" are often regarded as "ideological", says Terry Eagleton. For him this is because 'ideology is always a way of describing other people's interests rather than one's own' (Eagleton 1983:211). Elsewhere Eagleton stresses that 'Ideology is not in the first place a set of doctrines; it signifies the way men live out their roles in class-society, the values, ideas and images which tie them to their social functions and so prevent them from a true knowledge of society as a whole ... the imaginary ways in which men experience the real world' (Eagleton 1976:16, 17, 18). In the preface to the latter work, Eagleton affirms that literature is a vector of ideology when he says 'ideologies [are] the ideas, values and feelings by which men experience their societies at various times. And certain of those ideas, values and feelings are available to us only in literature.'

The link between literature and ideology, though subtle, is one that we must try to grasp. On the one hand 'vulgar' Marxists generally hold that literature is nothing but ideology in different form, that literary works are the expressions of the dominant ideologies of their time. But other Marxists counter this claim by asserting that a great deal of literature challenges the ideology it confronts. However, as one of the forms of social consciousness within the superstructure, literature has a unique relationship with ideology (Ngara 1985:21). According to Engels as quoted by Eagleton (1976:16) 'art is far richer and more 'opaque' than political and economic theory because it is less purely ideological'.

The fact is that the basic material with which the literary artist works is essentially ideological. But in creatively working on it, he gives the ideology a definite shape and form in a way peculiar to literary art. The finished fictional product, as art, distances itself from the ideology that gave it birth (Eagleton 1976:19). What such a creative work makes us 'see', 'perceive' or 'feel' (in imaginary ways) is the ideology of the world from which it springs. Yet the work can also transform that ideology when it interrogates, when it challenges it. Therefore, from an ideological conception of a world a creative work is born, but which work, depending on the class or social group origin of the artist, can react back upon and affect that ideology by proposing a counter or an alternative ideology. However, in some cases, the artistic creation can be homologous with the dominant ideology of an epoch.

If, as we have said, literature is a vector of ideology, that ideology is inscribed in a text's matter and manner, in the themes and forms that make up a literary work, for the 'true bearers of ideology in art are the very forms rather than abstracted content of the work itself.' And to this Eagleton adds that in choosing a form, 'the writer finds his choice already ideologically circumscribed. He may combine and transmute forms available to him from a literary tradition, but these forms themselves, as well as his permutations of them are ideologically significant' (*Ibid*:26).

Our discussion thus leads us to one conclusion: to be able to bring out the ideology of a literary text, one would do well to examine not only its themes and pre-occupations but its formal aspects as well. That is to say, in the spirit of authentic Marxist aesthetics, one should examine the dialectical relationship between content and form and how these are rooted in the social and general history of the epoch.

After this theoretical consideration, we now embark on the practical analysis of the three dramatic texts, beginning with Victor Epie Ngome's *What God Has Put Asunder*[1]. Victor Epie Ngome's play, at the literal level, is a tale of the unstable marriage between a girl called Weka and a man known as Miche Garba. Their wedding is solemnized by Rev. Unor probationally, without the matrimonial rings. The couple will live together and study each other for ten years at the end of which period, if they still desire to be husband and wife, the official ceremonies will be conducted.

However, with time, Weka discovers that Miche Garba is not a worthy husband. He maltreats and neglects her; he takes over and exploits the rich cocoa farms left by her father and squanders the money on his concubines. He does not tolerate the questioning attitude of Weka who is able to stand up to him.

When she can no longer bear Garba, Weka escapes with her children back to her father's compound. Garba pursues her there, but having failed to forcefully take her back, he takes the matter to court. And the court's verdict is that the couple will continue to live in physical separation though united in a 'simulated wedlock'; that the marriage remains subject to confirmation by husband and wife only, to the exclusion of any other third party; that it will become null and void once any of the two parties objects to it; and that until the confirmation is carried out under the supervision of the court, the couple will continue to live under physical separation.

The main theme emerging from the play is matrimonial incompatibility. The conjugal union between Weka and Garba is, at best, a precarious one and at worst an unworkable relationship. Besides leading an adulterous lifestyle, Garba is neglectful towards Weka. Worst of all, he is a polygamist whose other wives have been brought up on the principle of total submission to authority without questioning, a lifestyle inherently abhorrent to Weka whose upbringing in the orphanage has taught her to question things and not just to accept them docilely.

Garba's other wives accept his decisions meekly, willingly going along with whatever he decrees. In this respect Garba is even scared of his new wife because the intelligent and critical Weka is influencing these women to dare to stand up to him. Thus his general philosophy and philandering lifestyle remain insurmountable hurdles in the way of genuine domestic happiness as far as Weka is concerned.

A related theme is economic exploitation. Garba seems to have married Weka more out of economic consideration than out of real affection. He derives a great deal of profit from the coca farms but does not plough back any of it to develop the farms, nor does he use it to attend to Weka's physical and aesthetic needs.

At another level of economic exploitation, we find Garba and his closest collaborators feeding fat on the assets of the co-operative society, the wealth of the nation. He is the unconscionable General Manager of the co-operative society, from whose account he draws huge sums of money to support his sensual lifestyle with beautiful women in luxury hotels. Accountable to no one but himself, he is afraid of no auditors who are practically in his palm and can only investigate what he dictates to them.

Now, beyond the literal level, *What God Has Put Asunder* is a national allegory whose conjugal metaphor, within the Cameroonian context, relates to the uneasy political union between the Anglophone Cameroon and the Francophone part. Hence Weka (West Kamerun) stands for the English-speaking former Southern Cameroons, while Miche Garba (Ahmadou Ahidjo) represents the French-speaking La République du Cameroun.

We will handle the allegorical aspects of the play only generally, instead of going into their minute details. It therefore suffices to state broadly that Garba's neglectful but exploitative attitude towards Weka signifies the negligent attitude of the Francophone leadership towards the minority Anglophones in present-day Cameroon, an indifferent comportment that has come to represent a central grievance in what Anglophone Cameroonians have identified as the Anglophone Problem.

The allegorical Garba becomes the dreaded dictator, President Ahidjo, who, while he was alive, dominated Cameroon politics, the authoritarian bourgeois who tolerated no dissent from whoever. His rule over Cameroon, like Garba's absolute control over his submissive wives (Francophones) was a one-man show; he ruled by decree encountering little or no opposition at all.

The lavish party Garba throws to his wives in order to bamboozle them to opt for one indivisible family becomes the so-called 'Peace Revolution' of 1972. After skillfully manipulating the population of the Federal Republic of Cameroon, the crafty Ahidjo successfully got all Cameroonians to vote by 99.9% in favour of a unitary state rather than a federation, whereas only Anglophones had participated in the plebiscite of 1961 that led to reunification with the

Francophones. Under normal constitutional practices, only Anglophones would have taken part in the 1972 referendum. Ahidjo had known in advance that with the majority Francophones taking part in the consultation, the outcome was a foregone conclusion.

From the many references made in the play to separate physical habitation, it is clear that Weka (Anglophones) shows a preference for a federalist cohabitation, for within a federation Anglophones would be sure of more development of their region than under a unitary state. The scrapping of the federation by Ahidjo in 1972 has become the major source of what today is known as the Anglophone Problem, the totality of the Anglophone grievances against their Francophone counterparts, summed up in one word: 'Marginalization', despite the fact that much of the national wealth comes from their region.

In 1993 at an All-Anglophone Conference held in Buea with over 5.000 Anglophones in attendance, the Anglophones crystallized their grievances against the Francophones and enshrined them in the now famous 'Buea Declaration' part of which reads as follows:

> Our natural resources have been ruthlessly exploited without any benefit accruing to our territory or to its people. The development of our territory has been negligible and confined to areas that directly or indirectly benefit Francophones. Through manoeuvres and manipulations, we have been reduced from partners of equal status in the Union to the status of a subjugated people.
>
> The common values, vision, and goals which we share as a people and those of our Francophone partners in the Union are different, and clearly cannot blend within the framework of a Unitary State such as was imposed on us in 1972…
>
> The so-called 'Peace Revolution' of 1972 was a ploy by Francophones to use their overwhelming majority to alter the basis of reunification for which Anglophones, and Anglophones ONLY, had voted.
>
> (The Buea Declaration 2nd and 3rd April 1993, 9 – 10, 12 – 13).

Perspectives on Written Cameroon Literature in English

Even in the early 1990s, during the government-organized constitutional debate going on then, the Anglophones submitted a federal draft constitution that would guarantee their minority interests and ensure rapid economic, social and cultural development, and equitable distribution of the natural resources and, hence social justice. This was in contrast to the official government stand that privileged a unitary draft constitution.

The critical attitude shown by Weka as opposed to the acquiescent nature of Garba's other wives symbolizes the questioning spirit of Anglophones, in contrast to Francophone more deferential attitude to presidential authority. This indicates a fundamental philosophical difference in the world visions of the two major linguistic communities in Cameroon, an irreconcilable dissimilarity well-captured by Professor Godfrey Tangwa (1998:76):

> Generally, the most telling difference ... between *anglos* [Anglophones] and *frogs* [Francophones] has to do with their respective attitudes towards *authority*. For the latter, a person in authority can never be wrong. Recall that francophones were not bothered by the clause in Owona's proposed constitution which states that the President of the Republic cannot be held responsible for any of his actions. For Anglophones, by contrast, a person in authority, while being respected, is always keenly watched with ultra critical eyes and immediately and loudly denounced for any lapses.
>
> These differing attitudes between anglophones and francophones are directly reflected in their respective attitudes to fundamental human rights and freedoms. Francophones take arbitrary curtailment of their freedoms, state terrorism and wanton abuse of human rights as rather in the normal order of things. But these things are what have traumatized Anglophones in the past three decades, to the extent that, today, the vast majority of them would rather risk mass suicide than suffer a continuance of this state of affairs.

These unbridgeable differences between Anglophones and Francophones in Cameroon, poetically captured by the title of Ngome's text, seem to be rooted in their respective colonial legacies.

Professor Tangwa says he had been baffled by some aspects of the Francophone judicial system with regard to authority until he read the following from a book about the French by two British authors, Thatcher and Scot: ' "Under the French law of 1881 it is an offence to insult the President of the Republic … In Britain we consider it a corner-stone of our democracy to be able to insult anyone we wish" ' (*Ibid*). 'Should we substitute "francophones" and "Anglophones" in the right slots', concludes Tangwa, 'the above passage remains true in our own context' (*Ibid*).

After looking at some of the text's themes and pre-occupations at both the literal and allegorical levels, we can safely affirm that what Ngome's play makes us 'see' or 'perceive' is the social mentality, the dominant ideology of the world from which it springs, the historically relative structure of perception that underpins the power of the class represented by the dictatorial, domineering Ahidjo. And from the point of view of political ideology, all evidence points to the fact that the kind of ideology incarnated by Garba (Ahidjo) can therefore be best described, without any shred of doubt, as authoritarianism, a political ideology which, in the words of Andrew Heywood, is 'a belief that a strong central authority, imposed from above, is either desirable or necessary and, therefore, demands unquestioning obedience' (Heywood: 328). For everything around the allegorical Garba hinges on authoritarianism which tends towards assimilating resisting elements for the purpose of enforcing compliance and eventually stultifying and stifling criticism of any kind.

But Ngome's text is far from constructing a simple, passive reflection of the dominant ideology of the epoc of Ahidjo; on the contrary, it challenges the very ideology. For the critical attitude with which Weka is endowed, backed by her demands, her pre-occupations and her preferences as revealed by the multiple references to separate physical habitation, amounts to an interrogation of the dominant ideology of her time. The nature of the ideology espoused by Weka, at the symbolic level, can be qualified as federalism, defined by Heywood as 'A territorial distribution of power based on the sharing of sovereignty between central (usually national) bodies and periphery ones' (Heywood: 331).

But a genuine Marxist analysis of a text does not simply end at its ideological content, at a mere abstraction of its ideology and relating it to class struggle. There is the aesthetic dimension as well; for, after all the formal elements of literature are the words that make up the language in which that literature is written. Therefore, whatever ideology a text embodies is subtly inscribed in the words and techniques, in the content of the text. For, as Eagleton puts it, 'The languages and devices a writer finds to hand are already saturated with certain ideological modes of perception, certain codified ways of interpreting reality' (Eagleton 1976:27).

Similarly, the devices or techniques deployed by Ngome, such as the contrast between Weka's censorious attitude and the compliant spirit of Garba's other wives, the dramatic conflict between Weka and Garba, which is the main conflict of the text, the manner in which that dramatic encounter is carefully crafted to be resolved at the end so that Weka has an edge over Garba, the particular character traits that define Garba and Weka as distinctive human beings – all of these devices are ideologically resonant. They foreground before us the various characters and issues of the text; and as the characters come across to us through their roles, speeches and actions, or how they are perceived by other characters, we can discern their tone of voice, and therefore 'perceive' or 'see' their moral as well as ideological orientation.

In like manner, the language Ngome's characters employ is ideologically significant. For instance, when Garba proverbially declares that 'a cow can only browse within the reach of its tether' (23), or that 'a mistletoe only dies with the tree if it did not propagate its seeds to other trees' (24), he is voicing codified ways of interpreting reality. His proverbs can only be translated to mean that he is a smart bourgeois who wants to exploit his advantageous social position and intends to keep things as they are for his own economic benefit, an attitude of mind in harmony with reactionary authoritarianism. When he says of Weka that 'she is a bloody terror in that Goddamn house… Now she is teaching all my other wives to question whatever I do,' or when he asks his wives: 'We shall continue to be one, indivisible and happy family shan't we?' (52), his conservative, authoritarian view of the world, as well as his great fear of a counter vision of life becomes only too evident.

Equally ideologically saturated are the words used by Weka and the court. When Weka complains of Garba that 'he forced me to settle in with him ... [and] had been forcing my children to learn his own mother tongue and to forget mine with which they grew up; I must abide by the customs of his clan, not mine' (53), the divergent cultural as well as ideological interests of the two parties become obvious: Garba's is assimilationist authoritarianism as Weka's is an attempt to keep intact her cultural identity, since she would prefer that they 'live on as before – that is under separate roofs' (53). Weka's federalist disposition is one boosted by the final decision of the court which states that 'the couple shall continue to live in physical separation under the same condition provided for in the probation by the solemnization act' (58).

From the point of view of textual ideology, *What God Has Put Asunder* is not limited to authoritarianism and federalism. It can equally be explained from yet another ideological perspective ... that of racial Manicheanism, epitomized by Rev Gordon and Sister Sabeth, the authorities of the orphanage where Weka grew up (Southern Cameroons as a trusteeship under British administration). Ngome's text reflects, from the perspective of Gordon and Sister Sabeth, the construction of the Self and the Other. These European representatives of Empire set out to orientalise or 'africanize' Weka and the rest of the 'natives'. They view the world through the veil of racial hierarchy: Theirs is a superior race. Whatever is good and civilized is European, while the evil, the primitive, is African.

In their view a girl in Europe can marry through love, but in Africa she has to be coerced to marry against her will:

Weka: You told me that before, Sister Sabeth. But didn't you also tell me that back in your native England a girl only marries the man she loves?

Sabeth: Yes, but that's in England
Gordon: Listen, Weka, it took us centuries to establish all those civilities, and this is a totally different setting. This is Africa, for God's sake (7).

Now, all that we have done so far, with regard to Marxist explanation of *What God Has Put Asunder*, may look like an unreasonable request to some, a tall order of sorts; our composite reading of the text may look like an undue mélange of literary criticism with politics and economics. Well, a Marxist response to such criticism is that a full understanding of a literary text must take into consideration these aspects and even more; and that unless it does so, relating them to the base/superstructure model of society, it is not truly Marxist.

On the other hand a 'vulgar' Marxist view of Ngome's work might be that it is determined by the socio-historical conditions prevailing in the era of President Ahmadou Ahidjo. That is, of course, true, but it amounts to saying that the text is a simple reflection of those conditions. However, such an approach fails to take into account many other factors that mediate between the text and the mode of production in the epoch of Ahidjo.

In contrast to a 'vulgar' Marxist method, a genuine Marxist approach, in addition to all that we have analysed, will consider the social position, including the social group origin, of Epie Ngome. The fact that he is an Anglophone, and so of the minority group, that he is one of the finest products of the Anglo-saxon educational system, that he has written four other plays, that he is a journalist holding high positions within the national broadcasting system, that his academic career took him to several foreign universities in quest of higher degrees – these are elements worthy of consideration. They certainly influenced the type of play he came to write and the language he used.

Written in a critical realist mode, *What God Has Put Asunder* is structured in the manner of traditional drama, reminiscent of Shakespearean plays which were more or less the staple literary food of post-colonial students at the secondary and university levels, at times even in some senior primary schools. But because of the culture of ear and silence that marked the Ahidjo fear in Cameroon, Ngome could not afford to call a spade a spade, hence the allegorical form in which the drama is cast to protect himself from possible police harassment. For instance, according to the author, when this play was first broadcast in the early 1980s, 'My friends were prompt and unanimous in advising against a repeat broadcast – for my own safety, they said' (*Prefatory note iii*).

Some of the aims of journalism are to inform, educate and entertain. And Ngome's text, though definitely not a piece of journalism, draws on some of the goals of his profession: information, education and entertainment. The text embodies all of these, for it is a play that pleases while it teaches. The informational and instructional dimension has to do with the content that we have sufficiently discussed. The entertainment angle relates to the high dialogue value of the play, the wit and humour that exude from some of the characters, especially Weka and Emeka.

With regard to Emeka, two texts that Ngome appears to interrogate most are a popular Nigerian serial drama that took Anglophone Cameroon by storm in the 1980s, and Richard Sheridan's *The Rivals*, a play that was popular with the G.C.E. Advanced Level Literature students in the 1970s. Emeka's queer and amusing use of language reminds us of Chief Zebrudaya's English in the Nigerian soap-opera, on the one hand, and Mrs. Malaprop's malapropism in *The Rivals*, on the other, intertextual echoes that indicate a positive influence on Ngome.

The marital metaphor that allows for two levels of meaning, the literal and the symbolic, is an ingenious theatrical device employed by the playwright. Young Cameroonians without a sound knowledge of the political history of their country, together with non-Cameroonians may grasp only the literal level and yet be sufficiently satisfied with it: an exciting play on matrimonial problems and the related issues highlighted earlier; the witty repartee between Weka and Rev Gordon, and the malapropism of Emeka will still make for a great deal of humour and interest. Interesting characters like Garba, Emeka and Weka remain so with or without their allegorical garb.

However, the greater pleasure is reserved for the adult readers or audiences able to effect the necessary mental shift from the literal to the symbolic level of interpretation. And there is constant mental stimulation and titillation whenever a reader or member of the audience makes a political or historical linkage between a literal character or incident and a historical one.

As already hinted above, the play's dialogues have a high conversational value, the work of a stylist and a brilliant conversationalist versed in the art of talking, a dramatic attribute of great merit. It has the advantage of holding and sustaining the interest of both the readers and audiences. A Marxist justification for the overall artistic force of *What God Has Put Asunder* is that to write well is more than just a matter of possessing a good style. It is equally because Victor Epie Ngome has at his disposal ideological perspectives that can penetrate to the realities of his characters' experiences in various situations. Above all, his historical situation as a sensitive Anglophone allows him access to certain intuitions.

After everything, then, the relationship between the base and the superstructure is not a simple, symmetrical one. *What God Has Put Asunder* is not tied in a one-to-one way with the mode of production. There is a complex, indirect relation between the text and the ideological world it inhabits. Such a relation emerges from the text's form and content. In other words, the social and historical forces, together with the whole lot of factors examined already, have been mediated, through the agency of form, to arrive at the conjuncture of the elements we know as *What God Has Put Asunder*.

If, as we have seen, Ngome's text is a national allegory, an extended metaphor as it were, based on the ideological world under former President Ahidjo, Bate Besong's *Beasts of No Nation*[2], on its part, is 'a metaphor of national decay' (131) inspired by the ideological realities under the New Deal Regime. The raw material that Bate Besong, like many imaginative writers, works on is basically ideological. But he creatively transforms it, giving it a definite artistic shape and form. As Cliff Slaughter (1980:200) puts it, the artistic work 'constructs a mystification or particular way of obscuring the truth about its historical conditions of production.' Now, the completed dramatic artifact, as art, is less purely ideological than say economic and political theory, and thus differs from the original elements that gave it birth.

As such there is a sense in which it can be said to have therefore 'distanced' itself from the ideological world whence it springs. However, the drama can make us 'see', 'perceive' or 'feel' in imaginary ways, the nature of the ideology of that world. And this is due largely to the text's themes and pre-occupations as well as its styles, form and other mediating factors.

But before we come to examine the textual ideology in detail, the dramatic situation in this remarkable play, *Beasts of No Nation*, is this: On the one hand we have night-soil-men (NSM), the doomed carriers of mountains of fetid waste of Ednouay City Council asking for their freedom and professional cards; on the other, there is the

Mayor of Ednouay Municipal Council, Aadingingin, refusing to grant them these rights, complaining, instead, that the municipal administrators are faced with a huge economic crisis in their hands and working within an austere budgetary allocation, coupled with the rigorous demands of the Structural Adjustment Programme (S.A.P.).

The themes and issues emerging from *Beasts of No Nation* are economic, political, cultural and social. Ednouay is a city economically ruined by the bourgeoisie, the ruling class, led by Supreme Maximum Mayor, Comrade Dealsham Aadingingin. The strict demands of S.A.P., together with the wasteful flamboyant lifestyles of the big directors is taking its toll on the citizens, especially the night-soil-men. City Council money is shamelessly and recklessly pillaged, led by the mayor and his close collaborators, many of whom put up fabulous storey buildings and ride expensive, status-symbol cars like Jaguars, Italian Pajeros and Ferraris, and Mercedes 500.

The playwright pictures the municipal administrators not only as big looters but as big 'money eaters.' Money is seen as something edible, as food which is consumed and then passed out as waste matter – shit. And there is a great amount of this in the city. That is why Ednouay is considered the most expensive dung-heap in Africa. This accounts for why most of the Council's budget is reserved for the clearing up of waste, a colossal sum of 450 million out of 500 million set aside just for toilet tissues and disinfectants, leaving the other city projects the laughable, paltry sum of 50 million. Thus Ednouay City Council rulers are brazen, unconscionable embezzlers who not only spirit away the council's money into European banks, but are not ashamed to hide some of it in the ceilings of their homes.

In this regard, we bring in here an interpretation of the play by a Francophone government functionary who watched it when it premièred in Yaoundé. We will first quote a portion of B.S. Biatcha's letter in French, addressed to the Chancellor of the University of Yaoundé, followed by our English translation:

> … L'auteur soutient que les Francophones au pouvoir sont responsables de la crise économique parce qu'ils entretiennent la gabégie et les détournements des fonds. Parmi les francophones (frogs), un accent particulier est mis sur les Beti, amis et frères du

Président Biya, qui sont plus responsables de l'état actuel au Cameroun.

L'auteur affirme également, et ceci est la philosophie principale de la pièce, que 'les Anglophones au Cameroun, sont marginalisés et confinés dans les rôles indignes comme celui de 'ramasseurs' d'excréments.' Ils n'ont aucun statut propre et sont même dépourvus de toute carte d'identité professionnelle qu'ils réclament sans succès. Pour Monsieur Bessong (sic), l'Anglophone au Cameroun est considéré comme un traître et un esclave...

(Our Translation)
... The author defends the thesis that Francophones in power are responsible for the economic crisis because they are producers of waste and embezzlers of public funds. Among the Francophones (frogs) special emphasis is placed on the Betis, friends and brothers of President Biya, who are more responsible for the present state of Cameroon. The author equally affirms, and this is the central thesis of the play, that the Anglophones of Cameroon are marginalized and confined to undignified roles like that of 'carriers of excrement.' They do not have any professional identity cards which they are asking for in vain.

According to Mr. Besong, the Anglophone in Cameroon is considered a traitor and a slave...
(Quoted in Ambanasom 2003: 110 – 111; 113 – 114).

While Bate Besong and Epie Ngome are closer in ideological orientation, they come from two different dramatic conventions. But an aspect of technique common to their two works is the use of metaphor; the authors call one thing in terms of another. However, while Ngome's text is an extended metaphor that assumes the full status of an allegory, Besong's is allegorical only in a general sense, for the latter's dramatic style is distinctly different. A maverick and an avant garde, Besong is a playwright in a class all alone.

In contemporary Anglophone Cameroonian imagination and consciousness the word 'frog', a pejorative term used several times in Besong's play, stands for the Francophone. It connotes an irresponsible consumer of what others labour to produce, a thriftless, exploitative and even unpatriotic person. In the play the economy is generally under the control of the 'frogs', particularly the Supreme Maximum Mayor of Ednouay Council, Comrade Dealsham Aadingingin with his close bourgeois collaborators – 'the frater-mafia of greed, grab and graft' (118). Note the emotionally ladened and, therefore ideologically charged nouns in the quoted portion of the above phrase, especially the last three.

According to the author 'Ednouay is a fictional city' (82). However, if one spells 'Ednouay' from right to left, one has the political capital of Cameroon, Yaoundé. It is important to note that although the drama pulsates on every page with the Cameroonian spirit, the word 'Cameroon' itself does not feature anywhere in the text. The reversed 'Ednouay' becomes a metonymy, representing the whole of Cameroon, for in the words of Augustin Simo Bobda ([1994]:116), 'This term [metonymy] is closely related to metaphor; [it] consists in designating something by using the name of something associated with it.' Ednouay is also a synecdoche for Cameroon.

This technique is also indirectly at work in one word in the high-sounding name of the mayor of Ednouay – 'Dealsham.' If one splits this word into two, one has 'Deal' and 'sham', a noun and an adjective. If, however, we make the adjective qualify the noun, we have 'sham deal,' a cynical, pejorative epithet with a poetic ring to it that rings a bell to many Cameroonians. Besong's recourse to this technique and his evident insistence on the fictionality of 'Ednouay' might be an attempt to disguise his fundamental political criticism of the incumbency. The ineffectuality of his effort to camouflage his intention is underscored by his arrest and detention by the authorities immediately after this fiery play was premièred in Yaoundé in 1991, a fact confirmed by the following Press release signed by the Cameroonian novelist, Mbella Sonne Dipoko:

> Following the news that Bate Besong, playwright, poet, critic, and teacher, has been arrested and detained, friends, writers, students, sympathizers, lawyers etc have formed today, Saturday 25, [May]

> 1991, a COMMITTEE FOR THE RELEASE OF BATE BESONG.
>
> As a first step, a letter has been sent to the Government calling for his immediate release[3].

Another derogatory word featuring many times in *Beasts of No Nation* is 'Anglos,' which stands for Anglophones. It connotes slaves, traitors, enemies, renegades or the lowest of the social heap, indeed, the dregs of humanity. Anglos are the 'Night-soil-men' who, by extension, can 'also represent the workers without whom society will come to a standstill' (Abety 1996:255).

In vain Anglos ask for their freedom and also their identity cards. Aadingingin tells them to attach to their application form, the impossible fee of one million francs each, but which amount the third NSM intimates 'will immediately be embezzled' (113). These demands are issues of great symbolic significance. For they stand for Anglophone basic demands including their cultural identity. Without them the Anglophones run the risk of being assimilated into the greater Francophone culture. The stiff resistance put up against these demands by the bourgeoisie or the 'frater-mafia' in authority in the play speaks volumes for what was happening in the 1990s in the Cameroonian society with regard to pressure groups like Cameroon Anglophone Movement, CAM; All Anglophone Conference, AAC; Teachers' Association of Cameroon, TAC; General Certificate of Education Board, G.C.E.B; and the drawn-out war of nerves between TAC and the government over the G.C.E. Board issue, all of which are real symbols of Anglophone identity and culture.

When all has been said and done, the dominant ideology emerging from this text is bourgeois ideology, a term, in Heywood's words, 'denoting ideas and theories that serve the interests of the bourgeoisie by disguising the contradictions of a capitalist society' (Heywood 328). The bourgeois ideology is incarnated by the man with the overblown, suggestive name of the Supreme Maximum Mayor of Ednouay City, Comrade Dealsham Aadingingin and his close collaborators the 'frater-mafia of greed, grab and graft.' They constitute the bourgeoisie, the ruling class and the top brass of the government department. Their privileged positions give them access to millions or billions to toy with.

Among them are big directors of lucrative organizations and co-operations like SONARA, CELLUCAM, and AMACAM; from their midst emerge real estate developers who put up fabulous chains of storey buildings, which they then rent out to the government; some of them dominate the transportation industry with a fleet of luxurious buses. Should they be ill from gorging themselves with rich food and expensive wines, extraordinary medical care is given them; were they to die, they would be put in their golden caskets and interred in diamond-studded graves.

Owners of the means of production, these bourgeois, according to Narrator, are the 'beasts of no nation... and sensuous class who, some day will take the Ednouay nation hostage as a result of their inexhaustible greed' (131). And it is owing to their insatiable appetite for money that 'corruption is the national industry in Ednouay' (135). They get richer because the producers of their wealth, the workers, get poorer. To perpetuate and protect their interest, the bourgeois increasingly become cocooned in self-interested delusion. They must tell lies to the proletariat to conceal the fact of the latter's oppression and exploitation.

When the bourgeois ideology is confronted by radicalism mounted by the night-soil-men, the bourgeois attempt to appease the NSM by ascribing their economic woes to 'the rigours of the present crisis' (139). Otshama says, 'the crisis has spared no one' (135). In any case any attempt by the bourgeois to rationalize the economic misery of the proletariat is contradicted by the flamboyant lifestyle of the bourgeois themselves.

Although the radicalism that challenges the bourgeois ideology is out for fundamental change in favour of the night-soil-men, it is not inscribed in any classic Marxist terms. In other words, apart from advocating liberty and freedom as well as professional identity cards, the radicalism, beyond these demands, is not yet well-defined. But it is there, evident in the purposefully provocative and disgusting behaviour of the NSM with their smelling buckets of human excrement. For instance on page 102 we are told 'The Night-Soil-men raise their behinds to the audience and foul the air'! The radicalism is there, inscribed in the emotive language used by some of the characters, especially the NSM as well as in the stage direction provided by the playwright. We quote here only parts of two songs by the NSM in pidgin, and in English. From 'Song of the Prodigal'

(a) Goat di chop
For place weh
Dey be tie him (100)

....

So my dear frog
Brother wack
And burn
This damnbrubah
Ednouay (100)

(b) From (The Night-soil-men sing)
All: When you eat money
The way locusts
Eat tonnes of green
When frogs eat money
The way locusts
Eat tonnes of green (102)

(c) Solo: I fit bury
One thousand million
For my ceiling
I fit bury meme
Ten thousand million
For my ceiling (103)

Songs (a) and (b) highlight in strong emotional language and through the images of a goat browsing where it is tethered, and of swarms of locusts consuming tonnes of green vegetation, the issue of 'frogs' in authority capitalizing on their fortunate social positions to plunder the nation's wealth with reckless abandon. Fragment (c) quoted highlights the matter of stealing and hiding, by frogs, even in their ceilings, of huge sums of money.

The language of the play is not ideologically neutral; rather, it is suffused with ideological modes of perception as indicated by the following quotation in pidgin:

Cripple: Monkey will do
The dorty work
Gorilla go dey wack

> First (NSM): O me die man, innocent Anglo
> Monkey work gorilla chop?
> (106)

Here in 'Monkey work gorilla chop', we have a codified, proverbial way of interpreting reality: the idea of parasitism, of an individual feeding fat on the labour of another, in short, of economic exploitation. The Monkey does the dirty job, but it is the gorilla who reaps the fruit of the monkey's toil. It is obvious who the gorilla is, and who the monkey; the gorilla is the bourgeois, while the monkey is the worker (the Anglo).

Since the dramatist has 'no voice' in his own work because it is other characters doing the talking, the closest any dramatist comes to voicing an opinion in his own drama is in the stage directions. In the case of Bate Besong's stage directions in *Beasts of No Nation*, sometimes, there is strong and affective and, therefore, radical language employed, the kind that sometimes characterizes Besong the polemicist. For instance, in describing Aadingingin on page 138, Besong deliberately employs insulting, repugnant and repulsive language that makes Aadingingin appear in his most grotesque ugliness, a discourse that spells radicalism by any account and shows his negative attitude towards the man:

> *Comrade Aadingingin is a lumbering gargoyle of a mayor with a brooding brutishness. He is fat, extremely fat; the sort of bloated fatness associated with very juicy toad... Comrade Aadingingin like one of those who eat and drink too much has developed several ripe fleshy layers, pumpkin-like below the natural skin.* (138)

A dramatist at home with the modernist mode of discourse, Besong is a self-conscious playwright determined to break with the past. A militant author with an obvious innovatory dramatic technique, he is continually experimenting and searching for new ways of expression. In all his dramas to date Besong provides us with an admixture of the realistic, the historical, the tragic, the comic and the grotesque, all of this underlying a particular ideology or ideologies. He brings into his writing, in a recondite manner reminiscent of T.S. Eliot, his wide learning as well as lived and imaginative experiences.

His fame as a dramatist partly resides in the fact that he is also a published poet with a rare ability to use words to create powerful images and symbols with poetic resonance as he does in *Beasts of No Nation*. The following comment on Besong's poetry is equally generally appropriate for the technique he uses in his dramatic text:

> He is never content with simply talking about one thing only, but he must seek parallels, analogies or contrasts here and there, hence the highly allusive nature of his poetry… To read Bate Besong one should be ready for an allusive excursion into history, literature and the Bible. Ambanasom ([2004] 2002: 46).

Beasts of No Nation itself abounds in literary, Biblical and historical allusions. The title of the play – 'Beast[s] of No Nation' is an abusive phrase flung by an angry character at another in Chinua Achebe's *No Longer at Ease* (1960:138). In Besong's text Narrator uses it alternatively with the modified version 'Thieves of no nation' (90), in direct reference to the destructive, compulsive appetite of the bourgeoisie for money. The Narrator's and the author's strong antipathy towards the bourgeoisie becomes clear.

On his part Otshama's flattery of Aadingingin: 'Your Excellency is absolutely right. I never thought of that. It is surprising how Your Excellency thinks about everything', is a verbatim utterance from C. Achebe's *Anthills of the Savannah* (1988:19) and belongs to Professor Okong flattering the head of state in that novel. Here Besong uses this allusion to satirize the Ednouayans' (Cameroonians') exaggerated, sycophantic attitude towards the head of state.

In the play there are general allusions to sickness afflicting a people and the need for a cure. Specifically, there is an allusion to the wickedness and immorality of the people of the Old Testament and the punishment God metes out to them. For instance, when Narrator says:

> If I find in Ednouay
> Two righteous Directors
> Then I will spare
> All the place for
> Their sake….. (94)

He is alluding to the passage in Genesis 18:24-32 wherein Abraham pleads with God to spare the sinful City of Sodom which is eventually obliterated, anyway. There is also the subtle allusion to Romans 6:23: 'The wages of sin is death.' Besong uses all these allusions to point to the imminent or possible economic destruction of the City of Ednouay by the imprudence of the plundering bourgeoisie. The author uses parody and songs in pidgin to highlight certain themes and issues and to communicate more effectively with the audience.

As already stated, *Beasts of No Nation* is the product of the socio-historical conditions prevailing under the New Deal Regime. Besong, the author, is a University graduate and lecturer in English Literature, and one who has mastered, and has been influenced by the drama and poetry of difficult modernist writers like T. S. Eliot and Wole Soyinka. Eternally committed to the Anglophone Cameroon welfare, and himself a victim, in an immediate sense, of the system he flays and whose rulers he flogs, Besong is an angry writer whose diverse experiences and influences he harnesses and transmutes into art. His wide-ranging satire slashes at everything in its path: personalities and institutions in sports, history or politics, etc.

But it may be objected that Besong's modernist dramatic technique, although it reveals a rich and fertile imagination, sometimes engenders obscurantism, owing to inaccessibility of language and style. One can say, in Besong's defence, that his unconventional approach as such is, as Terry Eagleton says of Brecht, 'quite compatible with the widest uses of fantasy and invention' (Eagleton 1976:72). Besong is using realism in a new way, extending its range. He would probably agree with Brecht that 'our concept of realism must be wide and political, sovereign over all conventions… we must not derive realism as such from particular existing works, but we shall use every means, old and new, tried and untried, derived from art and derived from elsewhere to render reality to men in a form they can master' (Quoted in Eagleton 1976:72).

As we have seen, in *Beasts of No Nation*, the bourgeois are confronted by the oppressed, symbolized by the NSM. The latter actively and persistently ask for their rights and, towards the end of the play, even carry the struggle to the dreaded Mayor's office, storming it with their buckets of excrement, a radical act of ideological resonance. But this radicalism that challenges the bourgeois ideology is articulated in non-Marxist terms. However, when we come to Besong's next play, *Requiem for the Last Kaiser*[4], a work conceived from a socialist perspective, the bourgeois are challenged by a more determined radicalism expressed in a spirit that is clearly Marxist as it takes on a socialist coloration. The broad-based, conscientised progressive forces fighting the bourgeoisie now are fully aware of what they want, where they are going, and how to get there.

Requiem for The Last Kaiser consists of three fragments of scene, and two movements. The first fragment opens with a woman educating a student to take part in fighting the repressive forces in Agidigidi, and the second reveals that Atangana, a clergyman, collaborates with the reactionary regime of Akhikikrikii. The flashback in this fragment also reveals Abossollo as the security boss of the regime and therefore, one who controls the instruments of torture. He accuses Woman of subversion and of planning a coup d'état. But Woman says 'ours will be a popular uprising not a coup' (16). Atangana the Pastor cautions her: 'Be careful woman... Don't let the Devil mark you... Trust and obey' (16). In the last fragment, we see Akhikikrikii, the Head of State, in the company of his foreign friends and supporters: a Western Ambassador and a Swiss Banker, all of whom flatter him.

In the first scene of the first movement we meet the progressive forces, made up of unemployed academics like Akonchong and Gambari, Poet as Mandela, workers, voice of Woman, etc. There is a parody by the academics in which the regime is subtly satirized. The scene ends with Abossollo threatening critics and enemies of the regime. In the second scene of the first movement we meet the progressive forces again, including the leader of the market women, Woman and soldiers. We notice the education of the soldiers by Woman in the interest of the oppressed. There is the play within the play, wherein the academics play the role of head porters, etc. Here the cruel ways and weaknesses of the regime are subtly criticized and exposed. There is the reading of the revolutionary thesis by Akonchong, and then Abossollo arrives in a threatening mood with a gun, but he is disarmed by the people.

In the second and last movement we find the people – the progressive forces: the poet, former infantry men, women, workers, etc., surrounding Akhikikrikii's Marble Palace. There is a general revolt, and Ngongo, the chief praise-singer of the regime, confesses his crime against the people. Worst of all Abossollo too, without the army, abandons Akhikikrikii. But the Ambassador and the Swiss Banker still stick around him. However, deserted by his people, Akhikikrikii commits suicide and the people, the progressive forces, force their way into the Marble Palace.

The central theme of this play is the popular challenge to an authoritarian regime, or a popular uprising against a dictatorship. It is the education of the deprived and their stand against a tyrant. In fact, this theme is already didactically summed up by the author in the play's sub-title 'a drama of conscientisation and revolution'.

Conscientisation implies the education of the masses, especially the oppressed masses, in such a way that they become imbued with a heightened sense of critical consciousness. When oppressed people become conscientised, they tend to know more about certain issues and situations than they did before. They become more familiar with the inner structure of their society and the dynamics of the vicious system that has held them captive. The knowledge of this produces a change in behaviour in such a way as to make them now want to do away with the evil forces that have helped to cripple them. Thus for every vicious action, so to speak, by the oppressors, there is not only an equal and opposite, but, in radical terms, a superior opposite reaction by the oppressed, whose ultimate goal is the improved living condition of the masses.

This trend of reasoning reveals that Bate Besong has been influenced, consciously or unconsciously, by Marxist thought, at least as far as *Requiem for the Last Kaiser* is concerned. Marxism, the political and economic philosophy founded by Karl Marx and Friedrich Engels, holds that history is primarily determined by economics. It regards the history of any society, with the exception of that of primitive communalism, as the history of class struggle. Marxism stands strongly opposed to capitalism which it seeks to topple, replacing it with socialism.

But to be able to do so, Marxists must first educate the oppressed in the dynamics and nature of capitalism, the economic philosophy that upholds the private ownership of property and the means of production, and encourages individual initiative, spirit of competition and the profit motive or accumulation of wealth. 'Marxism's goal is the liberation of consciousness and freeing of praxis from bondage via revolutionary theory.' (Solomon 1973:14)

For a real revolution to take place the people's consciousness must be transformed; there must be a change of mentalities. The people must be prepared, educated and ideologically sound. And this pedagogical mission is essentially Bate Besong's intention in *Requiem for the Last Kaiser*, as implied by the subtitle: a drama for conscientisation and revolution.

Talking about literature and ideology, the Russian Marxist, Georgy Plekhanov, says no literary work is conceived in an ideological vacuum, that all art emanates from an ideological conception of the world (Eagleton 1976:17). The veracity of this statement can be illustrated from *Requiem for the Last Kaiser*, for the brief outline of the play above clearly bears this out. There are two distinct ideologies locked in a fierce confrontation. And here, as Rius says, 'ideology expresses and defends the interests of the classes in struggle' (Rius 1976:149). On the one hand we have an oppressive, exploitative and essentially capitalist or bourgeois way of life represented by Akhikikrikii and his tribal clique including the Western Ambassador and the Swiss Banker. Agidigidi is a neo-colonial state, and Akhikirikii, a neo-colonial agent, subjected to easy manipulation by his European neo-colonial masters. The consequence of this neo-colonial stranglehold on the state of Agidigidi is the cruel exploitation and pauperization of the masses for the benefit of the national bourgeoisie and compradors, and their foreign masters. The latter's survival depends on their keeping things as they are, admitting neither radical changes nor non-conformist tendencies. As a result, their administration is characterized by coercion, threat, imprisonment and torture.

On the other hand there are the exploited, the oppressed, represented by Woman, Student, Poet, workers, market women, the unemployed academics and former infantrymen. As a group they constitute the progressive forces, working for a change of the status quo. Their approach is basically radical, and their general attitude, socialist. They are out to seize power from the tyrannical minority and give it to the people. This comes through to the audience from the steady education given by Woman to the student and soldiers, in particular, and the sensitization of the masses in general.

Woman and Dr. Akonchong roughly represent theory; the student, soldiers and other workers, the potential for action. The ones represent reflection, the others, praxis. Thus brain and brawn become necessary for a successful revolution.

Iduote, the capital city, is the setting of the play. 'Iduote' is a word constructed in the same manner as 'Ednouay' in *Beasts of No Nation* is. That is, spelled from right to left, Iduote becomes 'Etoudi', the local name for the presidential palace in Cameroon, under the New Deal Regime. Iduote is thus a synecdoche for Yaoundé, the capital of Cameroon.

Requiem for the Last Kaiser is a product of its society, having been informed by the social, political and historical conditions of Cameroon under the New Deal Regime. Bate Besong fully subscribes to a central Marxist principle that literature is socially-conditioned. In his own words '... literature must be inspired by a historical myth-informed consciousness. It must embody in bold relief the specific historical features of the entire Cameroonian reality' (Quoted in Ngwane 1993:36). And his literary works are an exemplum of his words. His plays are artistic creations inspired by the Cameroonian experience. They are the transformation into art of social, political, economic, cultural and ideological issues pertinent to the Cameroonian reality.

Making allowances for the playwright's poetic licence and his fertile imagination, all that goes on in the neo-colonial state of Agidigidi is generally true of our present day society. Some of the statements made by the fictional Akhikikrikii like: 'The people understand me very well. I also understand them, Je vous ai compris' (1), belong to his historical counterpart. Even names like Abossollo, Atangana, Ngongo, etc, in Cameroon are easily identified with ethnic groups with close affinities to the dominant ruling class. The topicality, currency and, consequently, the sensitivity of Bate Besong's material can be seen from J.S. Biatcha's visceral reaction translated above.

Requiem for the Last Kaiser is a reflection and also reinforcement of the contemporary critical attitude of many Cameroonians who, thanks to a lively private press, are no longer afraid of sticking out their neck for political change. The significance of Besong's dramaturgy in Cameroon, like Bole Butake's, lies in the fact that his plays are an important aspect of the on-going process of political sensitization of Cameroonians in the wake of the wind of change from Eastern Europe in the late 1980s and the resurgence of multiparty politics in Africa, particularly since the last decade of the twentieth century. For with the coming of Gorbachev's *perostroika*, there was a loosening up of dictatorial grip on power by despots of mostly one-party regimes; there was a gradual liberalization of the press and a general goodwill to democratize and open up to multi-party politics.

Yet in many cases, especially in African countries, the external democratic pressure was not enough to force political rulers to change; internal pressure was also necessary, indeed indispensable, for any significant political change to be registered. For this reason, in Cameroon, political parties were formed and some forcefully launched in the face of stiff government resistance; social pressure groups and local human rights organizations also came into being; committed imaginative writers and outspoken independent individuals emerged. All of these progressive forces, like those in the play, had a common goal: to force the hand of a reluctant government to yield to the wind of change and to open up to a valid democratic process that would allow for the respect for human rights and social justice.

As an Anglophone Cameroonian, Bate Besong writes with the burden of the Anglophone Problem frequently on his mind. In *Requiem for the Last Kaiser* the issue of 'Anglos' being integrated into the larger Francophone society is raised in the parody scene where Gambari asks: 'Anglos what are your grievances against National integration then?'

On his part Akonchong says: 'We have recruited Frenchmen of sciences to civilize you yet your secessionist brains have rejected all medicines... What is your grievance ... Ph.D. Doctor... Too much English... Too much angalis-Biafré!' (34) In Cameroon the word Biafré or Biafran is a code term for Anglophones, and in *Requiem for the Last Kaiser* the unemployed academics, are 'pseudo-Biafrans'. This is made clear to the audience through an aside by Abossollo in the parody scene, with reference to Gambari and Akonchong, 'Pseudo-Biafrans are excellent in the evil art of mockery' (36).

Bate Besong draws on both the Anglophone experience and his personal plight; for, as a civil servant, he has been roughly treated by the system. The anger we find in his plays is partly the bitterness inspired by the frustration the man has known, not only as an Anglophone, but as a bruised individual. In Besong's own words: 'The Anglophone Cameroonian Writer must never forget his origins.

His writing must depict the conditions of his people, expressing their spontaneous feelings of betrayal, protest and anger' (Besong 1993:18).

As a realistic work *Requiem for the Last Kaiser* reveals a quality valued in Marxist criticism – that of 'the world-historical'. According to Georg Lukács, a realistic work is one rich in complex relations between man, nature and history. These relations embody and reveal what is most typical about a particular phase of history. What Lukács refers to as typical are the 'Latent forces that in every society are the most significantly historical and progressive and that expose society's inner structure and dynamics' (Eagleton 1976:28). The duty of the realist writer is to flesh out these typical trends and forces in sensuously realized characters and actions.

In this play these forces include the forces of oppression and exploitation, incarnated by Akhikikrikii and his clique with their neo-colonial masters, on the one hand, and the progressive forces made up of the exploited, on the other. When the oppressors, standing firmly in the way of change, are confronted by the oppressed, bent on routing out the tyrants, then there develops a tense situation likely to explode with serious repercussions. For, as Wole Soyinka says, 'he who makes peaceful change impossible makes violent change inevitable.'

In their sensuously fleshed-out forms, these characters are bound to generate actions and reactions likely to produce historically significant social outcomes imbued with the power of 'world-historical'; that is, events with the power to create or influence history. To the extent that these forces make things different, especially in favour of the masses as shown by their forceful and successful occupation of the Marble Palace, its former occupant having committed suicide, they are progressive. The progressive forces, the proletariat and others are quite aware that they are making history; that they are working towards a change, the change of the status quo. 'We want nothing! We have come to hear you die! Only your blood can cleanse this land!' (58)

A key principle in Marxist criticism is commitment of art to the cause of the proletariat, putting art in the service of pressing social issues. In all his writings: his poetry, polemical essays, drama and even in his lifestyle, Bate Besong reveals himself as a man profoundly committed to the welfare of his Cameroonian community in general, and the Anglophone environment in particular. He comes through to the reader as a man whose breast is full of the milk of human kindness, a fierce defender of the rights of the downtrodden. Indeed, he has come to symbolize the Anglophone hope.

All the issues and themes raised in his plays reveal that only a committed artist, a humanist, would be that concerned with the lot of suffering men and women, a suffering inflicted on them, tragically enough, by their own cruel kind with the collaboration of unfeeling neo-colonial masters. Yet, Bate Besong is not misty-eyed in believing that he has a magic wand to solve, instantly, the problems of his suffering people. He himself acknowledges the limitation of the committed writer:

> True, the power of the writer is not always strong enough to change the political and social situation of his time but his art can become a fighting literature, he can write works which are artistically profound and politically correct: he can write works of indictment and works that show how his world is and could be.
> (Besong 1993:18)

The committed artist alone may not have the power to bring about immediate political change. But he and the writers of other forms of political literature, a buoyant private press, the appropriate political opinion leaders and parties, can all effect meaningful change. 'The committed artist need not be a wheel alone, but he is an essential spoke in the wheel of socio-political change.' (Ambanasom 1996:225)

Requiem for the Last Kaiser is socialist in conception but modernist in technique (Matumamboh 1988:iii). The desire on the part of Besong to experiment, to look for more effective dramatic techniques, is still there. But greater emphasis is now on a more effective communication with the audience. Gone are the songs that were a feature in *Beasts of No Nation*. Then, they had served as thematic reinforcement, but now Bate Besong does not need them since he has incorporated his issues into clear statements and dialogues.

There is the flashback technique which is effective in that it throws more light on the character of Abossollo, Atangana and Woman. There is also parody for satirical effect. And the device of a play within the play makes for multiple role-plays, allowing the author to use certain actors to achieve comic and satirical effects otherwise impossible with the real actors without greatly modifying the context.

Thus we have Akonchong and Gambari, the unemployed academics, role-playing head-porter, but at other times they are Akhikikrikii and the Ambassador. Still there are times when Akonchong is condemning "Akonchong", his alter ego. The only difficulty likely to arise from such multiple roles is that if members of the audience are less wary to know exactly when a character is playing his central role and when he takes on someone else's, or is parodying somebody, the play will be confusing to them. Equally effective is the technique of using voices rather than the physical presence of the speakers. Voices can, from off stage, threaten Akhikikrikii in languague that would be impossible if the speakers were physically near the tyrant.

A profound Marxist understanding of Bate Besong's *Beats of No Nation* and *Requiem for the Last Kaiser* would take into consideration a number of factors like the social group origin of the author, his educational background and aesthetic orientation, the literary influences on him, his authorial ideologies and their relation to literary forms, and the linguistic devices and the techniques employed by the author. All of these elements are relevant to the base/superstructure paradigm. However, there is no simple, direct correspondence between the base and the superstructure, between Besong's works and the real history of his time.

There is but a complex indirect relationship between these texts and the ideological worlds they inhabit. Therefore, in constructing contrary, radical ideologies to confront the dominant bourgeois ideology, as we have seen, Besong, like Epie Ngome before him, succeeds in transposing, through the agency of form, the world vision of the progressive social group to which he belongs as well as other historical forces into the highly mediated dramatic piece we know as *Beasts of No Nation* and *Requiem for the Last Kaiser*.

From the perspective of overall textual ideology, we have seen what can be more or less termed competing ideologies (i.e. a dominant versus a less dominant but opposing ideology) emerging from each of the three texts analysed. In Victor Epie Ngome's *What God Has Put Asunder* there is authoritarianism versus federalism; in Bate Besong's *Beasts of No Nation* we have bourgeois ideology confronted by radicalism; and in *Requiem for the Last Kaiser* the bourgeois ideology is seriously challenged by a socialist ideology. All of these rival ideologies are what Emmanuel Ngara (1985) calls the authorial ideologies, whether or not the author is clearly leaning on one ideology or the other. And in the case of all three texts, we have seen that Ngome's and Besong's sympathies are on the side of the oppressed and exploited; that is to say, the authors espouse radical ideologies.

But, quite apart from these central ideologies, there is the 'Aesthetic ideology' which, in E. Ngara's words 'refers to the literary convention and stylistic stances adopted by the writer' (Ngara 1985:108). They can be defined, in literary terms, as romanticism, symbolism, expressionism, realism, formalism, socialist realism, modernism, etc. To go by this definition, then, the aesthetic ideologies coming out of the three texts are as follows: from *What God Has Put Asunder,* there is critical realism; from *Beasts of No Nation* we have modernism; and from *Requiem for the Last Kaiser*, we have a mélange of socialist realism and modernism.

In his review of Shadrach Ambanasom's *Education of the Deprived* of 28 April 2003, Chris Dunton, with regard to the author's treatment of textual ideology, says:

> What Ambanasom does offer is a very detailed textual exegesis of the plays under discussion, equally sensitive to the thematic terrain and to dramaturgy. The discussion is not especially searching in terms of the critique of textual ideology, but this is understandable in a book the task of which is documentation ... from a committed perspective, namely, the recognition of the political maltreatment of West Cameroon.[5]

We are grateful to Dunton for his observation, and receptive to his criticism. Action and reactions are what we need for growth; thesis and antithesis are dialectical dynamics necessary for a healthy synthesis. The accent placed on textual ideology in this article, even though concerning only three dramatic texts instead of the thirteen in the book[6] reviewed by Chris Dunton, is partly in response to his comment, and a model that can be extended to the remaining ten texts.

End Notes
1. Victor Epie Ngome, *What God Has Put Asunder*. Yaoundé: Pitcher Books Ltd. 1982. Page references to this play are taken from this edition.
2. Bate Besong, *Three Plays*. Yaoundé: Editions CLE. 2003. Page references to *Beasts of No Nation* are taken from this edition of *Three Plays* (2003).
3. See 'Press Release!!!' dated May 25, 1991 and signed by Mbella S. Dipoko: Place of the 'Release' is not indicated.
4. Bate Besong, *Requiem for the Last Kaiser*. Limbe: Presbook, 1998. Page references to the play are taken from this edition.
5. The African Book Publishing Record, *ABPR,* vol XXIX/1(2003):16-17, 17, 18.
6. Some of the material in this article is drawn freely from this book.

Works Cited

Abety, Peter. 'The Literary Podium and the Political Pulpit: Medium and Message in Anglophone Cameroon Drama' in Hansel Ndumbe Eyoh, Albert Azeyeh and Nalova Lyonga (eds) EPASA MOTO Volume 1, Number 3 (1996): 250-264.

Ambanasom, S.A. 'Pedagogy of the Deprived: A study of the plays of Victor Epie Ngome, Bole Butake and Bate Besong' in Hansel Ndumbe Eyoh, Albert Azeyeh and Nalova Lyonga (eds) EPASA MOT volume 1 Number 3 (1996): 218-227

__ __ __. *Education of the Deprived*. (A study of four Cameroonian Playwrights). Yaoundé: Presses Universitaires de Yaoundé, 2003.

__ __ __. 'Is Bate Besong's Poetry Too Difficult for Cameroonians?' in Abioseh Michael Porter (ed.) *African Literature Association ALA BULLETIN,* Vol. 28 Summer/Fall 2002 ¾ and *ALA Bulletin* Vol. 29 Fall 2003/Winter 2004 No. 3 ([2002] 2004): 242.

Barry, Peter *Beginning Theory: An introduction to literary and cultural theory*. Manchester and New York: Manchester University Press, 1995.

Besong, Bate 'Literature in the Season of the Diaspora: Notes to Anglophone Cameroonian Writers.' Keynote Address in Lyonga, Breitinger and Butake (eds) *Anglophone Cameroon Writing* pp. 15-18. Bayreuth: Bayreuth University, 1993.

__ __ __. *Requiem for the Last Kaiser* rev. ed. Limbe: Presbook, 1998.

__ __ __. *Three Plays*. Yaoundé: Editions CLE, 2003.

Bobda, Augustin Simon. *Watch Your English!* 2nd ed. Yaoundé: B and K Language Institute, 2002.

Dipoko, Mbella Sonne. 'Press Release!!!' n.p. dated May 25, 1991.

Dunton, Chris. A Review of Shadrach A. Ambanasom's *Education of the Deprived* in ABPR, Vol. XXIX/1 (2003): 16-17, 17, 18.

Eagleton, Terry. *Marxism and Literary Criticism.* Berkeley and Los Angeles: University of California Press, 1976.

___ ___ ___. *Literary Theory An Introduction.* Minneapolis: University of Minnesota Press, 1983.

Heywood, Andrew. *Political Ideologies.* 3rd ed. New York, N.Y.: Palgrave Macmillan, 2003.

Matumamboh, Alfred. 'The Supremacy of Bate Besong's Dramatic Art' in Bate Besong: *Requiem for the Last Kaiser*, rev. ed. Pp. i-iv. Limbe: Presbook, 1998.

Ngara, Emmanuel *Art and Ideology in the African Novel.* London: Heinemann, 1985.

Ngome, Victor Epie *What God Has Put Asunder*. Yaoundé: Pitcher Books Ltd, 1992.

Ngwane, George *Bate Besong Or the Symbole of Anglophone Hope.* Limbe: Nooremac Press, 1993.

Rius. *Marx For Beginners*. New York: Pantheon Books, 1976.

Slaughter, Cliff. *Marxism, Ideology & Literature.* London and Basingstoke: The Macmillan Press Ltd., 1980.

Solomon, Maynard. *Marxism and Art*: *Essays Classic and Contemporary.* New York: Alfred A. Knopf, 1973.

Tangwa, Godfrey B. *Road Companion to Democracy and Meritocracy: Further Essays from an African Perspective.* Bellingham: Kola Tree Press, 1998.

Good News Bible With Deuterocanonical Books. 2nd ed. Published by United Bible Societies, 1994.

7
THE EDUCATIONAL SIGNIFICANCE OF THE CAMEROON NOVEL OF ENGLISH EXPRESSION: FOCUS ON FOUR TEXTS

Cameroonian creative writers of English expression have adopted an imperial language, English, and the novelistic art form to serve the Cameroonian vision. Like many others, the four novels discussed in this article *The Deadly Honey* (2002) by Eugene J. Kongnyuy, *The Disillusioned African* (1995) by Francis B. Nyamnjoh, *Across the Mongolo* (2004) by John N. Nkengasong, and *The Death Certificate* (2004) by Alobwed'Epie are exploring, dramatizing and exposing the mores, and critiquing the social ills that plague the Cameroonian/African society. The world of these novels is an imagined real world peopled with characters who criss-cross one another's path, full-blooded characters caught up in the complex web of daily existence, involving their dilemmas, hopes and frustrations. Through their utterances, thoughts, feelings and emotions, these characters express themselves, and in the process, reveal their outlook and world-view. They articulate their views about certain issues or individuals in their communities or their world. In handling these virtual characters, the Cameroonian novelists artistically guide and shape our attitudes towards them, subtly persuading us to adopt the writers' point of view or ideological stance. Herein lies their pedagogic intention.

Set in Nso in the North West Province of Cameroon, *The Deadly Honey*[1] is the harrowing but eye-opening tale of how an ignorant but sexually active people blissfully invite death and disaster upon themselves. The 'axis of evil' involves the movement of young HIV-infected persons (mostly girls) from the city of Douala to the Nso rural community, itself immersed in sexual promiscuity. These 'young fresh' things from the city are eagerly and lustfully pounced upon by unwary village lechers; thereupon a wave of sexual scandals and abominations hits the community. Soon afterwards the libertines, one by one, become ill, manifesting various symptoms of an unknown disease; one by one they begin to die at an alarming rate. A plague of an unknown name and origin has struck the population; a curse of some sort has come upon the Nso people.

To fight the pandemic the natives turn to their tradition. They consult their *Sheys* and *Fais* and carry out acts of atonement; they perform sacrifices and rituals to their ancestors and gods and offer gifts to alienated kindred to pacify them, all in a bid to stem the ravages of the 'slim disease'. All the medicine men come together to unearth a buried 'evil' pot purported to have been the source of the frightful pestilence. But the net effect of these palliatives on the epidemic is nil.

In the hands of the novelist the deadly scourge becomes a device for exposing certain aspects of the Nso culture, and also for delivering a moral message to mankind, a means of revealing the best and the worst in human nature at a moment of an existential crisis.

Early in the novel, Rev Father Michael in a memorable and prophetic homily had warned his faithful that in the past God's anger against sinful mankind had come into effect through flood and slaughter; now, against the sexually promiscuous Nso people, it was likely to be effected through the 'deadly honey'. This sermon has an abiding positive effect on the young and beautiful Kila, the central female subject of the text. With the priest's powerful voice still resonant in her mind, Kila succeeds to keep away from lustful men until she duly gets married to Tumi, a business man from Douala.

But unknown to this innocent and faithful woman, Tumi is infected with the killer disease and determined to spread it to many people before he dies. And he does so, leaving behind him, when he dies after a humiliating suffering, a long list of 75 women he has infected, top on the list being his wife now pregnant.

The best moment in the narrative is the pleasant surprise the author has reserved for the reader on the penultimate page of the novel. It is one of the rare but happy probabilities of science of great moralistic resonance and is this: the faithful, innocent and devoted Kila, despite her marriage to the infected villain, Tumi, is found, upon medical examination, to be sero negative! The message or moral of the narrative is thus clear: while the reckless are swept away by the plague, fidelity to a single spouse can be an antidote against it; however, under certain conditions infected persons like Shatou can live positively with the disease. Like in Ngoran's *Nyuysham* the central theme of this novel is that the wages of sexual sin is death. Aids is real and is spreading among the sexually promiscuous like wild fire. At this rate it is likely to decimate whole communities.

Thematically speaking, then, this is a novel of high social significance as its educational value is quite obvious.

However, the Achilles' heel of the author is his occasional approximate use of language and the tendency towards bombast. One has the impression that the author is constantly consulting a thesaurus to impress the reader with sonorous Latinate words, rendering his prose, in places, stiff and pompous. We will quote here only two examples of the omniscient narrator's resort to verbosity:

a) The mellifluous conversation flew and just when they were at their glib discussion that coincided with the acme of hatred and phobia against all strangers, there was a knock at the door (15).

b) When their teacher had used that word for the first time, the class unexpectedly went into prolonged, side-splitting laughter and superfluous pell-mell that the teacher got sombrely ill-humoured and left the class morosely (23).

The educational value of this novel is highlighted by John Bimela Tume when, in the preface to the first edition, he affirms that 'The various Ministries of education and health will not hesitate to recommend this text for the school curricula, especially the G.C.E., as it carries within itself a moral' (iv). Indeed, *The Deadly Honey* is a work which, when well-edited, can be even more impressive than some other Anglophone novels. However, as it stands, it is marred by many linguistic gremlins that need to be expunged before it is fit for consumption by secondary school students, its targeted readership. Otherwise, while the text sets out with the laudable, didactic intention of eliminating the HIV/AIDS virus, it may, paradoxically, implant a different germ in students, i.e. the linguistic virus that language and literature teachers would like to discourage in young learners of English: their penchant for bombast, a tendency towards linguistic inflation and grammatical impropriety.

As for Francis B. Nyamnjoh's *The Disillusioned African*[2], it is set in Cameroon in the early 1990s in the context of contemporary world politics, and against the background of the wind of change that had blown from Eastern Europe in the 1980s. It is purportedly written during an imaginary visit to the United Kingdom by the Cameroonian hero-philosopher and putative author, Charles Keba. A philosopher by his own admission, Charles has gone to Britain 'to amass authority in philosophy' (5). He is understandably very pre-occupied with philosophical reflections or, in his own words, 'Philomeditations'. It is while in Britain to study philosophy that he writes four long, rambling, and critical letters to his friend back home in Cameroon, Franglotus Moungo. But the fifth letter is the one written to the readers by Franglotus Moungo.

The title of this work constitutes its apt theme: the disillusionment of Charles Keba. Charles' disillusionment is in several senses. He is disillusioned with himself for going to study African philosophy in the UK where there is no university with a department for that specialization; disillusioned with his experience in the Hospital for Tropical Diseases where he nearly died of a raging malaria bout while British medical doctors carried out forever their slow and annoying tests; disillusioned with the paradoxical attitude of the French, the fountainhead of 'Liberté, Fraternité et Egalité,' who rationalize monopartism in tropical Africa while encouraging multipartism in Eastern Europe; disenchanted with the inability of the African people to overthrow their dictators in the way Ceausescu and his consort were ousted in Eastern Europe; disappointed with the so-called African democratic ruling elite falsifying election results in their favour to remain in power; and disillusioned with the opposition parties that make no provision for decision-making with regard to the illiterate peasant masses, nor do they fight genuine corruption.

For all his disillusionment, however, Charles is more sympathetic and tolerant towards the suffering African masses. While he is more positive towards Africans caught up within the sites of cross-cultural encounters, he is definitely critical of African rulers and their impoverishing leadership; more critical of Africans ashamed of their African origins or of African apers who claim to be more English or French than these Europeans, but know next to nothing about their own culture. Charles is more condemnatory of American or European anthropologists with their stereotypical attitudes and beliefs about Africans; and more censorious of the hegemonic attitude of some Western powers, especially the French, eager to hold sway over certain parts of Africa. According to Charles, it would be better for Africans if competing European hegemonies were to operate in their societies than if there were only one dominant power, 'lest one good custom should corrupt the world,' to quote Alfred Lord Tennyson (Abrams 1971).

Consequent on this disillusionment is a related theme: the role of the intellectual in society. *The Disillusioned African* is a novel of ideas, and the most central idea, and one of its major themes, is the place of the genuine intellectual in emerging democratic African societies. Francis Nyamnjoh, in an artistic manner, i.e. through the letters of Charles and Moungo explores and articulates the role of the African genuine intellectual in societies where politics is still marked by the hegemony of the so-called democratic ruling elite who have virtually hijacked the wealth produced by the indigent masses. Though a minority, the political elite, through corruption and organized pillage, control the economic resources of their societies.

If Charles' imaginary sojourn and trajectory from Cameroon to Britain and back; if his movement from high, critical intellectualism and then down to earth is anything to go by, then what Nyamnjoh is saying is that the genuine African intellectual should go beyond being a mere egg-head; he must move from the high ivory tower of mere ideas to the hard realities on the ground. He must become altruistic by taking an active part in ameliorating the living condition of his people. And this will be best done through the sensitization, conscientization or education of the socially deprived, or the dregs of humanity, to become aware of their own socio-political potential. Once these people are politically conscious, they will initiate meaningful change in their society, leading to an improvement of their human condition.

As one follows Charles' sweeping critical intelligence from the first to the fourth letter, encompassing Cameroonian, African, British, European, and, indeed, world socio-cultural and economic issues, one cannot but acknowledge that here, indeed, is an intellectual with highly developed critical powers. Charles is really in his element talking about contemporary world socio-political issues, but what bothers him most is the human condition of the African struggling masses. The more one delves into Charles' critical discourse, the more one is reminded of Bernard Fonlon's model of 'the genuine intellectual' as spelt out in his book *The Genuine Intellectual* (1978).

The sensitive reader who follows Charles' searching, critical thought from Part One to Part Four of the novel, and carefully reads Moungo's letter (Part Five) to the readers, and noting what it says about Charles, will certainly realize that Charles has moved from the heights of high intellectualism and criticism to the local realism of his rural Menchum community. The university-level intellectual has logically put his scientific and philosophical knowledge, as advocated by Fonlon, to the service of his immediate community and humanity as a whole. Charles has 'decided to conduct the fight from the only angle he believed true change was possible' (149): from among the rural peasants of his Menchum locality, specifically 'the resettled but forgotten victims of the 1986 Lake Nyos Disaster' (*Ibid*).

The didactic significance of such a humanitarian act for anyone who aspires to the status of a genuine intellectual is thus obvious and best summed up by the concluding portion of Moungo's letter to the readers, many of whom may consider themselves as intellectuals:

> So he (Charles) teaches the peasants how to make political and economic capital out of their sweat and toil, and out of the ignorance and lazy habits of their urban-centred overloads.
>
> And it is for these reasons, dear readers, that I broke my promise to a friend at heart. I thought Charles had something to share with more than just a friend. It is my hope and wish that some of you might be inspired to work along similar lines, and that one day the situation will be well and truly better for the downtrodden and the forgotten bulk of our Darkened Continent (150).

If, in the educational sense, Charles Keba represents the hope of the deprived peasants of rural Menchum, in the same sense, it can be said that Ngwe, the central character in J.N. Nkengasong's *Across the Mongolo*,[3] is the symbol of Anglophone hope in the Federal Republic of Kamangola. Set in Cameroon around the mid sixties and the seventies, *Across the Mongolo* is a novel that highlights Anglophone subalternity within the Francophone hegemony in the bilingual Federal Republic of Kamangola. Because of the insurmountable obstacles he faces, Ngwe fails to obtain an academic degree at Besaadi University and emerges at the end of the story virtually bleeding from physical torture; however, he also comes out of his traumatic experiences wiser, with enough political education to become leader of the Young Anglophone Movement, an act of no mean educational significance.

After a sound secondary school education in the Anglophone state of Kama, the novel's central character, Ngwe Nkemassah, proceeds to the Francophone state of Ngola in the bilingual Federal Republic of Kamangola to acquire university education in Besaadi, the only university in Kamangola. But it is in Besaadi, within the hegemonic influence of the French language, that Ngwe meets his academic Waterloo.

To better appreciate what is happening in *Across the Mongolo*, the reader should bear in mind the socio-historical context in which the text was constructed. History has it that since 1961, the year of the union between the former French and British Cameroons, the effects of European colonial history, English and French bilingualism became a national policy in the Republic of Cameroon. At the turn of the 21st century the Anglophone Cameroonians number at least 4 million out of a total population of 15 million Cameroonians, constituting thus a linguistic and cultural minority.

In the text the friction between the majority Francophones and the minority Anglophones is therefore one constructed by the realities of the larger social context and based essentially on the psychology of numbers. It is a battle of complexes, more or less, wherein, impelled by their numerical strength, to go by Ngwe's narration and reasoning, Francophones feel that they should colonise and assimilate the Anglophones, that the dominant Francophone culture should lord it over the Anglo-Saxon culture. The narrator, as well as the author, sees this relationship in terms of master/slave binary opposition, with the Anglophone assigned the subaltern status of the inferior Other (65, 108, 163, 164).

This explains the hegemonic influence of French, particularly in the University of Besaadi where major courses are dispensed, and all examinations written, in French in a country that calls itself the bilingual Federal Republic of Kamangola. This would equally account for the hostility mounted against the Anglophone whenever he attempts to speak in English, whether it is in the District Officer's (D.O's) office, or in one of the university offices, or, above all, in the university lecture hall, of all places! (64-65).

One discerns in the attitude the Francophone imperial text that sets out to rewrite itself in the Anglophone inferior Other. But there is a big gulf between the 'pure text' and 'performance.' When pushed to the limit to explain himself in French in an office, Ngwe-blurts out only what can be termed barbarism committed on the French language: Je suis dit que' (61), literally translating the English 'I'm saying that'. This, of course, subverts the Francophone colonial 'text' that has produced an intolerable 'performance'. That is why the scandalized Francophone whom Ngwe is addressing urges him to go ahead with his English that had been shushed out of him, in the first place. 'Non, non, non. Continuez en Anglais' (61).

Unlike in the Anglophone citadels of academic excellence of Wysdom College and College of Arts where discipline, orderliness, hardwork, and merit are the cardinal values for success, in Besaadi, fraud, personal interest, gambling, injustice and disorder are the order of the day. In the novel Francophones ideologically 'textualize' the Anglophone as the inferior Other. Their orientalising attitude consists in perceiving him as a kind of comic freak whose behaviour gives rise to debasing appellations like 'anglofou, anglobête, esclave, salaud' etc.. (Ambanasom 4).

Ngwe goes through a great deal of humiliation, degradation and grinding frustration which inflict on him traumatic stress disorders that, several times, bring him close to a nervous breakdown before he is finally done in. But he draws on his great presence of mind and is determined to make it in Besaadi. However, for all his tenacity onto his ethic of hard work and honesty, after six years in the university, and even changing faculties, his academic endeavours end in failure, leaving him with zero degree.

Gradually, it dawns on him that his humiliation is not an isolated fact but one shared by other Anglophones; that the Francophone government in place has a hidden agenda for a subtle deconstruction of the Anglophone identity in the United Republic of Kamangola, with the university as the experimental nursery ground; and that the Anglophones co-opted into the government are there to destroy the Anglo-Saxon culture. It also becomes clear to Ngwe that the older generation of Anglophones have failed and that unless the young people do something to rescue the situation soon, the Anglo-Saxon swan song may well soon be sung. Consequently, he forms the Young Anglophone Movement (YAM) to help keep alive the Anglo-Saxon heritage, to fight for the Anglophone rights to full citizenship and not just to be 'some assistant somebody' (138). In short, YAM's goal is to uphold the Anglophone identity.

It is thanks to Dr. Ambo's connection that Ngwe finds himself at the reception in the residence of a junior Anglophone Minister in charge of Special Duties at the Presidency, Mr. Wankili, a pivotal episode in the text with regard to the Anglophone Problem and subalternity. It is here that Ngwe becomes more conscientised concerning the Anglophone condition of coloniality and inferior Otherness. The junior Anglophone Minister's outrageous declaration that his office will not be the place for solving petty Anglophone Problems (134) as well as the import of the conversation of two elderly Anglophone citizens, goes a long way to radicalize the young man. A statement from the conversation of the Anglophone citizens avers that the 'Francophone government uses our Anglophone brothers to destroy us, to ruin our heritage, to assimilate us, to clearly wipe out Anglophone traditions from the face of this country' (135).

That conversation marks a turning point in the life of Ngwe; he will never be the same person again. Its immediate effect on him is his resolve to form the Young Anglophone Movement (YAM), aimed at educating the Anglophones about their rights and full citizenship, and to wean them from being contented with any second class status or 'an assistant citizen' (142). Such an education will produce Anglophones proud of their Anglo-Saxon legacy and not traitorous sellouts and apologists for the majority Francophone culture. Among the Anglophone traitors must feature Nkwenti, the Anglophone clerk who refuses to speak English to Anglophones, or the Anglophone police officer who instructs his Francophone colleagues in French to maltreat Ngwe better, or Junior Minister Wankili who declares publicly that he has nothing to do with 'Anglophone'.

These and similar Anglophones, eager to be associated or identified with the majority Francophone culture, facilitate the execution of Babajaro's assimilationist ideology. Since YAM's fundamental intention is to subvert such an ideology, Ngwe, its fountainhead, becomes the sure target of Babajaro's dreaded police, from whom Ngwe has had a close shave. It is symbolically significant that at the end of the text, though physically and psychologically tortured and traumatized, the hero is still alive. He is the symbol of Anglophone hope. According to the Prince of Concealed Secrets, 'This child is of the powerful breed... His anguish is the beginning of his mission in the world, a mission to rescue his people trapped into slavery in a faraway land' (199), a declaration whose importance is even more heightened by its rhetorical placement: located in the text's penultimate page and paragraph.

Alobwed'Epie's *The Death Certificate*[4] is a national allegory of great resonance which, like Bole-Butake's dramatic parable, *And Palm Wine Will Flow* (1999), is set in a fictional African country called Ewawa. The text's anti-hero is Mongo Meka who, whether dead or alive, remains the subject of interest for most of the narrative, and this because of his pivotal, if unpatriotic, function in the novel.

A native of the First Province and doubling as Treasurer General and Acting Director General of the Central Bank, Mongo Meka is the keeper of the keys to these financial institutions. He therefore enjoys unlimited access to cash at any time. Being an unconscionable individual, however, he embezzles the whopping sum of FCFA 550 billion, most of which he stashes away in a Parisian bank under the name of his French wife, and then fakes up death in a road accident in a neighbouring country, in a bid to forestall a possible prosecution for denuding the national treasury.

His death is mourned, and he is duly buried, with a certificate of death having been established in his name. Taking Meka's death in earnest, however, his widow, Antoinette Yvonne, remarries, this time, a French man, Roger Girard, a development that threatens Meka's machinations, forcing him to come back from the land of the dead to embarrass the living, with his ghostly reappearance. He initiates costly law suits against the French couple with the intention of putting them asunder. However, Meka is hoisted with his own petard, as his stratagem becomes a boomerang. His death certificate being genuine, Meka is legally considered dead, and the man now 'masquerading' as Mongo Meka, an impostor! To further compound Meka's discomfiture, his alienated wife dies in a cyclone at sea in Australia, leaving her French husband the inheritor of Mongo Meka's FCFA 350 billion in her account, legally putting the money far beyond Meka's reach, a dramatic turn of events that impels the now impoverished and fugitive Meka to commit suicide in France.

There is the hegemony of citizens of the First and Second Provinces in all spheres of influence. They head key ministries, major lucrative companies and organizations, key financial institutions, the army, the gendarmerie and the police, etc. Their identifying terms are the kinship idioms of 'sons and daughters of the soil', or brothers and sisters of the First Province. What is at work here is the 'ethnicisation' of politics, since tribal Manichaeism is everywhere manifest. Perceiving themselves as the superior Self, fellows from the First and Second Provinces orientalize those of the peripheral provinces as the inferior Other (Ambanasom 8).

As I see it, tribalism as practised by the fellows of the First and Second Provinces of Ewawa is the theory and practice of ethnic politics; those of their elite charged with the management of public affairs are ruled and dominated by feelings of ethnic consideration. Since the elite in authority deal with power and economics, power in sharing resources, often scarce resources, they are bound, sooner or later, to betray their ethnic inclination when confronted with difficult questions as to who has what, when, and how much. They are constrained by strong, selfish ethnic attachment to give preference to people from the same area like them when giving out positions, posts, contracts or scholarships. They hardly therefore reason or reflect on the adverse consequences of their act. With ethnicity thus exalted, nepotism, favouritism and tribalism are accentuated in the novel.

The central theme that emerges from the text, dwarfing all the other themes, is that of organized pillage and unconscionable squandermania by members of a single tribe. These citizens manage public, money-generating institutions as if they were their private enterprises, running them wastefully; the money generated is spent as if the spenders are in a contest, i.e. as if they are striving to grab the trophy for the greatest squanderer, for the biggest spendthrift. The wastrels consume money as if the world is going to end tomorrow.

They dole out huge sums of money to relatives, friends and loved ones; they lavish impossible sums of money on themselves to sustain their wasteful, concupiscent lifestyles; they put a great deal of money into gigantic, ostentatious projects; they erect fabulous castles in the middle of the tropical forest; some go on expensive shopping sprees in Europe; others, like the Director of the Farmer's Cooperative Bank, (48), turn many expensive government vehicles at their disposal into their private cars to run their errands. The novel evokes huge financial figures that can make one dizzy; in places the sheer size of these figures is simply staggering and unfathomable.

A lifestyle like this is the central source of the corruption for which many African countries have become notorious today. Alobwed'Epie, in a way, rewrites Bate Besong's *Beasts of No Nation*

(2003) a dramatic piece which holds that corruption in 'Ednouay' has become 'an industry' wherein '...frogs eat money.
The way locusts
Eat tonnes of green' (102).
A behaviour like this cannot go on forever without obvious negative consequences; if it persists unchecked, it is bound to breed, sooner or later, untold unsavoury effects.

The central narrators: Mula, Nchinda, Musa and Ndjock are the characters through whom Alobwed'Epie carries out the education of the deprived and the marginalized. It is thanks to the kind of language with which he invests the discourse of the putative authors that citizens from the peripheral regions can become conscientised about the havoc wrought on the national economy by a profligate ethnic group. The financial recklessness of the latter is pushing the country onto the brink of revolution and chaos as evident in the apocalyptic discourse of the narrators. Alobwed'Epie, through the agency of the educators of the marginalized, makes this clear thanks to their disturbing, symbolic language.

In this regard addressing Mula early in the novel, Nchinda says: 'These fellows of the First Province are going to rake this country bare... This country is jubilating on a volcano of mismanagement, corruption and embezzlement. There's pus in our boil, it will burst' (12). The very idea of a possible violent reaction that this provocative squandermania may give rise to is reiterated on page 51. On his part, Musa, talking to Mula, says:

> For one thing, our leaders according to you are amassing wealth, they are depriving the common man of the bounty of our country. If this continues, they will become Louis XVI of France, his nobles and the clergy. It may be that's the situation we are living now with the way mere Directors flash 70.000.000 Frs. Pajeros around. So, ours may be in fact, the feudal system, now, 25 years only after independence. If, as you advocate, we should fight against the shackles of the system, then of course, we shall be reliving the experience of the storming of the Bastille and its consequences (51).

Musa re-echoes this perspective on page 192: 'We are brooding on an active volcano', which thought comes close to being practically enacted in the opening paragraph of the penultimate chapter of the text, as the whole nation is seething with anger and hatred against the denuders of the national treasury: 'The hatred had taste and smell. It was solid, as a bulldozer and moved like flowing lava. It hung in the air, on walls, everywhere. It was total' (295).

Thus through these unsettling, colourful representations of reality, Alobwed'Epie is subtly educating, sensitizing the common masses on what they can do. Therefore, the possibility of violence is real, but it is only an alternative option for a new society. Another figurative representation would suggest that a new society can still be constructed through an inclusive peaceful forum of national reconciliation, suggested by Marie-Claire's father. Talking to her in a discourse full of allegorical significance, he says the cleansing of FramMki, Marie-claire's defiled son, is not an individual affair, but one that involves the larger community: "The cleansing will require an assembly of the elders of our two communities" (303).

However, any such gathering will not come easily, in view of the strong antipathy of some of those who matter; for, according to the Minister of Territorial Administration (M.T.A), for instance, 'Only over our dead bodies can natives in the form of traditional doctors put us on trial. They can go to hell. Zero cleansing' (304). Should this declaration signify the possible failure of the peaceful option, imaginatively proffered by the author, then the novelist is left only with the revolutionary choice.

Judging from our discussion, then, these four novelists are visionaries who handle their common subject matter, the Cameroonian society, with intelligence and concern, as they imaginatively explore it, with its future in view. Eugene Kongnyuy's focus is the socio-cultural plain. He subtly urges a change for the better, in the sexual habits of his immediate Nso Community, in particular, and Cameroon, in general. If Kongnyuy's accent is on the promiscuous comportment of Cameroonians, the emphasis of the other three writers is rather on the higher socio-political ground. Here they imaginatively explore counter ideologies to subvert the prevailing hegemonies for possible alternative dispensations. With Alobwed'Epie and Nyamnjoh, it is radical education for critical consciousness with which to deconstruct the conservative ideology of the neo-patrimonilists; with Nkengasong, it is federalism versus assimilationist authoritarianism. It is, therefore, the intention of the novelists to instruct and persuade the readers to view things radically as they (the authors) do, for a meaningful social deconstruction of Cameroon.

End Notes
1. Eugene Kongnyuy, *The Deadly Honey*. Yaoundé: AMA-CENC, 2002. Page references to the novel are taken from this edition.
2. Francis B. Nyamnjoh. *The Disillusioned African*. Limbe: Nooremac Press, 1995. Page references to the novel are taken from this edition.
3. John N. Nkengasong, *Across the Mongolo*. Ibadan: Spectrum Books Limited, 2004. Page references to the novel are taken from this edition.
4. Alobwed'Epie, *The Death Certificate*. Yaoundé: Editions CLE, 2004. Page references to the novel are taken from this edition.

Works Cited

Alobwed'Epie. *The Death Certificate*. Yaoundé: Editions CLE, 2004.

Ambanasom, Shadrach A.A Review of John N. Nkengasong's *Across the Mongolo. The Post* 24 Jan. 2005, 4.

___ ___ ___. A Review of Alobwed'Epie's *The Death Certificate. The Post* 7 Feb. 2005, 8.

Abrams, M.H. Gen. ed. *The Norton Anthology of English Literature*. Sixth Edition. New York. London: Norton, 1996.

Besong, Bate. *Three Plays Plays*. Yaoundé: Editions CLE, 2003.

Fonlon, Bernard. *To Every African Freshman or The Nature, End and Purpose of University Studies*. Victoria: Cameroon Times Press, 1969.

___ ___ ___. *The Genuine Intellectual*. Yaoundé: Buma Kor, 1978.

Kongnyuy, Eugene J. *The Deadly Honey*. Yaoundé: AMA-CENC, 2002.

Nkengasong, John N. *Across the Mongolo*. Ibadan: Spectrum Books Limited, 2004.

Nyamnjoh, Francis B. *Mind Searching*. Awka: Kucena Damian, 1991.

___ ___ ___. *The Disillusioned African*. Limbe: Nooremac Press, 1995.

Shadrach Ambanasom

8
DECONSTRUCTING GENDER HIERARCHY: A STUDY OF MARGARET AFUH'S *BORN BEFORE HER TIME*

A literary fact about Cameroonian imaginative writing of English expression is that it is generally phallic. For instance, a feminist reading of the Anglophone Cameroonian novels will reveal that, nearly all of them, by male writers, embody embedded biases that betray their social determination in patriarchy. It is in the context of this patriarchal landscape that we must situate the significant publication, *Born Before Her Time* (2003), a novel by Margaret Afuh.[1] The view espoused in this article is that the text, *Born Before Her Time*, from an ideological point of view, is Margaret Afuh's fierce attack against patriarchy; in it she undertakes to deconstruct gender hierarchy in favour of gender equality.

According to Elizabeth Goodman (ed. 1996:x), 'Feminism is a politics: a recognition of the historical and cultural subordination of women (the only world-wide majority to be treated as a minority), and the resolve to do something about it.' Anyone in today's globalized world, who seriously reads Margaret Afuh's *Born Before Her Time,* if he is not a rare Neanderthal man, must readily concede that feminism is an issue in the text; and that the latter, an imaginative product of a contemporary woman, has been constructed within the context of feminist awareness. There is, therefore, no doubt that Afuh must be numbered among feminist authors who, in the words of Goodman, 'have a political agenda in the writing of their work' *(Ibid)*. Such cognizance demands that for a meaningful examination of Afuh's text, one needs to apply the feminist critical perspective, defined by Goodman as 'an academic approach to the study of literature which applies feminist thought to the analysis of literary texts and the contexts of their production and reception' *(Ibid)*.

Set in Batibo, in Momo Division, in the early 1960s, this female *bildungsroman* is the story of a brave girl, Abo, betrothed to an old man, Worewum, before she was even conceived[2]. When she is born, her marriage to Worewum becomes a *fait accompli*, a fulfillment of a pledge made by her father, Mbacham, in gratitude to Worewum for saving his life, during a boyhood incident, from a swarm of stinging bees. Thus at the tender age of 14, Abo is forced into the house of Worewum, a man in his early sixties. However, she successfully and courageously fights her way through obstacles that would have daunted many, to eventually marry John, the young man of her choice, putting forth significant defiance against an age-old practice that has dehumanized women.

Unlike her male contemporaries whose texts provide little narrative space for female subjectivity, Afuh's female protagonist is at the centre of her master narrative. Indeed, from the ideological perspective, the novel she has chosen to write is quite appropriate for her intention; for the *bildungsroman*, from its German origin, means a novel of education and development of a young person, especially from adolescence to adulthood. The young person, in this case a girl, grows up and discovers herself, her identity and conceives her mission in life and embarks upon it seriously.

Florence Stratton (1994) makes a point when she posits that a sexual allegory is at the basis of the organization of the structure of African colonial or post-colonial societies: 'an allegory of male and female, good and evil, superiority and inferiority' (15). The closer one looks at *Born Before Her Time*, the more one notices how deeply-rooted male supremacy is, at least in Momo Division, and the more one tends to believe that Margaret Afuh falls among those feminists who undertake an imaginative critique of the 'heterosexual matrix that organizes identities and cultures in terms of opposition between man and woman' (Jonathan Culler 1997:128).

Another term for male supremacy is 'patriarchy' which, in Andrew Heywood's words is 'commonly used in a broader sense to mean quite simply "rule by men" both within the family and outside' (Heywood 2003:246). He adds that 'feminists believe that the dominance of the father within the family symbolizes male supremacy in all other institutions. Many would argue, moreover, that the patriarchal family lies at the heart of a systematic process of male domination in that it reproduces male dominance in all other walks of life' (*Ibid*).

To carry out her novelistic intention, Afuh provides her narrative with well-selected situations as well as carefully conceived characters, endowing her heroine with historical subjectivity, while showing sensitivity to her male characters. She could have adopted an antagonistic approach to character portrayal by simply standing gender hierarchy on its head, valorizing her female characters while discrediting or stereotyping the male ones as, indeed, some female writers like Flora Nwapa and Grace Ogot before her have done. But this would hardly have settled the gender problem; it would merely have reversed rather than resolved it.

Afuh's approach essentially entails the juxtaposition of two broad categories of characters: the progressives or those who represent modernity versus the conservatives, defenders of tradition. The upholders of modernity are Abo and John, heroine and hero respectively, including the Rev Sisters of the Catholic Church and the younger generation; the conservatives include the parents of the young lovers as well as the jilted Worewum and his wives. By the time the novel ends, the scale of the argument will be tipped in favour of the progressive forces who support mutual respect between man and woman. But before then, Afuh effectively demonstrates the functioning of gender hierarchy in its cruel treatment of the women folk.

In Mbacham and Ebod Api, respectively father and mother of Abo, we have sexual archetypes. Mbacham is the conventional head of the family, sure of himself and his secured position, and confident in the fact that he can never be contradicted by his wife in any decision he takes over his daughter. Ebod Api is the ideal, compliant wife, humble, subservient and obedient to her husband, maintaining a low profile whenever the men are around or engaged in important discussions: 'She feared and respected her husband and when the latter took the decision to offer their daughter to Worewum, she went along with it very happily and went on to convince her unwilling daughter' (27).

This gender hierarchy is replicated in Worewum's home where he is the undisputed lord over his five submissive wives led by Ebodnjei whose duty is to educate and tame the rebellious sixth wife to submit herself to the will and sexual desires of their husband as demanded by tradition. The gendered ideology of male domination is equally supported even by John's Christian parents who oppose his interference in Worewum's marriage to Abo. According to them, it is normal; it is the way of tradition and nothing can be done about it. Indeed, in their Christian view, John would even be committing adultery to know a woman now someone else's wife.

To subvert this formidable monster that is tradition, then, Afuh positions Abo and John, the heroine and hero, constructing the former as her female subject, while making enough room in her narrative for the central male character, John. Her female subject is present in the narrative. We see and follow her everywhere she goes; we notice her every action and are taken into her mind.

Through these young lovers Afuh launches a scathing attack against patriarchal authority. The heartlessness of the latter is nowhere better illustrated than in the 'slaughtering', so to speak, of Abo on the slab of reactionary ideology of male supremacy, as she is bound, hands and feet, by her own parents and carried like a goat and dumped on Worewum's bed.

While there and still in chains and suffering from multiple wounds, Abo is effectively raped by old Worewum and left more bruised: 'Worewum watched on impatiently, with twinkling eyes as Abo was laid on his bed. When this noble job had been done, Mbacham walked out with dignity and his wife followed humbly behind, closing the door on Abo and Worewum' (27). A 'noble job,' indeed! And when it was logically concluded, the brutal reality dawned on the victim: 'Fear gripped her heart as the truth dawned on her. She was on Worewum's bed. Yes, she could remember everything now. He had taken her by force, in fact, raped her and left her all bruised and broken' (29).

Could anything be more inhuman and degrading than this? Where is the humanity in a system that would permit parents, with easy consciences, to deliver up their own daughter for such physical and sexual violation, for unspeakable brutality in the name of male prerogatives? The objectification and commodification of the woman, in this context, becomes complete; within this particular patriarchy, Afuh would seem to be saying that women have become mere objects, commodities, to be carried and sold to the highest bidder, in this case, the rich old man.

The Anglophone Cameroonian text that Afuh appears to interrogate most is Joseph A. Ngongwikuo's *Taboo Love* (1991) whose main narrative equally involves two transgressive young lovers, Jam and Iyafi, facing an even more powerful gerontocratic patriarchy within the Mukomangoc society. The consequence of their sexual act is death, for no man can make love to a *Wintoc the wife of His Highness, the Foyn* and go free. Prior to the dreadful fate awaiting them, Iyafi recalls similar savage treatment inflicted on girls by their parents. One memorable example is that of Nabi, virtually carried by her own parents (female relations) to her husband's house. 'As she would not open her thighs the women forced them open and called on Timti [the hated husband] to jump in and consummate his marriage' (Ngongwikuo: 18). This and other intertextual echoes are affirmatory. They foreground women's marginal status in a male dominated society, a practice paradoxically sustained, in part, by women themselves.

When we intimate that Afuh's text deconstructs gender hierarchy, we are far from suggesting that it destroys gender hierarchy completely. Deconstruction, according to Jonathan Culler, can be

> simply defined as a critique of the hierarchical oppositions that have structured Western thought: inside/outside, mind/body, literal/metaphorical, speech/writing, presence/absence, nature/culture, form/meaning. To deconstruct an opposition is to show that it is not natural and inevitable but a construction, produced by discourses that rely on it, and to show that it is a construction in a work of deconstruction that seeks to dismantle it – that is, not destroy it but give it a different structure and functioning (Culler:127).

The dialogic tension within Afuh's text becomes evident in the conflicting discourses of modernity and tradition, inscribed, respectively, in the utterances of the pair of defiant, young lovers and the older generation. In matters of the heart the former fearlessly face the latter. The discourse of the young is invariably marked by rebelliousness. Abo and her mother do not see eye to eye on the question of her marrying Worewum. In her resistance Abo is frank with her mother:

> 'Mother, I am sorry but I shan't marry this old man. You shouldn't choose a husband for me. I have to make my own choice. After-all I'm the one to marry him and live with him and ...'
>
> 'Hei! Stop that nonsense. That's why your father never wanted you to go to school. Is that what they teach you in school? To go against your parents' wish? My own father chose my husband for me and that has been the custom: that parents choose husbands

for their daughters. You are not going to change the order of things,' Ebod Api fumed (21).

Such a patriarchal discourse, forcefully articulated by a woman without complexes, is emblematic of the extent to which the notion of male supremacy is embedded in the people's psyche and regarded as an absolute by the traditional society. That would explain why Ebod Api is scandalized by her daughter's daring attempt to challenge patriarchy, in the circumstances, an audacious and apparently futile act in our view, analogous to that of a Shakespearean Hamlet contemplating taking up 'arms against a sea of troubles' (Shakespeare: *Hamlet* III i). But the bold daughter is not browbeaten at all as she retorts in a threatening manner:

'Mother let me warn you. If you force me to marry this old man, I'll kill myself before he lays his hands on me'... 'I will fight till the end. I must' (21, 22).

We find the same defiant mood in John's declarations when he too faces his parents, or when he is engaged in his interior monologues. In places John sounds like the legal defender of women's rights. In vain Tabita warns her son not to think of Abo any more:

> 'Don't go near her. You shall be responsible for what Worewum does to you. We love you. You are a good boy but you know Abo was promised to Worewum even before she was conceived.'
>
> 'That is the more reason I should stand by her. And I mean to stop such wicked customs. A girl should have the right to, at least, help in choosing her husband. I am going to Abo right now. A time will come when lovers will discover each other and march hand in hand into happiness while parents watch on' (48).

When he leaves his mother, John becomes engrossed in his thoughts as he laments the fate of other girls in situations comparable to Abo's.

> He thought of other thousands of Abos who had gone the same way to their slaughter house of a marriage to old and weak grandfathers while they were yet children. They were forced to carry out the enormous tasks of womanhood on the bruised shoulders of childhood.

'No, Abo will not suffer such a fate. I will see to it' (48,49).

But, against his father's argument, John delivers his greatest defense of the women's rights, his most impassioned oration in favour of women's concerns:

Father... It is high time men treated women in this village like human beings... Everyday girls and children are handed over to old men on platters as gifts or payments for one debt or the other. I could go on and on with incidents of such injustices. For God's sake, these women are your mothers and your children's mothers. They have souls and feelings equally as men. I hope a time will come when women will live hand in hand with their husbands as two complementary parts and not like master and slave. Slave, you hear that? That's what these helpless creatures have been reduced to (56, 57).

The utterance is a furious attack against patriarchy, a conservative system that exalts men and humbles women. It is a discourse that favours deconstructing gender hierarchy while valorizing gender equality; for it holds women to be equal to men and not their slaves. We consider it the central pronouncement, the key ideological statement, of the text, one that embodies the author's feminist vision of life inscribed in gender equality. Here John is a feminist serving as an important mouthpiece for the author. It is symbolically significant that the progressive discourse is ascribed to a young male character with the future in his favour. For it amounts to saying that the conservative male practices of today will no longer be tolerated in the future.

As he lurks around Worewum's house in an attempt to save his love from the old man's grip, John 'longed for a time when wives will live in love and understanding with their husbands discussing their problems and sharing ideas as he read in Father's house' (73). In an introspective mood three pages previously, he had told himself that 'He would show Pa and his in-laws that times had changed with the advent of education and Christianity in the clan. It was high time they know that women had feelings and would love just as passionately as the few white couples around' (70). School and church, education and Christianity, important agents of change, are seen here as liberating forces working in favour of the young people in matters of love.

Following Abo's escape from Worewum's compound to find safety and protection with two Rev Sisters, in a neighbouring enemy village, controversial, collective reactions are swift and blunt. To many conservatives Abo is a bad example of a girl acting against her father's wishes. Others apportion greater blame to her father who had blundered by exposing his daughter to the corrupting influence of the heady ideas brought by the schools and the church. In contrast, liberals, especially the young generation, hail Abo who has become a role model.

In the final analysis the influences of Western culture help to make it impossible for Worewum to accept Abo as a wife: 'I can't even accept her now. She is polluted with your ideas and way of life' (137). With Worewum out of their way, it becomes clear to the young lovers that their marriage is just a matter of time. Their happy sentiments are spontaneous, as in the following exchange:

> 'When we start working we shall have a grand church wedding – what do you say?' 'Wao,' cried Abo. 'What do I have to say? You are my lord and master. I shall follow you anyway like a sheep.' 'No. I do not want to be your lord and master. I want an intelligent, loving wife with a mind of her own to share my life and all'. (139)

In this passage, while Abo surprisingly sounds conservative, as she wishes to submit herself to her husband 'like a sheep,' John, true to his progressive principles, refuses to lord it over her as the older generation are doing now. He would prefer for a wife a woman more or less on an equal footing with him, a 'loving wife with a mind of her own to share my life and all.'

With the intervention of the Catholic Church to whose faith Abo has now been converted, the marriage of Abo and John is solemnized after Worewum's dowry on Abo has been refunded. 'After this the couple moved forward to stand before Father Peter for the exchange of the marriage vows and rings. "What God has put together, let no man put asunder," concluded Father Peter' (146). Through the agency of the young lovers, the novelist thus undertakes to dismantle the hegemony of patriarchy, reinscribing it in equality between men and women.

Afuh's novel opens *in medias res*, with Abo already in chains in Worewum's house, a device of technique wherein a narrative begins with a crucial event instead of the first chronological episode of the story. Even though the narrative perspective of the text is that of the omniscient narrator, much of the story is focalized from the consciousness of the heroine, especially through the effective use of the flashback technique, some of which occurs while she is in solitary confinement from which she is planning an escape.

Afuh's sensitivity, sympathy and objectivity are seen in the way she constructs not only the female characters but the male ones as well, especially John, to match her female subject. In a sense it could be argued that the text is a twin *bildungsroman*, for while it is the story of the education, growth and development of young Abo, it is equally that of the teenage John, thus the narrative of two young people who fall in love and come to discover their mutual historical mission: that of breaking with the traditional past, of carrying out an onslaught against a monstrous tradition long sustained by a callous patriarchy. The evocation of the powerful love between the young people as well as their strong sentiments against the gendered ideology is very realistic.

As she does with Abo, the author makes us follow John and listen to his declaration to Abo, his arguments with his parents, and his conversation with Abo's mother. Above all, she takes us into his mind to follow the trend of his thoughts as he lurks around Worewum's compound at night in his attempt to rescue his 'imprisoned' lover. In John, Afuh has constructed a realistic likeable character, likely to be a role model to her male readership, while Abo would similarly appeal to many an adolescent girl.

Though the thesis defended in this article is one that places more emphasis on the ideological than on the aesthetic dimension of *Born Before Her Time*, we consider it appropriate, before we conclude the discussion, to briefly comment here on Margaret Afuh's condition of coloniality, an interesting phenomenon evident in her text. She is a post-colonial subject whose text is written in an imperial language, English. But the intimate and immediate circumstances of her life that constitute the subject matter of her work are Cameroonian (African), a reality bespeaking her hybridity. A hybrid subject emerging from a situation of a superimposition of a conflicting European language and culture upon hers, Afuh is thus a child of two worlds: the one by virtue of her British colonial educational upbringing, the other by her close attachment to her Moghamo tradition.[3] Her text therefore appropriately celebrates diversity, difference and hybridity.

From a purely linguistic perspective, Afuh's rural Moghamo characters, in normal circumstances, should actually be speaking Moghamo, a language the author herself speaks but does not write. As she is capable of writing rather in English, her rural characters are made to speak in English, but an English refashioned to reflect the thoughts, speech patterns, rhythms and idioms of Moghamo native speakers.

Any informed student of literature in English reading Afuh's text will instantly recognize it for what it is: a post-colonial text belonging not to English literature but to literatures in English, and one in which, to go by the flavour of their language, the characters (Cameroonians) are speaking, living, and interacting with one another in a unique provincial setting. For instance, part of a discussion based on the attempt to persuade the jilted Worewum to take back his dowry on Abo, is conducted thus:

'You forget that she is my wife even now?'
'Be prepared to have your bride price back.'
'Fongang Abo-Atuh?' shouted Tangang, jumping to his feet and addressing each elder by his title.
 'O – e,' the others responded
'Ekwabi.'
'O – e!'
'Ikwafugho…!'
'O – e!'
'Afuka…!'
'O – e!' (129)

Here we have a practice, common in African oral literature, wherein elders are addressed, in some traditional societies, not directly by their names but by their titles, involving a lively exchange between an oral performer and the audience. As for the term 'bride price', it is the African rendition of the English concept of 'dowry'; 'bride price' will strike a native speaker of English as a bit odd even if he or she understands what it means in the African (Cameroonian) context.

Afuh's characters use proverbs which though phrased in English, embody metaphors and images drawn from an African rural environment and experience: 'She is a rotten palm nut indeed. Both the pulp and the kernel are bad' (82); 'Mbacham was blowing fire with water in his mouth' (91); and 'Our people say a toad does not hop about at noon for nothing' (140).

As the villagers celebrate Abo and John's wedding, they are served food items from their rural setting: 'Outside, the local guests were served with beans, and plantains... cocoyams and vegetables. The food was pushed down their throats by cups and cups of raffia palm wine' (146).

The celebration of the wedding of the young people marks a romantic high point in their lives, and emblematizes the triumph of hybridity over 'purity', for Abo and John are post-colonial subjects who, because they have been influenced by the ideas and values brought by the schools and the church, can no longer lead the kind of traditional life known to their parents. By the same token, Western influences do not automatically transform them into Europeans, to abandon their culture completely. They strike a balance between the two spaces, the imperial space and the indigenous space, creating a 'third' hybrid space, neither purely one nor the other, but a bit of both. The consummation of their relationship begins with a traditional betrothal and wedding (140-142), before culminating in the 'grand church wedding' (143-146).

After everything, then, *Born Before Her Time* thematizes the cruelty of patriarchy or male chauvinism which victimizes Abo, the female subject, whose feminist ideas are ahead of her time, hence the text's title. She asserts her individuality as she takes upon herself to challenge an age-old, conservative tradition. Her unequivocal feminist stance amounts to a counter discourse, confronting the prevailing discursive patriarchal practice. As already intimated, feminism thus becomes a central issue in the novel. However, placed within the spectrum of feminist views, Afuh the novelist would emerge as neither a conservative nor a radical but a moderate. Indeed, her moderate feminism comes close to womanism, a brand of black feminism. According to C.O. Ogunyemi (1988:65)

> Womanism is black centred; it is accommodationist. It believes in the freedom and independence of women like feminism; unlike radical feminism, it wants meaningful

union between black women and black men and black children and will see to it that men begin to change from their sexist stand.

In Abo and John, Afuh Margaret has constructed an archetypal couple with mutual respect. From their successful wedding, her text accentuates not a vertical but a horizontal relationship. It highlights an egalitarian union between a man and a woman, upholding gender equality.

The text's overall aesthetic effect is, however, slightly vitiated by some editorial shoddiness, evident in a number of linguistic and grammatical blemishes, some of which betoken the author's hybridity within the context of post-coloniality. On the whole, however, *Born Before Her Time* is more than redeemed by the author's artistic strengths seen in her deployment of effective techniques as well as having at her disposal a feminist ideological perspective that allows her adequate perception of her issues and the deep penetration of the realities of her characters. A lone[4] feminist voice in the Anglophone Cameroonian patriarchal wilderness with reference to prose fiction, *Born Before Her Time,* assumes a paradigmatic status, foregrounding an issue that resonates with contemporary feminists in Cameroon, in particular, and Africa and the world in general.

End Notes

1. Margaret Afuh, *Born Before Her Time*. Bamenda: Patron Publishing House, 2003 (with an introduction by N. Patrick Tata). Page references to the novel are taken from this edition.
2. A truncated version of this article was published in *The Post* of Monday, March 21, 2005 p. 9, under the little 'A Woman Writes Back: A Commentary on Margaret Afuh's *Born Before Her Time.*'
3. Ms Margaret Afuh is actually bilingual in English and French. Although an English-speaking Cameroonian with a British colonial educational upbringing, she has also studied French in Cameroonian schools and in Créteil (Paris) France.
4. There are at least six published Anglophone creative women writers. There is Azanwi Nchami with her novel *Footprints of Destiny* (1985); there is Anne Tanyi Tang with her collection of plays, *Ewa and Other Plays* (2000); there is, of course, Margaret Afuh with her novel *Born Before Her Time* (2003); there is Comfort Ashu, specialized in children's literature, e.g. *Ayamoh's*

Days at School, Kantana's Days at School, Nobility Differs From Wealth (2004), etc; there is Ma Fese, equally specialized in children's literature; and there is Emelda Ngufor Samba with a commissioned dramatic piece on HIV/AIDs entitled *The Boomerang* (2005). Two other Anglophone Cameroonian women critics who have also produced creative works are Joyce Ashuntantang with a collection of poems and Eunice Ngongkum with her collection of short stories. There are other women writers whose works I have not laid hands on but who will be documented by other researchers. However, of all these women, Margaret Afuh is the only one who has produced a novel in which patriarchy and the resolve to fight male chauvinism are central issues.

Works Cited

Afuh, Margaret. *Born Before Her Time.* Bamenda: Patron Publishing House, 2003.

Ambanasom, Shadrach A. 'A Woman Writes Back: A Commentary on Margaret Afuh's *Born Before Her Time.*' *The Post* (21 Mar. 2005): 9.

Culler, Jonathan. *Literary Theory.* Oxford and New York: Oxford UP, 1997.

Goodman, Elizabeth, ed. *Literature and Gender.* London and New York: Routledge, 1996.

Heywood, Andrew. *Political Ideologies: An Introduction.* 3rd ed. Basingstoke: Palgrave Macmillan, 2003.

Ngongwikuo, Joseph A. *Taboo Love.* 2nd ed. Yaoundé: Editions SOPECAM, 1991.

Ogunyemi, Chikwenye Okonjo. 'Women and Nigerian Literature.' in Yemi Ogunbiyi, ed. *Perspectives on Nigerian Literature 1700 to the Present. Volume One.* Lagos: Guardian Books Ltd, 1988 60-67. M

Shakespeare, William. *The Complete Works.* Ed. Peter Alexander. London and Glasgow: Collins, 1951.

Stratton, Florence. *Contemporary African Literature and the Politics of Gender.* London and New York: Routledge, 1994.

9
THE ANTI- HEROES OF L.T. ASONG'S FICTION: FOCUS ON FIVE NOVELS

The most prolific Cameroonian novelist writing today in English is Linus T. Asong, and his seven published novels, within the last decade of the 20th Century, must be seen by literary scholars as an impressive contribution to the development of Anglophone Cameroon literature. This paper is concerned with only five of them, namely *Stranger in His Homeland* (1997a), *The Crown of Thorns* (1993a), *A Legend of the Dead* (1991), *No Way To Die* (1993b), and *Salvation Colony* (1997b). The order of analysis of the texts reflects a logical sequence of the novels within Asong's fictional corpus. For instance, though published four years earlier than *Stranger(s) in His Homeland*, *The Crown of Thorns* is actually the sequel to the former novel, while *Salvation Colony* is the sequel to *No Way To Die*. This article defends the thesis that Asong's main characters in the five novels are anti-heroes, carefully conceived, in each case, to make him accomplish special artistic effects and convey a particular authorial vision (Ambanasom 185).

In the conventional sense the hero of a novel should evince some or all of the following attributes: courage, dignity, decency, honesty and an essentially kind disposition. He should be one, even with a flaw, who inspires respect, admiration and even love from both virtual characters and readers alike. Often when faced with adversity such a protagonist puts up a reasonable fight or resistance. Conversely, the anti-hero is one who lacks all or most of the above qualities. In other words, he often possesses but their very opposites.

In the hands of Asong anti-heroism becomes a significant device of technique. And the term "technique," in literature or art in general, means "the working methods or special skills employed by a writer or artist in producing a work of art... how something was done" (Holman 1980:441). Drawing on T.S. Eliot's insight, Katherine Lever says "technique" is "any selection, structure, or distortion, any form or rhythm imposed upon the world of action" which enhances and enriches our understanding of such a world. In this regard, she goes on, "everything is technique which is not the lump of experience itself" (Lever n.d.: 88).

Thus, technically speaking, choosing to construct his novels around anti-heroes is a deliberate rather than an arbitrary artistic decision on the part of the novelist. For it involves, with reference to his central male subjects, a careful selection, construction or distortion of the characters, meticulously building them up and then cutting some of them down to size, debunking, demystifying them in accordance with his aesthetic goal or authorial vision. Therefore, character, in this case, the anti-hero, is a device of technique just as any of the following devices of technique: contrast, leitmotif, irony, symbolism, digression, or narrative perspective, etc.

In *Stranger in His Homeland (1997a)* Asong has conceived an anti-hero, Antony Nkoaleck, who, despite his high level of academic attainment, (he holds an MSc. in political Science) is very ignorant of the norms of his society. The result is that, for all his good intentions, he behaves like a fish out of water because he is a stranger to the ways of his society. His individual norms stand opposed to those of his society, a fact that gives rise to some interesting ironies of situation and disastrous anti-climaxes exposing him to ridicule and humiliation.

After five years of study abroad, Antony Nkoaleck comes home full of honesty, enthusiasm and idealism to change his society. His proud uncle, Anuse, toils and moils to ensure that Anthony is the cynosure of attention and given royal treatment. To this end he reserves one of his rooms for the graduate. There he will sit in a throne-like chair to receive visitors who will be formally introduced to him through an interpreter. He will not speak in the local vernacular nor will he eat local food.

However, Antony lets down the uncle; for he is found eating a local dish *abe-nchi* with riff-raffs, a group of dirty, naked children with running noses. Besides, Antony does not care about the special treatment Anuse wants to give him. He feels people can see him anywhere. 'Let them see me anywhere they want. If it does not bother them, it should not bother me' (*Asong 1997a:* 52). Anuse decides not to bother himself to give his nephew any more red-carpet treatment.

However, the desire to parade the graduate's abilities remains strong. In Chapter Eleven the entire Biongong tribe plans a grand reception in honour of Antony. All the guests and VIPs are seated, and food and drinks served. Then comes the moment when the tribesmen expect to hear some good words from their illustrious son, their black white man, words that will be expected to echo throughout the town, thanks to the magic of the microphone, and uttered in the awe-inspiring white man's language concerning this great son's fabulous experiences in the land of the white man. Yes, the Biongong have a chance to show off to guests from other tribes, that they too have a son who has been abroad, one greater than theirs who have spent only a few weeks in Nigeria, a neighbouring country.

However, the great irony of situation is that when he starts addressing the people, Antony does everything the wrong way. First he avoids using the microphone. He starts off in English quite all right, but soon slips into a jarring language, neither English nor the vernacular, but a combination of both, which to him is the local language! He is advised to stick to English, but then what he says is not what his people want to hear. Indeed they are ashamed of his frank declarations. Each statement he makes is a gaffe. And Antony glides from one blunder to another, hardly aware of the prejudicial effect of his verbal indiscretion on his listeners:

> I am not a white man, for all I know. I do not speak through the nose and do not even feel the need to do such a ridiculous thing... I am from Cape Coast and Legon in Ghana. Ghana is a black man's country. It is in Africa. The people there are even blacker than you and I...
>
> I am staying in my aunt's house. A mat house. And I was using a wooden comb, something we had long stopped using in this country which you think is backward. Please, I hope I have made myself quite clear. You make me feel so guilty and ashamed to think that I have ceased to be one of you - that I have suddenly become a God, just because I have gone to a University outside the country (*Ibid:* 92-4).

Antony has certain principles by which he lives, a set of ideas through which he comprehends and interprets reality. He says to his friend Dr. Mandieg, 'A man should have a guiding principle. Some philosophy of life. A formula for living, Doctor', (*Ibid*:226). A page earlier he had said, 'I have a principle, never to deceive myself or anybody else'. There would be nothing wrong in Antony holding onto these principles were his society ready for them. But where the beautiful ones are not yet born, it would be difficult, if not impossible, for the likes of Antony to make moral inroads in such a society. One tends to agree with Dr. Mandieg that in 'human society principles should be constantly readjusted… to guide you to live happily' (*(Ibid*: 226). No man is an island; Antony must mix with other human beings; his fortunes and destiny are inevitably linked to those of other human beings.

In other words it is one thing to fashion out a neat code of conduct, but quite another to have it work in a society of complex human beings. When Antony the 'been-to' tries to address his tribesmen in an honest fashion, when they want to project him as a demi-god, he runs into trouble with them. His so-called truth or frankness does not square with truth or frankness as the Biongong understand it.

Antony scoffs at Eru's life of sex and alcohol. But when he becomes frustrated he himself violates his own code of conduct and takes to drinking and womanising, doing exactly what he had condemned in Eru. To justify his rejection of Vickey, his first wife, Antony resorts to outright lies and blatant falsehood, jettisoning his own precepts of truth and honesty. When he is dismissed from the civil service, he throws overboard his principles as he tries to falsify his marriage certificate without his wife's consent.

Antony adopts honesty, truth and fairness as a moral code of conduct in an imperfect society. But it is neither necessary nor desirable to always insist on being honest at all times. Though the truth will often set one free, it hurts sometimes. And under circumstances when truth would rather hurt, diplomacy or discreet silence would be preferable. But Antony knows none of these subtleties, and insists on being honest, regardless of the circumstances.

These and many more instances reveal Antony as one who hardly inspires much admiration or respect from his own people or from the readers. This is a man who boasts that he wants to change his society but who ends up being changed by that society, a man who upholds truth as a principle but ends up violating it, a character who stands for honesty but ends up being dishonest, etc. Antony, to some extent, is a man of confused values, one who 'fails to live up to the status of a hero' (Nyamndi 8).

In exploring the character of this anti-hero Asong subjects him to a series of humiliating experiences some of which are clearly meant to deflate his ego and debunk his ideas. In this regard Asong is saying that to be able to make a significant impact on his society, an individual needs more than just academic knowledge. He should understand that society very well and be part and parcel of it and sensitive to the feelings of the people who surround him on a daily basis. Academic knowledge alone does not really make one educated. With all his academic qualification, Antony still appears woefully ignorant with regard to the norms of his people. He lacks the vital, realistic contact that would make him positively functional in his community. His bane is blind idealism.

The anti-hero in *The Crown of Thorns (1993a)*, a sequel to *Stranger in His Homeland,* is Alexander Nchindia, a rebel prince forced to be a ruler against his very instincts, the young man who in the earlier novel is chosen by the king-makers against his wishes and in clear violation of the will of the late Paramount Chief Fuo Ndee. Here is a man who throughout his early life has not dreamt of being considered qualified to rule a people. He is suddenly thrust into prominence to be a traditional ruler, and this in disregard of the rightful heir to the throne, his half-brother Antony Nkoaleck. The main catalyst behind this action is the District Officer who has intervened forcefully to influence the Council of Elders to shove aside Antony Nkoaleck in favour of Nchindia. One of the Elders, Ngobefuo, in reference to the gravity of the crime they have thus committed says, 'This is spittle which we have spat above our heads. One day it will fall back to foul our faces. We shall never wash our hands clean' (Asong 1993a : 38). This metaphorical statement will turn out to be a prophetic pronouncement, indeed, and one pointing to a curse that will end up destroying the soul of the tribe. For to disregard the will of a dying man like the great late Fuo Ndee, the Paramount Chief of Small Monje, who before dying designates Antony Nkoaleck as his successor, is to commit an abomination in strict traditional terms. Thus Ngobefuo foresees their act as a boomerang that will destroy them.

Alexander Nchindia clearly refuses to be chief. 'His objections are conveyed in several confrontations which he has with the Council of Elders and the flagrant manner in which he continuously flouts the traditions of Small Monje' (Chia-*et al* 174).

He actually escapes but is caught and forced to wear an uncomfortable crown; no wonder it becomes the crown of thorns. Despite Nchindia's strong antipathy to being made chief, the Council of Elders and the District Officer (D.O.) remain impervious to his protestations. And, as if to reward them for forcing a crown onto his head, Nchindia is openly rebellious and psychologically determined to flout the royal code of conduct. He commits royal blunders and gaffes, and does not respect any royal consideration.

We are therefore presented with a classic situation of the making of an anti-hero: a chief or traditional ruler who refuses to behave like one, but prefers to be like an ordinary citizen pursuing his common interests and desires. Nchindia's unroyal behaviour is underscored by such acts as wearing jeans and casual clothes on ceremonial occasions, smoking cigarettes rather than using the royal pipe, quarrelling publicly, or coming close to fighting with ordinary citizens, turning a deaf ear to the seasoned advice of the Council of Elders, disregarding royal retinue during his outings, sleeping in hotels frequented by thieves and harlots, suspected of philandering with women of uncertain virtues, rejecting the queen chosen for him, and marrying an outcast.

All these are very serious crimes, indeed, especially in an area where tradition prescribes strict royal behaviour. Yet the people of Small Monje are willing to go an extra mile with their wayward chief, in the hope that he may turn over a new leaf. Unfortunately this is not the case. The nadir of Nchindia's disrepute is reached when he 'succumbs to the seduction of conformist degeneracy' (Kashim 216), and assists the D.O. in the stealing and selling to a foreigner of *Akeukeuor,* the god of gods, the spiritual symbol and the soul of his own people. And the people's verdict is final: the wages of Nchidia's sin is death! Nchindia, the D.O. and their accomplices are rounded up and murdered by the enraged natives. One cannot find a better anti-hero than Nchindia. A ruler driven onto a throne but who, as a consequence, rebels against his subjects in every act he carries out.

Yet we cannot really blame Nchindia for what he does. Traditionally speaking, his half-brother and not him has been groomed for the throne. He knows that if he accepts the throne while his brother is still alive, he will appear to have usurped what has been somebody else's right. That is why he feels strongly against being coerced to be chief, and psychologically revolts against the approach adopted by the king-makers.

You cannot hustle somebody into a role he loathes and expect him to do well, especially in a role that goes with grave responsibility. To the Elders of Small Monje who allow themselves to be influenced by the dictatorial D.O. Asong the novelist seems to be saying: 'Serves you right'. This is what you get for forcing a crown onto the head of a wretch against the wise words of Fuo Ndee. Indeed, Ngobefuo's prophetic 'spittle' has begun falling back to foul the people's faces.

A sequel to *The Crown of Thorns, A Legend of the Dead* (1991) continues from where the former ends. In the aftermath of human and material destruction in Small Monje, there is an urgent need to resolve the crisis and restore order: to bring the culprits of the homicide to book as well as to fill the vacant throne. In this regard competing interests emerge. On the one hand, there is Marcus Anuse, a rich prince of Small Monje, now living in Likumbe, who attempts to corrupt his way to the throne through the venal Governor Abraham Isaac; on the other, there are the kingmakers, led by Ngobefuo, who have settled on another and more respectable son of Small Monje, Beckongcho, as their choice for the traditional office. To ensure Anuse's success the governor orders the eventual elimination of the elders of Small Monje, and imprisons Beckongcho.

However, the Minister of Territorial Administration, Aliou Ndam Garga, informed by Beckongcho of the true situation of Small Monje, intervenes, taking the problem into his hands. He appoints Beckongcho as both the Senior Divisional Officer (SDO) and Paramount Chief of Small Monje and Bimobio, two sub-districts and strange bedfellows, already secretly united through a dubious deal by the late D.O., and the late Chief. But what is conceived as an ideal solution to the Small Monje crisis, the dual functions of Beckongcho, only turns out to be his undoing; for it is impossible for Beckongcho as a true traditional ruler to co-exist with Beckongcho the SDO, emblem of an unethical governmental administration. The seeds of Beckongcho's eventual downfall and the cause of his own cruel, untimely death, have thus been sown. The unscrupulous governmental administration overreaches itself when, following Beckongcho's mysterious demise, it decrees the area around his palace unfit for human habitation, therefore making it impossible for the indigenes to mourn their ruler, provoking thus the justified rebellious anger of the internal and external elite of this accurst administrative unit.

A school teacher who throughout his educational career has enjoyed a leadership role, Beckongcho is the only central character in all of Asong's fiction who inspires respect and admiration from both the virtual characters and the readers. From the impeccably clean environment of Beckongcho's home and the orderliness in his house, the reader can infer discipline and order in the man's character. A man of principle, Beckongcho has a list of moral codes that guides his behaviour (58-59).

He has already distinguished himself as a genuine, patriotic son of Small Monje. Concrete proof of his concern for his people is that while a head teacher in Ngeung-ale, in Sowa, it is thanks to Beckongcho's vigilance that the discovery of the loss of Akeukeu or is known. For all this, however, Beckongcho remains essentially proud and intransigent, qualities evident when he becomes both the SDO and Paramount Chief. At this time also, given his difficult circumstances, Beckongcho who has never been associated with corruption begins to yield to it, to a limited extent, particularly when he bribes to have his ailing and imprisoned uncle, Anuse, released, or when he taxes both Small Monje and Bimobio to pay for the destruction caused by Small Monje alone.

However, if Beckongcho is generally constructed as a respectable character, there are situations wherein he is subjected to indignities in a manner peculiar to Asong; for, technically speaking, from the point of view of overall structural conception, Asong's novels are invariably constructed around a pattern of ironies of situation at the expense of the central protagonists. In such contexts certain incidents turn out disastrously, contrary to normal expectation. This is thus the basic artistic design, form or rhythm, imposed by Asong upon his fictional world, which otherwise would have been a shapeless chaotic lump of experience.

We begin with the first of these situations, which comes from Chapter 16 when Beckongcho pays a grandiose royal visit to his subjects in Likumbe. Marshalling diabolic sophistry, casuistry and sheer insult (206-212), and coming at the end of a list of speakers for the day, Anuse, the most prosperous prince of Small Monje, pillories Beckongcho, now petrified, with a bowed head out of shame; he is compelled by a peculiar set of circumstances to sit through Anuse's tirade of abuse against him. This calculated insult is partly couched in metaphorical expressions like *To open one's mouth and talk,* and *to let one's ears hear something* (207), which, the omniscient narrator volunteers to explain to the reader, means that Anuse considers the SDO and Paramount Chief something of an idiot or a fool!

This is in marked, ironic contrast to the pomp and flourish with which Beckongcho arrives at the meeting and the deferential treatment and respect given him (194-195). Thus a meeting that starts on an upbeat note and followed by flattering speeches, unexpectedly ends on one of anti-climax; the great leader revered at the beginning of the meeting, is the very leader humiliated at the end of this chapter by Anuse. At the end of Anuse's verbal barb, according to the author, 'There was silence, abrupt, long, dismal. The kind of very heavily charged silence which can be said to follow the blatant exposure of *a villain who has always masqueraded as a saint* (213) (My emphasis).

As far as Chief Beckongcho is concerned, this is the first calamitous instance of irony of situation. Beckongcho's next humiliation is at Anuse's funeral where, for all his great rank and royalty, no modicum of respect is shown him as he struggles to address the alienated mourners unwilling to listen to him. Some even accuse him: 'Murderer, murderer' (297). In an oblique comparison between Anuse and Beckongcho, the latter is even subtly attacked by a choir in the opening line of their song, 'I am married to Jesus, Satan leave me alone' (296). Here, then, Beckongcho forfeits his people's respect because, as an almighty SDO and chief, he cannot be completely exonerated from Anuse's death.

Other instances involving catastrophic irony come close at the end of the text, the most significant being the handing over ceremony. Chief Beckongcho, the outgoing SDO, is to hand over to the incoming SDO. Splendidly dressed in a manner befitting a paramount chief, Beckongcho arrives at the ceremonial grounds in great fanfare and in a palaquin carried by four of his subjects. The singing of the national anthem, already in progress, has to be interrupted and resumed only after the chieftain has alighted.

After the brief ceremony, a few speeches follow, concluded by that of the Secretary General who 'went on to say the one thing he should never have said at the particular time and to those particular people' (340), and in these people's view the anticlimactic utterance is a scandalous breach of protocol. In effect, the Secretary General says: 'I want to insist that there is no higher authority on this land on which we are standing now, than the government whose representative is the SDO... So nobody, I say nobody, whatever he thinks of himself, should ever arrogate to himself the respect and honour due to the Head of State or his representative' (340). Beckongcho's mortification is total, and his people are in a state of sullen rebellion; there is confusion, which bewilderment is compounded by the misinterpretation of Beckongcho's hasty departure to attend to nature's call. In a disgraced, confused but dramatic fashion, Beckongcho leaves the premises just as he had arrived, in a kind of drama.

The disastrous manner in which that occasion ends will be read by the authorities as a subversive signal from Beckongcho for his people to rise against the governmental administrative system. And the mysterious death of Beckongcho, whose body is found under a pile of bricks behind his palace, is the direct consequence of the interpretation of that hasty and suggestive departure by the ruthless administration.

In these and other instances, then, and for all his respectability and dignity as a character, Beckongcho cuts a rather pathetic figure as a traditional ruler. Like any sensitive human being, he is affected by the dishonour; he suffers from his humiliation. But unlike with a Shakespearean Othello or Hamlet, the readers hardly suffer with Beckongcho, a fact that marks the difference between a tragic hero in the Aristotalean sense and what is generally known as a modern (anti-) hero.

Another anti-hero is Dennis Nunqam, the main character of *No Way to Die (1993b),* a victim of fate and unique circumstances, who is misunderstood and later rejected by friends and relatives. Dennis is a man living below the poverty line and eking out his livelihood as a small office messenger in a tiny co-operative. He has been crushed by fate and has withdrawn into himself. To friends, relatives and well-wishers he is a baffling psychological case.

Dennis has a weird prophetic sense of insight into his destiny. After a few personal disasters he becomes certain that no matter what he does or what someone else does for him, he is doomed to fail in life. Indeed so certain is he of his own sense of failure and of the futility of his efforts that Dennis regards himself as a 'bird of ill-omen' that 'would never rise above the level of a vagabond, an ex-convict, a dish-washer' (Asong 1993b:222). Whatever he does under pressure from friends, he does so as if to say O.K. let me comply just to satisfy you. But know that you're wasting your time.

Destiny, a power beyond Dennis's control, seems to be ordering events in his life for the worse; the scales are heavily weighted against his chances of happiness. We should briefly summarise the five instances of fateful coincidences that have stood in the way of Dennis's aspirations. In each case the victim referred to is Dennis:

- A brilliant secondary school student is confronted with poverty; the latter succeeds in sending him away from school.
- A talented artist is awarded a scholarship to study in the U.S., but close to the time of departure, he learns to his greatest shock that the daughter of the Minister of Information and Culture has gone in his place!
- An ambitious Cameroonian artist is helped by a British citizen into Britain to study art, but at the London Airport he is repatriated and thrown into jail because his passport is not regular.
- A nonchalant artist is persuaded by a well-wisher to study and register to write the General Certificate of Education examination, but his registration is ineffective because his money order has been stolen at the Post Office.
- An even more apathetic artist is comforted by his friend with the hope that he has been more effectively registered for the next examination session, but now all hell breaks loose in his host family as a nerve-racking domestic quarrel reveals ugly family secrets, leading to Dr. and Mrs. Essemo washing their dirty linen in public. And all this because of the troubles of the ill-starred anti-hero. Dennis cannot bear the idea of living and knowing that his woes have ruined Dr. Essemo's marriage. This thought, together with Dennis's self-persecution and death instinct, ends up making death the only way out for him. He attempts to commit suicide but fails.

In isolation these are credible coincidences. But when imaginatively strung together, perhaps not in quick but gradual succession as they really appear in the novel, they produce a distinct pattern; they convey the unmistakable impression of a view of life essentially pessimistic, an outlook of the world that appears to hold that human life is controlled by a non-beneficent Providence, that man is sometimes ruled by a power that does not always care about the welfare of his creatures, a Providence who mostly gives them suffering and sorrow instead of joy and happinness.

In my opinion this is the thesis that the novel seems to be designed to illustrate, making it a classic *roman à thèse*. The thesis is reinforced by Dennis's own declaration towards the end of the novel when he says, 'I Dennis Nunqam Ndendemajem, I had been sent to show man his other side, his back side, the side of shame from which everything human ought to shrink' (*Ibid*).

When we meet Dennis at the beginning of the novel he is already a frustrated man, barely scraping a living to sustain his family. The frustration has come about as a result of the first three fateful coincidences above. Indeed, after the third coincidence, Dennis said, 'That was what wiped laughter from my face and from my life' (49). It is thanks to the technique of flashback that we come to learn about Dennis's past. His wife Manda says of him, 'I had married a man who was too poor to maintain a constant supply of soap to wash his children's clothes, a man who was too poor to buy Dunlop mattress; a man who could not afford zinc for the roof of his house or cement blocks for the walls' (*Ibid*:15).

It is at this point in the novel that a former schoolmate of Dennis's, Max, now Dr. Max Essemo, a prosperous medical doctor, comes in as if sent by God to rescue Dennis. He offers to give Dennis a good education to the highest level possible at his own expense, and to keep Dennis's family on a regular financial allowance. It is his intention to completely transform Dennis from 'nothing to something', an expression that produces a shock effect on Dennis who feels that, miserable as he is, he is still a man all the same, that he is not 'nothing'.

Dennis thus feels hurt by Dr. Essemo's arrogance and presumption. He asks his wife, 'Manda am I nothing; am I not married with two children, boys who will continue to live after we have died? Do we not eat three times a day?... If people tell you that I am nothing, tell them that I am something. If they want to make NOTHING INTO SOMETHING tell them that they want to make SOMETHING into nothing' (*Ibid:*14).

Dennis's relatives cannot understand why he does not receive such a generous offer with open arms. They think that by being critical of Dr. Essemo's generosity, Dennis is exhibiting an eccentric behaviour. His friends and relatives work behind his back and arrange with the kind doctor to transfer him from Mbongo to Menako the capital city where he will be educated. But there is a curious irony in the sense that while the family, friends and well-wishers of Dennis are labouring to turn him from 'nothing' to 'something', the man has made up his mind not to change into anything.

Dennis has therefore rebelled against his rich friend because he has not accepted him for what he is, or has not come to discuss with him like a close friend to know what he (Dennis) would like to do in life. The following are Dennis's reasons for not co-operating with the man who came to help him. The reasons are found in *Salvation Colony (1997b)*, the sequel to *No Way To Die*:

> If Dr. Essemo really wanted to help me he should have looked for an opportunity to talk to me personally, to ask me what I can really do and how he could help me realise that goal within my own limits. This he did not do. He announced it to my entire family that he wanted to make me a doctor. And just because I had nothing, nobody thought I was worth listening to. They held meetings behind my back, arranged with my wife and my in-laws to ship me to Menako... (Asong 1997b:90). My friend did not think that a poor man could think for himself. He believed that the rich man could think and act for the poor man. I don't know how to put it, but his goodness killed me. I became a prisoner of his generosity. It made me meaningless in front of every single human being. I saw no future for myself. *(Ibid*: 117)

The great moral emerging from Dennis's justification of his 'strange' behaviour is that a man should never be underestimated; every sane human being has an ego to defend. Because he has been reduced to 'nothing', Dennis is psychologically determined to frustrate all the well-meaning plans and projects aimed at making him 'something'. Therefore, he does not co-operate with the expensive tutors hired to teach him, but daydreams away his time or engages in 'meaningless' drawings when he should be reading his books. We are, therefore, not surprised that he makes no progress at all in his studies in Menako.

Dr. Essemo's wife, Gertrude, wages a psychological war against what she considers a parasitic nuisance brought in to enjoy her husband's wealth when her own relatives are not even allowed to stay with them. She cannot understand how a married man with children can be made to depend entirely on another. Largely because of Dennis, Dr. Essemo's marriage is destroyed, a fact which so upsets Dennis that he does not find life worth living anymore. A main character who in the face of difficulties attempts to commit suicide cannot be a hero by our definition. Dennis is a man regarded by his uncle as a curse to the family, by his children as an embarrassment, by his wife as a puzzle, by Gertrude as a pest and a drone, and by his friends and tutors as an enigma. There we have our classic anti-hero, a man who takes no initiative to engage himself in any worthwhile activity outside his passion for art.

Yet, Dennis is not mad but simply a victim of a peculiar set of circumstances that cannot be fully apprehended by his acquaintances. Of his apparent eccentric behaviour he says: 'Sometimes when I sat like this and did things which surprised people, it was not madness. The things which had happened to me had not happened to anybody else' (Asong, 1993b:51).

It is rather strange that even Dennis's medical friend who should have known better does not adopt early enough a scientific (i.e. psychological) approach to solve the Dennis-puzzle. When Dr. Essemo thought that wealth alone was all that was necessary in solving Dennis's problem, he made a technical blunder, simply making a bad case worse. True, Dennis was miserable, but prior to Dr. Essemo's mistake, the man in Dennis had not yet died; he died after this miscalculation. This is an anti-hero novel of great significance.

Our last anti-hero who happens to be a villain is Rev Pastor Shrapnell, the main character of *Salvation Colony* (1997b*)*, the sequel to *No Way To Die*. Rev Pastor Shrapnell is the founder of Salvation Colony, the exclusive community of members of a Cameroonian religious sect. It is made up of the scum of the Cameroonian society, the dregs of humanity that society has turned its back on. They include the blind, the lame, the barren, ex-convicts, divorcees, murderers, rapists, saboteurs, arsonists, etc. One of them is the despised and rejected Dennis of the earlier novel. These are people who have irrevocably turned their back on their world of sin.

Rev Shrapnell gives them spiritual fulfilment and a sense of self-worth. He makes them feel that despite their infirmities they are important for being useful and productive. Shrapnell poses as an angel, indeed a demi-god. He is called 'Our Father', with implied divine attributes. A reformed and transformed Dennis says of Pastor Shrapnell that 'Our Father is our saviour. He brings joy to the sad, heals the sick, makes the blind to see, the deaf to hear, the lame to walk' (Asong 1997b: 97). Actually, Shrapnell does not perform any miracles in the way that Christ did in the Bible; unless, of course, one is speaking metaphorically. His brand of miracles may be limited to the rapid numerical growth of his converts and the material prosperity of the colony. Kind, jovial and generous he is available to his flock at all times.

If this were all about Rev Pastor Shrapnell, he would be an angel in human form indeed. But there is another side to the man, the unpleasant side. This is made evident with the ominous arrival of two nosy journalists, Cosmos and Istromo, bent on looking for a scandal to hang around the neck of the creator of the Colony, Pastor Shrapnell, because, according to them, there are often ugly scandals behind many religious sects.

Eventually their suspicions are confirmed; Shrapnell does turn out to be scandal itself. The journalists dredge up one scandal after another and publish them in their newspaper, *The Naked Truth*, sensational material eagerly consumed by the outside world. The facts reveal Shrapnell as a rapist, a dismissed medical practitioner, a counterfeiter and a bogus pastor. Posing as a devout spiritual leader, Shrapnell is a hardened criminal and a devil in disguise. His colony is built on counterfeited money secretly produced by him and smuggled into a bank outside the Colony. Confronted with the incontrovertible revelations about him, Shrapnell decides to end the Colony on his own terms. He prepares a poisoned last supper for his closest collaborators and disciples, but is forced to taste of the poison first and die. Dennis Nunqam, who has since become second in command to Shrapnell, takes over control of the Colony, and its spiritual life continues.

A deep reflection upon this novel will leave the thoughtful student of literature with the impression that *Salvation Colony* is a thesis novel. As defined by C. Hugh Holman (1980:443-444), a thesis novel is one 'that deals with some social, economic, political, or religious problem in such a way that it suggests a THESIS, usually in the form of a solution to the problem… The French term *roman à thèse* is sometimes used instead of thesis novel.' *Salvation Colony* as a thesis novel, is one written on a religious problem: the danger of sect fanaticism. Therefore, people should be sceptical of any sect leader claiming godhead and the ability to lead them to spiritual salvation. The thesis put forward is that religious sects pose a grave danger to society; for a brilliant criminal like Rev Pastor Shrapnell, the anti-hero of the book, can assume the innocent mien of a religious leader to commit an atrocity in society. Pastor Shrapnell is virtually deified by his devotees who completely surrender themselves to his control. It is against such unconditional loyalty to influential but potentially dangerous religious actors that L.T. Asong's novel seems to be warning us. The horrendous example of the mass suicide of Jim Jones's faithful followers in Guyana in the late 1970s is still fresh in the minds of many readers, and the Rancho Santa Fe horror of March 1997 is co-public with the discoveries of *Salvation Colony*.

Shrapnell's otherwise laudable achievement is marred by the fact that he is an evil genius, a fugitive from justice masquerading as a pastor. His Salvation Colony is built on the fruits of crime, on the type of foundation that gives rise to an evil empire, one built on sleazy, slippery sand and not on a solid, moral rock. Villainy is, therefore, Shrapnell's bane.

All things considered, one can conclude, from the point of view of positive contribution to life in their various imaginative societies in general, that the five anti-heroes are to some extent non-achievers. They are scorned, despised and even circumscribed by their society, and are not completely free to behave as they would have liked to. With the exception of Dennis these anti-heroes resort to dishonesty at critical moments in their lives; Dennis and Nchindia are considered indolent and lacking in courage and dignity. The subtle authorial perspective emerging from the five novels of anti-heroism is one wherein, in two of the texts (*Stranger in His Homeland* and *Salvation Colony*), the author ascribes the failure of the protagonists to major flaws in the anti-heroes themselves, while in the other three works (*The Crown of Thorns*, *A Legend of the Dead* and *No Way to Die*) he attributes their downfall largely to societal misunderstanding of them.

Works Cited

Ambanasom, Shadrach A. 'Introducing Linus Tongwo Asong: A Major Talent of Cameroon Fiction in English' *African Literature Association ALA BULLETIN* vol. 29 No. 3 (2004): 185-188.

Asong, Linus T. *A Legend of the Dead* North America Edition. Regina: Patron Publishing House, 1991.

— — —.*The Crown of Thorns*. Bamenda: Patron Publishing House, 1993a.

— — —. *No Way To Die*. Bamenda : Patron Publishing House, 1993b.

— — —. *Stranger in His Homeland*. Bamenda : Patron Publishing House, 1997a.

— — —. *Salvation Colony*. Bamenda : Patron Publishing House, 1997b.

Chia Emmanuel N. and Charles Atangana Nama. "A Sociolinguistic Appreciation of Asong's *The Crown of Thorns*", *Epasa Moto* vol. 1 Number 3 (1996): 167-176.

Holman, H.C. (ed) *A Handbook To Literature*. 4th edn. Indianapolis: The Bobb's Merill Company, 1980.

Lever, Katherine. *The Novel and the Reader*. New York: Appleton-Century-Crofts, Inc., n.d.

Nyamndi, George. 'An Overview of *Stranger in His Homeland*', *The Post Weekender*. Friday, April 24, 1988: 8.

Tala, Ibrahim Kashim. 'The Impact of Social and Cultural Change in the Novels of Linus Asong', *Epasa Moto* Vol. I Number 3 (1996): 211-216.

Shadrach Ambanasom

10
TWO OPPOSING TRENDS IN MONGO BETI'S FICTION: A STUDY OF *REMEMBER RUBEN* AND *PERPETUA*

Most of Mongo Beti's fictional works are pre-occupied with the colonial situation; they dramatise the conflicts of colonial situation and the reactions of individuals to these conflicts. The two relatively recent works that are the subject of this paper, *Remember Ruben* (1980) and *Perpetua and the Habit of Unhappiness* (1978) constitute, from the view point of history, a fictional pair bestriding the threshold of history: the one is set in the later phase of colonialism, and the other in the early stage of neo-colonialism. The spirit of militancy and social consciousness dominates both novels, bringing to the fore the fierce social commitment of the author. The thesis defended in this article is that, *Remember Ruben and Perpetua*, from an ideological perspective, are Mongo Beti's classic illustration of the inevitable radicalization of the colonized subjects by the inhuman colonial exploiters.

It is clear from these works that Beti's aesthetic goal is to use his art to serve the cause of his oppressed and exploited people, to place his fiction at the service of the struggle and liberation of his compatriots from French colonial and neo-colonial influences. Evidently two opposing trends emerge from each of the two novels: the forces of oppression and exploitation versus those of struggle and liberation. In both novels the choice of characters and human situations is dictated, for the most part, by these ideological considerations.

By its very nature a vicious exploitative system, colonialism is an extension of political and economic control over an area by an occupying state, often with organizational and technological superiority. In most cases, for economic and social reasons, the nationals of the occupying state migrate to the colony for the improvement of their lot. For the colonizers to realize their objective, the colonized subjects must be subdued or assimilated to the colonizers' way of life. But contradictions within colonialism are its own undoing; negative factors inherent in colonialism help to stir up angry reactions to it on the part of the colonized who seek to topple it to attain their independence. And for all its military might and technological superiority, the colonizing nation does not always find it easy to subdue all the colonized subjects, especially the conscientised ones.

In this regard *Remember Ruben* is a fictional classic in which one finds oppressive and exploitative colonialism being fiercely and frontally challenged by radical nationalism which begins, first, as critical reflection and trade unionism. The first part of this article will be concerned with the examination of the confrontation between the forces of oppression and exploitation and those of struggle and liberation as depicted in *Remember Ruben*; the second part will be devoted to the analysis of the very antagonism, but this time, under neo-colonialism in *Perpetua*.

Set in a French colony in sub-Saharan Africa, *Remember Ruben* is a fictional confrontation between the European colonialists and the colonized Africans. To go by the names of some of the characters, the colony in question is Cameroun. The confrontation begins with marauding colonial forces capturing Mor-Zamba in the village of Ekoumdoum and taking him to a big prison labour camp in Oyolo-Camp Gouverneur Leclerc, named after the white official ruling the whole country (colony). The prisoners in the camp are subjected to hard, physical labour. Abena leaves the village to liberate his imprisoned friend from colonial forces, but having failed to do so, gets recruited into the colonial army and is sent to Europe to fight on the side of France in the Second World War. At the end of the war the prisoners in the labour camp are released and Mor-Zamba moves on to Toussaint L'Ouverture, the African Quarter of Oyolo City.

Like in many other colonial situations in the African continent, there is a clear, physical, racist demarcation between the European colonizers and the colonized Africans. That is, they are locked in restrictive habitation, what some would call "the geography of exclusion." In the cities of Oyolo and Fort-Nègre there are distinct living quarters for blacks and Europeans. In both cities the blacks live respectively in Toussaint L'Ouverture and Kola-Kola, neighbourhoods characterized by filth, hovels and teeming, jobless black populations, including demobilized soldiers. The European quarters, by contrast, are clean, well-built, well-lighted and with well-tarred roads. In Marxist terminology the Europeans, in this context, are the 'bourgeoisie' while the colonized Cameroonians are the "proletariat." The quoted terms are explained by Friedrich Engels in the following words:

By 'bourgeoisie' is meant the class of modern capitalists, owners of the means of social production and employers of the wage-labour; by 'proletariat' the class of modern wage-laborers who, having no means of production of their own, are reduced to selling their labour power in order to live (Beer ed. 1955:9).

Every morning the blacks, in their thousands, leave their quarters to sell their labour, 'to beg for the meanest livelihood' in the European quarters. But in this essentially capitalistic system wherein the profit motive is paramount, 'Humanity disappears in the treatment of men by each other, and is replaced by an inhuman drive for profits' (Popkin and Stroll 1969:87). The remuneration of the blacks is thus not commiserate with their services. They are 'offered the yoke' (*Remember Ruben*, 94). The whites are uneasy with the growing black population in Toussaint L'Ouverture where, perhaps scared by the ominous sound of the name of the Haitian famous slave-liberator, they see in the black masses the emergence of 'some future black terror' (*Ibid:* 81).

And there does emerge a future black terror from the black quarters. According to Mor-Zamba it is at this time in the history of the colony that trade unionism is born. The president of all the trade unions in the colony is Ruben, a shadowy but charismatic personality who is to be the bête noire of the European colonialists. A structure put in place to fight for the interest and defend the rights of the working black masses, the trade union movement will later become a crucial umbrella organization for the channeling of political grievances. For about two years, in Toussaint L'Ouverture, for all their misery, the blacks live in a type of euphoria until the colonial administration becomes brutal.

Here we should summarize the series of harsh and provocative measures by means of which the colonial administration intends to subdue the colonized subjects, but which ironically help to radicalize the latter: The Labour Centre of the black workers is closed down; a police commissariat and a prison are erected in its place. This is the beginning of a bloody confrontation between the youth of Toussaint L'Ouverture and the police, the starting point of conflicting relationships between the base and the superstructure. Many young people are picked up and thrown into jail for innocuous crimes, some as simple as merely yelling 'Long Live Ruben' (*Ibid*: 87). In Kola-

Kola, not pleased with the rising popularity of Ruben, the police capture and torture him with murderous intentions; Ruben is rescued by students led by Dessalines and Mor-Zamba. The colonial administration slams a ban on the production and sale of local beverages; Ruben orders a resumption of the production and sale of the drinks. He is charged with an outrage against the 'highest representative of the republic in the colony' (*Ibid*: 168) when he accuses the Governor of collusion with private interest in the colony.

The Popular Progressive Party, the PPP, is born. According to the narrator Ruben 'had realized that priority must be given to political action, whose success was the necessary condition for the real transformation of the fate of the African workers' (*Ibid*: 169). Elections are conducted in the colony, and the people of Kola-Kola vote massively for Ruben, but there is heavy rigging as Ruben's name does not feature among the winners! Ruben suggests that in future elections the administration and the PPP should co-operate, but is rebuffed. Ruben declares election results null and void, and the Governor declares him a wanted man. The administration dissolves the PPP and destroys the Labour Centre in Kola-Kola. Permanent buildings are requisitioned and transformed into police stations linked by telephones. Ruben is killed by the colonial administration. However, Hurricane-Viet (Abena who has since returned from Europe) replaces him. He bombs petrol service stations and scares away administration commandos who leave behind guns which are then picked up by Rubenists. As Independence is only a few months away the revolutionaries and the forces of the colonial administration are poised for a major showdown over Kola-Kola. Hurricane-Viet declares 'I've kept myself alive all these long years for this moment above all others' (*Ibid*: 246) and that 'Africa has been in chains, so to speak, from eternity; whenever we liberate her will be soon enough... The struggle will be long, very long' (*Ibid*: 252).

In *Perpetua* we are in an independent republic headed by Baba Toura, and the expected confrontation over Kola-Kola has since taken place with the result that many Rubenists have either been killed, imprisoned or forced into exile. Essola, a former PPP detainee, gains his release from one of Baba Toura's prisons in a northern concentration camp after signing an undertaking that he would now militate in favour of Baba Toura's party, the African Union. He gets to his village only to discover that while he was away in detention, his

163

favourite younger sister, Perpetua, who had been 'sold' into marriage by his mother, had died in pregnancy. The whole novel takes the form of a quest, Essola's quest, from all those who knew her, of how Perpetua lived and died in her pregnancy.

At this point it is necessary for us to remind ourselves of some of the statements made in *Remember Ruben* as carried by the pamphlet of the external leaders of the PPP concerning Baba Toura. There Baba Toura is said to be a 'perfect screen' behind which the colonialists will continue to govern and everything will go on as before. We will have independence, but nothing will be changed (*Remember Ruben,* 217). 'With Baba Toura… the agent of colonialism and imperialism, hiding behind Baba Toura… will continue to hold him prisoner in his own land. The people will continue to walk naked and die of hunger in a country bulging with resources' (*Ibid*: 218).

Now, if we test these declarations against the practical realities prevailing under Baba Toura's government as depicted in *Perpetua*, we will notice that they are not airy, theoretical nonsense, that though the streets of the young independent republic are not littered with corpses of starving nationals, the citizens of this nascent nation are suffering from many deprivations, nevertheless. We will notice that though independent, Baba Toura's country is still indirectly under foreign domination. In other words it is now a neo-colonial state, and Baba Toura a neo-colonial stooge or leader of the national bourgeoisie.

According to Essola, just before independence he had seen in Ntermelen many watch-dogs of French colonial interests, known in official bulletins as 'French Overseas Forces,' in endless motorized patrols that instilled terror in peasants. Now, some six years later, 'it seemed to him that the obsessive presence of those responsible for public order was denser… than it had been then. On foot and scattered through the mass of people, or in groups in vehicles they were a conspicuous demonstration of strength' (*Perpetua*, 3). Therefore, in *Perpetua,* we are no longer talking of any persistent, open encounter between the two ideologies as noticed in the earlier novel.

Here the armed forces of the new Republic have won their battle against the revolutionaries and Rubenists who have been wiped out. Essola learns this upon leaving prison:

> As soon as Independence was declared, he was assured, the handful of militants still active had been denounced, tried and found guilty of terrorism by the courts of the new Republic, paraded from village to village, and then shot in the town square. The mutilated body of one of them had been left on show in his own village until it began to decompose. (*Ibid*)

The ex-PPP detainee equally learns that since 1962, Baba Toura, at the behest of the French psychologists working for him, had adopted a ruthless stand against anyone still attached to the memory of Ruben. The people had been cautioned to steer clear of politics, now a taboo subject dreaded by them as though it were leprosy.

As we did with colonialism earlier, we should attempt a working definition of the term 'neo-colonialism,' the ambiance or setting of *Perpetua*. According to Frantz Fanon, after a colony has achieved political independence,

> The national bourgeoisie steps into the shoes of the former European settlement: doctors, barristers, traders, commercial travelers, general agents, and transport agents... The national middle class discovers its historic mission: that of intermediary... of being the transmission line between the nation and a capitalism, rampant though camouflaged, which today puts on the mask of neo-colonialism. The national bourgeoisie will be quite content with the role of the Western bourgeoisie's business agent, and it will play its part without any complexes in a most dignified manner (Fanon 1968:152-3).

Neo-colonialism, simply put then, is the practice wherein a former colony now politically independent is, however, still economically controlled from abroad by a more developed country or by foreign multi-national companies. The directors of these corporations usually are local intermediaries answerable to their foreign bosses.

Baba Toura's country is now politically independent. The white Governor has gone away; Baba Toura the 'black Governor' is now in charge. But economically speaking not much has changed because colonial economic structures are still in place all over the country, controlling key economic sectors. These colonial economic structures, largely foreign-owned, are the things that Ruben had fought to change. Had he succeeded, he should probably have introduced some form of socialist economy, privileging collective or government ownership and management of the means of production and distribution of goods. The economy would have been in the hands of nationals. But because Ruben was executed, the foreign economic structures during colonialism continued after independence since it was Baba Toura, the choice of the colonialists, who became President. This, we gather from the rare conversation that Perpetua had had with her mother.

> 'Why didn't your Ruben become Governor, then?'
> 'You know very well, mother, the whites killed him because if he had been Governor, as you put it, they [the colonialists] would have had to give everything back to us: the cities, the shops, the market stalls, the offices, the trains, the airports, the big houses, everything. But with Toura, as you see, they've kept everything' (*Ibid*: 16-3-164).

This shows that the economy of the young Republic is in foreign hands, a classic definition of neo-colonialism; thus, Baba Toura is a 'perfect screen' behind which the colonialists have passed to maintain a firm grip on the country.

Those 'psychologists' working for Baba Toura and advising him to keep a heavy hand on his people in the name of 'necessary salutary harshness' for the sake of peace and stability, a condition *sine qua non* for the safety of foreign business interests, are symbolic of foreign, 'technical' advisers that would have been found in all ministries of the new President's government. Surely the 'psychologists' are not there for the welfare of Baba Toura, nor, much less, for the interest of the citizens of the country. The technicians are there to defend the interest of the European business community.

With just a little sum of money, foreign businessmen can bamboozle venal local bourgeois to sign away their patrimony with no qualms, as the Forest Officer does with logging companies destroying and depleting the forests (*Ibid*: 49-51). This exploitation, facilitated at lower levels by local compradors, is equally effected at higher levels by the highest personality in the land himself, Baba Toura, the pliable tool in the hands of his neo-colonial masters, who have placed 'psychologists' in strategic ministries to guide him on policies. That is why, according to Zeyang, Baba Toura can claim that the presidency is his business alone and no one else's; certainly Baba Toura is answerable to no one else but to his masters who put him where he is.

The exploitation and oppression of the population is also carried out by petit bourgeois as seen in the medical field where free drugs sent to the hospitals for distribution to the needy are sold by medical officers and politicians for their own profit. The few who benefit from free treatment are high-profile personalities, especially military or police officers, or their family members. Pregnant Perpetua painfully discovers this when she goes for medical consultation at the clinic (*Ibid*: 111-114). She and other pregnant women stand in the sultry sun for the whole day at the hospital without receiving any medical attention, while members of the privileged bourgeois class are being served.

In general, then, under Baba Toura life for the common citizen is hell; in many respects it is much worse than during colonialism. There is a nation-wide curfew putting an end to movement after certain hours; the ubiquitous presence of police and military men instills fear into citizens; and there is the annoying pass which a citizen has to obtain to be able to move from one part of the country to another. And, as Perpetua's mother complains, this is not always easy to do:

> 'You have to grease the palm of the man in the office who gives you the pass and the policeman who can still arrest you even if you've got a pass. It's never-ending. Why did Massa Baba Toura have to spoil everything and make it all so complicated? It was so much easier when the white-men were in charge' (*Ibid*: 162).

There are concentration camps all over the country to take care of rebels or Rubenists. A party official of the African Union need only invoke the phrase 'political provocation' or any of the following words: 'subversive', 'communist', 'Rubenist', against an individual for that person to be arrested instantly and thrown into jail. The regime, though it cannot afford a tablet of quinine or aspirin to help a poor pregnant woman, is in possession of the latest technology in torture. Zeyang bitterly complains that his sweetheart would not have died if those in position of authority had not misused free drugs put at their disposal. 'Perpetua would probably not be dead if this wretched country had not been completely deprived of medicines since Baba Toura came to power' (*Ibid*: 51). It would be ridiculous, under such a dictatorship, to talk of the respect of human rights, for they are grossly violated.

In *Perpetua*, therefore, because of the overwhelming military might now at his disposal, Baba Toura and the forces of oppression and exploitation have succeeded in neutralizing those of struggle and liberation. If under colonialism the forces of oppression and exploitation had as their main target Ruben, the man to be eliminated, under neo-colonialism their policy appears to raze to the ground any object that moves in the name of Rubenism. They have become more dissuasive and ruthless.

For all this, however, the forces of struggle and liberation are far from being completely wiped out. True, they cannot match the military might of their adversaries, but they exist to resist them all the same, with this difference, that they have revised their strategies. Overpowered as they are, they have gone either underground or into exile to carry out the war against Baba Toura in another form – by means of guerrilla warfare, or through the diplomatic option. But the forces of oppression continue to pursue them.

As recent as two years ago they successfully smoked out and executed radical Bifanda the greatest revolutionary and freedom fighter, second only to Ruben himself 'just when he was setting up a new guerrilla front in the south-east' (*Ibid*: 58). Before his untimely death this PPP theoretician and holder of a Ph.D. had written a radical anti-imperialist pamphlet targeting international capitalism, the very neo-colonial forces that have been shoring up Baba Toura's regime for their own selfish interests. Part of the revolutionary pamphlet ran thus:

> Witnessing as they do processions of bloodshed and hypocrisy in the midst of which imperialism has established, succours and sustains Baba Toura, protector of the colonial monopolies, guarantor of the cartels, guardian angels of international capitalism, how in the long run can the men of the backwoods retain their respect for two thousand years of so-called Christian civilization? No one has the right to claim they are invested with a civilizing mission in Africa,

except the Africans. To get up a chosen people to lead another, as stricken by some obscure curse, is merely to entrust the tender candour of youth to the perverse, envious and disgusting egoism of age. This is a lesson that history forever reinforces. In terms of education, what kind of example have our self-styled teachers given by their daily behaviour over the last hundred years, for the edification of their pupils who forever fail to pass the tests they set? Can plunder and bloodsucking uphold the education authority of a barbarism for which no profit is too low or too disgusting?

And since today oppression wears the mask of 'co-operation' let us also say, adapting the famous quotation, that what is called 'co-peration' is nothing but the pursuit of colonialism, by the same means, but in different words (*Ibid*: 56-57).

As if they have been fated to lose more ground to Baba Toura, PPP militants suffer an additional setback in their external wing when their key supporter in Accra, Ghana, President Nkrumah, the person who had provided sanctuary to their leaders in exile, is overthrown. This sad news, plus the equally disheartening report that Bifanda had been captured... and ... 'decapitated by Baba Toura's henchmen under the command of an Israeli technical assistant' (*Ibid*: 165), threw the hooligans and the general population into despair and 'a frenzy of drink, sex and backbiting' (*Ibid*).

The mass behaviour of the general population here shows that, to some extent, they are sympathizers of the PPP. But since politics, particularly radical politics, has become a taboo subject; since the regime has 'agents provocateurs' all over the place to denounce the slightest anti-Toura sentiments or pro-PPP sympathy; since the streets are full of police and military people ready to crush any critic of the regime; the people decide to turn their anger either inward, inflicting untold psychological harm unto themselves, or outward, channeling their frustration into equally self-destructive acts like a frenzy of uncontrollable drinking, sex and slander.

Indeed alcohol, in general, is a boon to the regime; it is a distracting and befuddling beverage for people who would otherwise have been fomenting trouble for the government. Alcohol and Baba Toura are one. Right from *Remember Ruben* the impression the reader has had regarding Baba Toura and alcohol is that the latter is a drunk, having been referred to several times as 'Massa booza' (Master Boozer), 'Le Biture', with indications of his having gone to Europe for treatment for alcoholism.

His regime is very tolerant of the production, sale and consumption of alcohol – beer, whisky and local illicit gin, a permissive policy certainly financially beneficial to the beer industry and the New African Brewery, a sector controlled by the neo-colonialists. For one must remember that at this early stage of neo-colonialism, a company like the New African Brewery is 'African' only in name; it cannot be owned by an African. It is the property of some white tycoon; however, under neo-colonialism it may have, as window-dressing, an 'African Director', answerable to his European overlord.

The social significance of Mongo Beti's two major novels resides in the fact that they place him on the enviable pedestal of socio-political criticism. *Remember Ruben* is in the forefront of anti-colonial protest with regard to African literature in general, while *Perpetua* takes the front seat among novels of post-independence protest against neo-colonialism. In terms of historical setting the latter novel covers the first decade of political independence (c. 1960-1970). The neo-colonial era in Africa generally dates from 1960 to the present; it is a period involving the fundamental struggle between the forces of exploitation and oppression, and those of struggle and liberation. The period reveals, in the words of Ngugi wa Thiong'o, "a society built on a system of robbery and theft corresponding to the two antagonistic positions of the robber and the robbed, of the parasitic and the creative, in the social production of wealth" (Ngugi 1981:124). In other words the confrontation is between Western capitalism, with its African compradors, on the one hand, and the African working masses, including progressive forces and intellectuals fighting for socio-political change, on the other. It is a struggle that, with Mongo Beti, began at the dawn of independence and is far from over yet.

How right was Huricane-viet when, at the end of *Remember Ruben* he had, with uncanny foresight, predicted the long duration of the fight! 'Africa has been in chains, so to speak, from eternity: whenever we liberate her will be soon enough. Our struggle will be long, very long' (*Remember Ruben,* 252). Mongo Beti thus places the national struggle within the broader context of the liberation of the African continent.

The political character of Beti's fiction, which he has made an instrument of radical change, therefore becomes clear. This peculiar temper of his work is what probably pushed Dorothy Blair to describe Beti's story of Mor-Zamba in *Remember Ruben* as 'the pretext for a political tract' (quoted in Moore, 1980:212), a clear criticism of Beti's art.

Does this mean that Mongo Beti uses the novelistic genre purely for political ends? Or that he is only a literary dilettante dabbling with this artistic form to push ahead his political propaganda? When one looks at these works closely, it does seem at times that Beti places great stress on the political dimension of his fiction, especially as revealed by the radical literature produced by the PPP revolutionaries, or Bifanda the theoretician of the Revolution. There are times when the reader feels that Baba Toura (former President Ahmadou Ahidjo) comes off much worse in Beti's fiction; moreover, that he is treated with the spite, scorn, hatred - and the words are not strong enough - of one who wants to settle a political score with a personal enemy. At moments when the novelist makes Baba Toura appear an idiot, an imbecile, a drunk, and a lecher, his prose does appear to be unworthy of him. But these are rare moments, indeed.

However, looking at Beti's fiction from a purely ideological perspective would be telling only half the story; the ideas, themes and issues treated in his works are only the framework on which the mortar and the bricks of the fictional creations are artistically worked. Both novels are moving human stories, well-told, deploying different narrative techniques.

Remember Ruben is the story of Mor-Zamba who, as the name indicates, is destined to play a prominent role in the history of his time: a wrestling champion in his village, two-time prisoner at the hands of colonial authorities, rescuer of the nationalist leader, capturer of the colonial spy, and finally, chief of his native Ekoumdoum. The novel consists of a variety of interesting characters like Mor-Zamba the man of destiny, Abena the soldier of fortune, Jean Louis the colonial spy, Robert the worldly African preying on Niarkos the colonial cocoa-merchant, himself defrauding cocoa-farmers of the real value of their cocoa, etc. If Ruben and Abena tend to be shadowy characters, it is because sometimes revolutionaries have to be that way to avoid early death. They lead a kind of risky life, being constantly the targets of their enemies.

On its part, *Perpetua* is a passionate and moving story of Perpetua, a brilliant girl sold into early marriage where she suffers and dies in her third pregnancy at the age of 20. The story, pieced together by Essola, is told by all those who knew and loved Perpetua, an array of lively narrators including Crescentia, Anna Maria, Zeyang, Martin, etc. But the story of Perpetua is also one of allegorical or symbolic significance.

The forcing of Perpetua into marriage in order for her mother to pamper her drunken son, Martin, with the dowry collected, and the ruining of Perpetua through torture and debauchery symbolize the destruction of the Cameroon for which Essola suffered six years' incarceration, from which he came out to find the moral and economic decline under Baba Toura (Moore, 1980: 214). No wonder Essola vents his frustration on his drunken brother, Martin, who represents for him Baba Toura. By killing Martin, Essola symbolically kills Baba Toura. 'Essola "assassine" Baba Toura à travers un de ses citoyens qui lui semble réunir toutes les contradictions du système' (Ndongo, 1988 : 159).

In general, then, Mongo Beti is a skillful artist who projects his political message without vitiating his art ; therefore, he maintains a fine balance between his matter and manner. He is a propagandist who is, first of all, an artist.

Works Cited

Beer, S.H. (ed.) *The Communist Manifesto.* Karl Marx and Friedrich Engels. Arlington: AHM Publishing Corporation, 1955.
Beti, Mongo. *Perpetua and the Habit of Unhappiness.* Trans. John Reed & Clive Wake. London: Heinemann, 1978.
_____. *Remember Ruben.* Trans. Gerald Moore. Washington D.C: Three Continents Press, 1980.
Fanon, Frantz. *The Wretched of the Earth.* New York: Grove Press, 1968.
Moore, Gerald. *Twelve African Writers.* Bloomington: Indiana U P, 1980.
Ndongo, Jacques Fame. *Le Prince et Le Scribe.* Paris: Berger Levrault, 1988.
Ngugi, wa Thiong'o. *Writers in Politics.* London: Heinemann, 1981.
Popkin, Richard H. and Stroll, Avrum. *Philosophy Made Simple.* London: W.H. Allen, 1968.

11
PEDAGOGY OF THE DEPRIVED

Introduction
Marxist critics have convincingly established the fact that every literature is essentially socially-conditioned, and that every major literary work is a reflection of the spirit of the society of which it is a product. This principle is generally borne out by the plays of three Anglophone Cameroonian writers: Victor Epie Ngome's *What God Has Put Asunder* (1992), Bole Buake's *And Palm Wine Will Flow* (1990) and Bate Besong's *Requiem for the Last Kaiser* (1991).[1]

For, treating cultural, economic and political issues pertinent to either Anglophone Cameroon, in particular, or all of Cameroon, in general, these playwrights subtly educate, and side with, those who do not have enough access to the social product of their country, nor the material base for adequate development of their intellectual, cultural and economic potentials.

To know how they have done this we will examine the content of each author's work, beginning with that of Victor Epie Ngome. And we will adopt what I call the matter-and-manner approach in doing so. This means that the first part of the article will be concerned with issues and themes (Matter), and the second part with aspects relating to dramatic technique (Manner).

MATTER

Victor Epie Ngome's *What God Has Put Asunder*[2]
At the literal level, *What God Has Put Asunder* is the story of Weka, a child brought up in an orphanage under Rev. Gordon and Sister Sabeth. When Weka reaches nubile age, two suitors ask her hand in marriage: one of them is Mr. Miche Garba, and the other Mr. Emeka who grew up in the orphanage together with Weka.

Despite Emeka's solid claims over Weka as a childhood friend, Mr. Garba has his way, but Weka accepts him reluctantly. Their marriage is solemnised by Rev. Unor, probationally, without the matrimonial rings. The couple will live together and study each other for ten years, at the end of which period, if they still desire to be husband and wife, the official ceremonies of the wedding will be conducted.

But during the probational period Weka discovers that Miche Garba is no good. He maltreats and neglects her. He exploits the rich cocoa farms left by Weka's father and squanders the money on his concubines. He does not tolerate Weka's questioning attitude.

When she can no longer stand Garba, Weka escapes with her children back to her father's compound to rebuild his dilapidated house and their shattered lives. Garba pursues her there, threatening to forcefully take them back to his house. Once more the matter is brought to court for a decision. And the court's decision is that the couple will live in physical separation although united in a 'simulated wedlock", and that the marriage remains subject to confirmation by husband and wife only, to the exclusion of any other parties; that the marriage will become null and void once any of the two parties objects to it; that until the legal confirmation is carried out, the couple will continue to live under physical separation but to show decency and decorum towards each other in order to avoid an unfortunate intervention by the court.

The main theme emerging from the play is the incompatibility of the couple Garba and Weka. Theirs is an uneasy union: at best it is a precarious marriage; at worst, an unworkable one. Weka cannot put up with Garba's philosophy and philandering life style.

The other theme is economic exploitation. Garba seems to have married Weka largely out of economic interest. For he takes over and exploits the cocoa farms left by Weka's father, deriving enormous wealth from them without ploughing back some of the profit to develop the farms. At another level of economic exploitation we find Garba feeding fat on the wealth of the co-operative society, the wealth of the nation. He is the unconscionable General Director of the Co-operative Society. With cheques to this or that girl, with mounting hotel bills to settle in support of his sensual lifestyle, Garba dips his hands into the co-operative funds with reckless abandon, eventually draining them dry of cash.

There are also the themes of adultery and neglect. Garba's life style is a classic manifestation of adultery and total neglect of Weka, whether emotionally or financially. Yet it is thanks to the wealth brought in by Weka that this politician and general manager leads a comfortable but irresponsible life style. These then are some of the solid and valid issues embodied at the surface level of the play.

But within the Cameroonian context the play and its themes have a greater symbolic significance. For instance, the marriage metaphor relates to the political union of Anglophone Cameroon and the Francophone counterpart. Hence, Weka stands for the former Southern Cameroons, and Garba for *La Republique du Cameroun*; Weka's parents represent the British Government that relinquished responsibility over Southern Cameroons; Rev. Gordon and the orphanage stand for the UN trusteeship mandate over Southern Cameroons; the Louis mentioned in the play is France; Emeka is Nigeria etc.

Garba's neglectful but exploitative attitude towards Weka represents the attitude of the Francophone leadership towards Anglophones in present day Cameroon, a behaviour that has come to represent the central grievance in what Anglophone Cameroonians have identified as the "Anglophone Problem in Cameroon". Now, if one transfers the literal themes discussed above to the symbolic level, they will make an important aspect of the Anglophone problem as outlined at the All Anglophone Conference and enshrined in the famous Buea Declaration of 2nd and 3rd April 1993, a tiny section of which reads thus:

> Within these thirty-two years, our Union accord has been violated. We have been disenfranchised, marginalized and treated with suspicion. Our interests have been disregarded. Our participation in national life has been limited to non-essential functions. Our natural resources have been ruthlessly exploited without any benefit accruing to our territory or to its people...

The ultimate social relevance of *What God Has Put Asunder* to the Anglophone community lies in the fact that it has contributed in no small way to the overall education of the Anglophones. Of course, it may be too much of a claim to suggest that the present state of the critical consciousness of the Anglophones is the work of a single play alone. The play is only part, albeit an important part, of a larger process that came in with the limited freedom of press.

The robust Anglophone private press and enlightened Anglophone political opinion, together with literary works similar to those treated in this article are equally partners in the whole process of the education of the Anglophone masses, in the pedagogy of the deprived. At the literal level, therefore, *What God Has Put Asunder* pleases while it teaches; but at the symbolic level it pleases and teaches even more. To some extent, the play has given a clear sense of direction to Anglophone Cameroonians. It has helped bickering Anglophones, to use words similar to those of Jesse Jackson, to move from battle ground to higher ground and seek common ground. It has been part of the process that produced the historic All Anglophone Conference.

Bole Butake's *And Palm Wine Will Flow*

Our second play that also plays a major part in the education of not only Anglophone Cameroonians, but of Cameroonians as a whole, is Bole Butake's *And Palm Wine Will Flow* (1990). But in the sense that there is a story moving steadily and rising to a climax before subsiding to a gradual end as in Epie Ngome's *What God Has Put Asunder*, there is no such thing in *And Palm Wine Will Flow*. However a story of some sort there is, since there are people, ideas and action in the play. The setting is an imaginary fondom in the grassfields, and the dramatic situation involves two camps juxtaposed more or less, two different approaches to life.

On the one hand we have the Fon, the epitome of pleasure and hedonism, surrounded by stooges, bootlickers and flatterers. He dispenses favours generously to fawners, promoting some to higher nobility, but tortures and brutalizes the dissenters. Palm-wine and drunkenness are worshipped. On the other hand there is Shey Ngong, the Chief Priest of Nyombom, the moral pillar and the epitome of spiritual values. He is critical of the Fon and strongly opposed to his lifestyle. He scornfully turns down appeals made to him to pay respects to the Fon.

The result of Shey Ngong's arrogance towards the Fon is the seizure of his wives' farm lands, which are now given to Kibanya, recently raised to higher nobility by the Fon. There is a plan underway by the Fon to destroy the sacred grove where Shey Ngong worships Nyombom. But the gods and ancestors of the land cannot sit by idly while the land is desecrated by immoral and mediocre elements.

The Earth-goddess makes a terrible pronouncement - there will be a drought and earthquake, including other unnatural occurrences. On his part Kibaranko, the destructive spiritual force, lays bare the Fon's Palace while the Fon takes to his heels. The women make a horrible concoction which they intend to force the Fon to drink. Later they pronounce death on him. His death puts an end to the tradition of Fons ruling the village single-handedly, in total disregard of their councillors. Henceforth the village will be ruled by a council of elders led by Shey Ngong who will be replaced as soon as he himself shows signs of not going by the people's wishes. From now onward power will come from the people, and not from any self-seeking, power-hungry, ambitious dictator. Power to the people.

From the point of view of themes, the play deals with dictatorial rule in a local fondom, examining the use or misuse of power. It is a study of unconscionable leadership, with equal focus on the fostering of mediocrity and hedonism. But above all, the play expresses the need for people with the moral conviction to keep up the fight against all the forces of evil in this world. A central thesis of the play is that if this fight is carried out with courage, conviction and determination the result will ultimately be victory for the forces of good, a victory in which the women play a very crucial role.

The social significance of *And Palm Wine Will Flow* must be situated within the context of contemporary world politics with particular reference to developing countries following the wind of change from Eastern Europe in the late 1980s. For, with the coming of Gorbachev's *glasnost* and *perostroika* there was a loosening up of dictatorial grip on power by dictators of mostly one-party regimes; there was gradual liberalization of the press and a general goodwill to be more democratic, to open up to multi-party politics.

Yet in many African countries the external democratic pressure was not enough to force the political rulers to change. Internal pressure was indispensable for any significant political change to be registered. Consequently in Cameroon, for instance, political parties were formed and some forcefully launched in the face of stiff government resistance; socio-cultural pressure groups as well as local human rights organizations came into existence and outspoken independent individuals emerged. All of these people had a common goal: to force the hands of a reluctant government to yield to the wind of change; to embrace a more valid democratic process that will allow for the respect of human rights and social justice.

Among these pressure groups were committed creative writers like those discussed in this article. And when we talk of committed writers, we mean people who, by their natural disposition and upbringing, have come to write sensitively, showing great concern for the lot of suffering humanity; they are people who write with the intention of improving the human condition, of contributing towards the general welfare of the greatest majority.

With regard to commitment in literature there are certain themes or burning issues which, when treated by a literary artist, cannot leave such a writer indifferent. African societies are still to rid themselves of ills like neo-colonialism, corruption, capital flight, capitalist exploitation, greed, torture of political enemies, tribalism, embezzlement of state funds etc. Now, a playwright or a novelist who writes with full conviction on any of these themes cannot help but take sides, however indirectly. If he examines, explores, and develops these issues experientially and convincingly he will be seen, in the final analysis, to be advocating a certain line of behaviour, to be propounding a certain ideology. He may side with the regime in place or with its victims. In most cases, however, such a writer's ideology is on the side of the victims of the social or political ills. Such is the case with Bole Butake and the other writers studied in this article.

Therefore the struggle in *And Palm Wine Will Flow* is not just a struggle between two individuals in isolation; it is a struggle between two approaches to life: the repressive, exploitative, unaccountable and irresponsible lifestyle versus a more just, moral and responsible governance. It is a struggle between a powerful minority that owns and controls nearly everything versus the suffering and powerless majority deprived of the comforts of life. That is why in the end the women and all the people take sides with the forces of good, symbolized by Shey Ngong, against the exploitative and arrogant Fon.

Nalova Lyonga once said that as a committed writer Bole Butake "is always a step ahead of reality."[4] And this reality can best be seen within the context of the contemporary political process in Cameroon. With reference to the wind of change mentioned above, Bole Butake was writing in the broad context of a certain political climate. In Cameroon a certain questioning awareness and some subtle social trends were already emerging. There was a general feeling that the dominant style of governance that had kept

Cameroonians subservient and docile for many years would sooner or later be intolerable. There was a feeling that the present was pregnant and likely to give birth to a child with a different outlook, that the past would no longer be the future.

Given the humane disposition of the playwright and the types of issues raised in his play and the forcefulness with which he explores them, the logic of the play's ending does not surprise us. And to some extent it is a prophetic ending in the sense that the play fore-shadowed the launching of the main opposition party in Cameroon, the Social Democratic Front, (S.D.F.), a party that stands for social justice and equal opportunity, and whose motto is: Power to the People! *And Palm Wine Will Flow* was published in 1990 and had its grand premiere on March 27, of that year. Two months later, on May 26, the SDF was launched in Bamenda in the face of stiff government resistance.

When this play was performed in some parts of Cameroon to audiences that subscribe to the principles that political parties like the SDF believe in, it became, and still is, popular. Its popularity is largely due to the fact that it heartens the disadvantaged or the deprived and gives them a sense of direction. It tells the people, albeit artistically and thus subtly, what to do or how to go about bringing political change. The play therefore becomes a crucial weapon in the process of the pedagogy of the oppressed, in the education of the masses for critical consciousness.[5]

Bate Besong's *Requiem for the Last Kaiser*

Physical torture of political enemies, a common theme in Bate Besong's works is to be seen in *Beasts of No Nation* which, because of limitations of space, cannot be discussed here. The play is so virulent in its attack on Francophone Cameroonians that a senior Francophone government functionary who watched its premiere in Yaoundé could not help but give an equally violent reaction. The quotation is a personal translation of the original French version of a letter addressed to the Chancellor of the University of Yaoundé, where the play was performed:

> It is a clear political pamphlet directed at the regime in power, that is held responsible for the economic crisis through corruption, favouritism and capital flight to foreign Banks. The author holds the thesis that

Francophones in power are responsible for the economic crisis because they are producers of waste matter, and embezzlers of public funds. Among the Francophones (frogs) special emphasis is placed on the Betis, friends and brothers of President Biya, who are more responsible for the present state of Cameroon.

The author equally affirms, and this is the central thesis (philosophy) of the play, that the Anglophones of Cameroon are marginalized and confined to undignified roles like that of "carriers of excrement." They do not have any good status and are even deprived of any professional identity cards, which they are asking for in vain.

According to Mr. Besong, the Anglophone in Cameroon is considered a traitor and a slave. The play ends with an appeal for rebellion and the disregard of the present authority. At the end of the performance, the playwright took to the stage to publicly declare that the future of Cameroon is uncertain and that chaos can set in at any time, especially from the other side of the Mungo. Consequently, he appealed to the audience, for the most part Anglophones, to get themselves ready to carry out their choices.

After putting up with this play, I had to get up by way of protest, accompanied by the Chief of Service for Students' Associations and Cultural Clubs, to quit the hall just at the time when Mr. Besong was concluding his fiery exhortations.

While we were leaving the hall I was booed in these words: "Man no run and "Owona," "Owona." I think, in my opinion, that at the time when the government is exerting great and constant efforts to make Cameroon a united country in which the two communities co-exist in all brotherliness, it is abnormal and unacceptable that intellectuals should promote divisions and conflicts. In any case, the University ought not to be the forum for such ill-intentioned ventures.

Unfortunately, the programme of theatre activities conceived by the Ministry of Information and Culture did not allow us to preview this play, a copy of which I bought at the exit of the hall.

On reading it, I even discovered that some passages have been altered by Mr. Bole Butake to make the play more current and critical. This experience which, I must admit, is shocking and disappointing enough will help me to be more vigilant and diligent with regard to all other cultural activities that will take place on the University Campus. (Jean Stéphane Biatcha[6])

Though we will comment on the dramatic technique later on, it suffices to observe, in passing, that the "shit" imagery in *Beasts of No Nation* is a strong and significant symbol of the putrescence that has overwhelmed the society. The Bate Besong we find here is similar to Ayi Kwei Armah, the angry author of *The Beautyful Ones Are Not Yet Born* whose overriding imagery is equally filth. Equally important is the image of carriers of shit, the Night-soil men, a metaphor for slavery.

In this play, unlike in *The Most Cruel Death of the Talkative Zombie*, the oppressed are given a voice. They actively and constantly stand up for their rights, and at the end even carry the fight right into the office of the dreaded Mayor, storming it with their buckets of shit, an act of great significance: To get something from a reactionary regime you must fight for it; you must be ready to risk your life for it.

As for *Requiem for the Last Kaiser*, it consists of three scene fragments and two movements. The first fragment opens with a woman educating a student to take part in fighting the repressive forces in a fictional country called Agidigidi, and the second reveals that Atangana, the clergyman, collaborates with the reactionary regime of Akhikikrikii. The flashback in this fragment also reveals Abessolo as the security boss of the regime and therefore one who controls the instruments of torture. He accuses the woman of subversion and of planning a coup d'état. But the woman says, "ours will be a popular uprising, not a coup" (p. 19). Atangana, the Pastor, cautions her: "Be careful woman... Don't let the Devil mark you...Trust and obey." In the last fragment we see Akhikikrikii, the Head of State, in the company of his foreign friends and supporters: a Western ambassador and a Swiss Banker, all of whom flatter him.

In the first scene of the first movement we meet the progressive forces made up of unemployed academics like

181

Akonchong and Gambari, Poet as Mandela, workers, voice of Woman etc. There is a parody by the academics in which the regime is subtly satirized. The scene ends with Abessollo threatening the critics and enemies of the regime. In the second scene of the first movement we meet the progressive forces again, including the leader of the market women, the Woman and soldiers. We notice the education of the soldiers by the woman in the interest of the oppressed. There is the play within the play scene wherein the academics play the role of Head Porters, etc. Here, the cruel ways and weaknesses of the regime are subtly criticized and exposed. There is the reading of the revolutionary thesis of Akonchong, and then Abessollo arrives in a threatening mood with a gun, but he is disarmed by the people.

In the second and last movement we find the people - the progressive forces: the poet, former infantry men, women, workers etc., surrounding Akhikikrikii's Marble Palace. There is a general revolt, and Ngongo, the Chief Praise-singer of the regime confesses his crime against the people. Worst of all, Abessollo too, without the army abandons Akhihikrikii. But the Ambassador and Swiss Banker still stick around him. However, deserted by his people, Akhikikrikii commits suicide and the people force their way into the Marble Palace.

The central theme of the play can be said to be the popular challenge to a reactionary regime, or a popular uprising against a dictatorship. The play is about the education of the deprived and their stand against a tyrant. In fact, this theme is already didactically summed up by the author in the play's sub-title - "a drama of conscientization."

Conscientization implies the education of the masses, especially the oppressed masses, in such a way that they become imbued with a heightened sense of critical consciousness. When oppressed people become conscientized, they tend to know more about certain issues and situations than they did before. They become more familiar with the inner structure of their society and the dynamics of the vicious system that has held them captives. The knowledge of this produces a change in behaviour in such a way as would make them now want to do away with the evil forces that have helped to cripple them. Thus for every vicious action, so to speak, by the oppressors, there is not only an equal and opposite, but, in radical terms, a superior opposite reaction by the oppressed, whose ultimate goal is the improved living condition of the masses.

This trend of reasoning reveals that Bate Besong has been influenced, consciously or unconsciously, by Marxist thought, at least as far as *Requiem for the Last Kaiser* is concerned. "Marxism's goal is liberation of consciousness and freeing of praxis from bondage via revolutionary theory" (Solomon, 1973: 14).

It is this pedagogical mission, which is essentially Bate Besong's intention in *Requiem*, that makes the application of a Marxist critical approach to the study of this play inevitable. The Russian Marxist, Plekhanov has said that no literary work is conceived in an ideological vacuum; that all art emanates from an ideological conception of the world" (Eaglelton, 1976:17). The veracity of this statement can be clearly illustrated with *Requiem*, as we have already seen from the synopsis. In this play, two distinct ideologies are locked in a fierce confrontation, the one oppressive and exploitative, and the other, the pauperized masses.

Requiem becomes a product of its society, informed by the socio-political malaise that surrounds its creation. Making allowance for the playwright's poetic licence and his fertile imagination, the picture he paints is a symbolic representation of contemporary society. He gives his work the force of topicality and sometimes uses direct and recognizable references. Bate Besong writes carrying the yoke of being an Anglophone and struggling for his identity and, in the course of this, that of his people. In dealing with this issue as well as others including power politics and domination, Bate Besong evidently defines himself as a humanist, committed to the cause of the suffering voices. He adopts a strident, even vituperative voice to castigate those who despoil the state, but he is never naive to think that the revolution is for tomorrow. He (Bate Besong, 1993: 18) is only too aware himself of the limitations on the writer, as he says:

> the power of the writer is not always strong enough to change the political and social situation of his time but his art can become a fighting literature, he can write works which are artistically profound and politically correct. He can write works that show how his world is and could be.

However, it is evident that the committed writer alone may not have the power to bring about immediate political change, but he and the writers of other forms of political literature, a buoyant private press, the appropriate political opinion leaders and parties can all, together, bring about effective political change. The committed artist need not be a wheel alone, but he is an essential spoke in the wheel of socio-political change. This is where the works of Victor Epie Ngome, Bole Butake and Bate Besong, become important in the emergence of an Anglophone and nationalist consciousness in contemporary Cameroonian literature.

MANNER[7]

The danger with these committed writers is that they may sacrifice their art for their message. In other words, are they not likely to sacrifice technique for sententiousness? To answer this question let us once again look at these works from the point of view of the exploitation of dramatic technique.

Victor Epie Ngome's *What God Has Put Asunder* is a five-act play, structured very much like Elizabethan drama, with the story-line gradually and steadily developing through scenes and acts towards a climax in act three, before tapering off from act four and ending in act five. Structurally, therefore, this play follows a traditional Western form with a well-constructed plot, fairly delineated characters who develop psychologically using realistic dialogue. The metaphor of marriage which is used by the playwright hammers home the message rather strongly, especially as it is seen from the point of incompatibility. But the greatest pleasure to be derived from this play is the shift in interpretation from the literal to the symbolic level. Yet, Victor Epie Ngome does not allow the deceptively simple framework provided by contemporary Cameroonian history to cripple his play. Rather, he exploits this material creatively, imbuing it with an internal logic which is forcefully his. His characters are lively, natural and spontaneous even though it is evident that they represent types.

Like Epie Ngome, Bole Butake's *And Palm Wine Will Flow* can be examined at both the literal and symbolic levels, with his local setting being an excuse to make jibes at the micro system. According to H.N. Eyoh, the play's localized setting becomes-a microcosm of the world. (1992:2). The Fon's extravagant lifestyle and his heavy-handed governance become representative of that observed at the level of state.

Butake's *And Palm Wine Will Flow,* however, differs from Epie Ngome's *What God Has Put Asunder* in style because it integrates music, dance, and mask, and rather than limit itself to well-flowing dialogue, exploits invocations, incantations and is replete with proverbs. *And Palm Wine Will Flow* has a richer local flavour than *What God Has Put Asunder*. Eyoh (1992: 2), again, describes Bole Butake as "a fine craftsman at once avant-garde and traditional, or traditionally avant-gardist."

Bate Besong is, however, more innovative stylistically than Ngome and Butake. His plays can hardly fit within any known form of dramatic literature. His plots are akin to Samuel Beckett's, underscoring the inanity of human existence. He provides us with an admixture of the realistic, the historical, the tragic, and the comic, all of this underlying a particular political ideology. His characters are drawn from amongst the lowest of the low, like the Night-soil men of *Beasts of No Nation* who are pitted against the highest of the land. The battle is one of political domination and rebellion, yet nothing seems to happen in these *shitologician'* plays, other than the portrayal of "shit." Bate Besong has no respect for the three unities of time, place and action. These are not important. For him, it is the workings of the inner minds of the masses which are in conflict with the oppressive forces that is essential. Bate Besong makes for difficult reading because of his abstruse style and rather adventurous use of dramatic technique, but this is exactly what makes him compulsive as we strive to discover what makes him tick. Gilbert Doho (1993:98) has described Bate Besong's style as extremely militant - "style de guerre."

What is certain about the three dramatists under study in this paper is their commitment to changing their societies and the urgency with which they feel this need. They each bring into their dramaturgy stories which are at once ordinary and symbolic, but whose messages cannot escape us. They have become the spokespersons of a silenced people, fighting to seek an identity for their community.

End Notes
1. Originally this article had examined Bate Besong's three published plays: *The Most Cruel Death of the Talkative Zombie* (1986), *Beasts of No Nation* (1990) and *Requiem for the Last Kaiser* (1991). But because of limitations of space, I

have had to cut out the portion on the first two plays, retaining only that on *Requiem for the Last Kaiser.*
2. Victor Epie Ngome, *What God Has Put Asunder.*
3. The Buea Declaration, 9. (3 April 1993).
4. Nalova Lyonga, Theatre Review: Bole Butake's *And Palm Wine Will Flow*, Production Programme, 1992.
5. The phrase "pedagogy of the oppressed" is borrowed from the title of Paulo Freire's Book, *Pedagogy of the Oppressed* (1983),: New York, Continuum, (translated by Bergman Ramus).
6. Letter addressed to the Vice-chancellor of the University of Yaounde by Stéphane Biatcha. c.f *Challenge Hebdo*, no. 0045 of 31 October to 6 November 1991:11.
7. This part of the paper was abridged for reasons of space.

Works Cited

Besong, Bate. *Requiem for the Last Kaiser*: Calabar, Centaur Publishers, 1991.

__ __ __. "Literature in the Season of the Diaspora: Notes to the Anglophone Cameroonian Writer". Lyonga, et al. (eds.). *Anglophone Cameroon Writing.* WEKA, (1993) 30:1, pp.

Butake, B. *And Palm Wine Will Flow*: Yaoundé, SOPECAM, 1990.

Biatcha, J. S. "A la Haute attention de Monsieur le Chancelier de l'Université de Yaoundé relative a la representation de la pièce intitutée Beasts of (sic.) Nation de Bate Besong *Challenge Hebdo* No. 0045 (31 Octobre au 06 Novembre 1991). 11.

Declaration of the All Anglophone Conference: The Buea Declaration, April 3, 1993.

Doho, Gilbert. "Théâtre et Minorité: Le cas du Cameroun". Lyonga et al. (eds.) (1993) pp. 93-

Eagleton, T. *Marxism and Literary Criticism*: Berkeley and Los Angleles: University of California Press, 1976.

Eyoh, H. N. "Commentary on Yaoundé University Theatre's production of *And Palm Wine Will Flow.*", Production Programme, 1991.

Lyonga, N. "Theatre Review: Bole Butake's *And Palm Wine Will Flow*", 1992.

12
ANATOMY OF A SHORT STORY: AN ANALYSIS OF BOLE BUTAKE'S "THE WAY OF THE CITY"

Bole Butake is a prolific writer; so diverse are his creative talents that he has published in nearly all the literary genres. A literary critic in his own right, Butake is today largely known as a prominent Cameroonian theatre arts practitioner, that is playwright/director. Some of his imaginative works, polemical essays and public pronouncements reveal him as an intrepid and irrepressible social critic, concerned with the Cameroonian commonweal. Varied as his gifts are, few people know that Professor Butake's first love in creative writing was in the short story, the angle from which I will zoom in on him. Hence my presentation is entitled "Anatomy of a short Story: An Analysis of Bole Butake's 'The Way of The City'".

It is the story of how a delinquent debtor, Ngong Tashi, attempts to hide behind the curtain, in the family single room, when his creditor, Tata Makow, arrives to ask for his money. But the hiding debtor is betrayed by his toes peeping rather uneasily from under the curtain separating the bed from the rest of the room. After waiting for about forty minutes and talking with the debtor's wife, Tata Makow, out of sheer pity for the desperate debtor and his poor family, decides to waive the debt. But before he takes his leave of the family, the creditor stuns Ngong Tashi's wife and child in the following words: "If he ever returns to collect his toes, which I am seeing under the curtain next to the table, tell him that he should consider whatever he is owing me as having been paid".

A bald statement like this is, indeed inadequate, except for the most minimal appreciation of Butake's well-crafted story. The brief summary conveys little or nothing of the language, drama and interior thoughts of the characters involved; little or nothing of the compelling single effect, or the high sense of suspense the story so effectively generates; and little or nothing of the intrigue and subtle humour skillfully worked into the story, and revealing the author's wit.

The story possesses the classic elements of a good short story: plot, conflict, suspense, surprise and focus on a single character, in this case, Tata Makow. Like any good short story, 'The Way of The City' reveals a lot in its introduction. It begins with the setting: a sloping, disorderly neighbourhood for low-income city dwellers around the hours of five and six in the evening; it introduces the main characters, Tata Makow and Ngong Tashi; it presents the conflict or the problem: Ngong Tashi unwilling to pay his debt; and establishes the point of view, that of the omniscient narrator, who can unlock people's hearts and reveal the peculiar nature of their mental landscape. Thus by the end of the first three paragraphs, the reader is aware of the setting, the main characters, the conflict and the narrative point of view.

After the introduction the story moves swiftly, involving all the characters, to the climax, when Ngong Tashi, upon being told that his creditor is presently on the way to his house, dashes, only partially dressed, behind the curtain, instructing his wife to play her normal role: "Kongla, the usual thing, eh?" When the creditor comes in, the debtor's wife, who is busy mixing her paste, lies that her husband has gone out. Tata Makow then sits down and is determined to wait for his return.

From here nothing, by way of action, happens to advance the plot of the story. However, there is an occasional conversation between the creditor and the debtor's wife. But, above all, there is a great deal of internal monologue, on the part of the interlocutors, to fill up the intervals of odd silence between them. At such moments each is absorbed in his or her unique mental universe. The creditor swears to himself and is determined to see how the peeping toes will disappear without their owner giving himself up; the debtor's wife asks herself whether she has suddenly become the debtor to be so badgered by Tata Makow with his basket full of questions. She equally confides to herself that she would have revealed some better marital truth about the grand deception played on her by her lying husband were the fool not hiding behind the curtain. The son of the debtor tells himself that he will not leave his mother alone in the presence of the visitor who may decide to beat her up while his father is unable to come to her rescue!

This section of Butake's work, by the way the bulk of the story, is the most interesting. In it we find Butake's urbane humour. The overall tone of the story is comic. And the deliciousness of the humour resides in the fact that it is subtle; it is underwritten. It should be noted that only Tata Makow has spotted the peeping toes, and each time the debtor's wife provides an answer to some of his questions, he casts a furtive glance at them to check whether they have disappeared. And he does so five times, but the toes are still there.

It is also in this section of the story that the element of suspense is highly sustained. The reader keeps on asking himself or herself what will happen to the toes and when they will come out. How will the war of nerves involving the creditor, the debtor's wife and the man with the peeping toes end? And when it suddenly ends it takes everybody by surprise, with the exception of Tata Makow who has been secretly holding the Joker. For when he decides to forgive the delinquent debtor whose presence in the room he is aware of, the debtor's wife and son are stunned, the debtor himself is transfixed, and the reader pleasantly surprised. What a fine short story!

The Way of the City is exquisitely told, and my analysis cannot do it justice. In the control of the intrigue, suspense, swift dénouement, and surprise, it is a beautiful short story, well conceived and vividly textualized. In the dialogue hardly a word is wasted. The beautiful effect thus produced on the reader is not gratuitous. It is conscious but subtle art at work; it is the result of artistic devices skillfully employed by Bole Butake, including, as I have said, the use of suspense, conflict, subtle humour as well as the incorporation of flashback, interior monologues and dramatic irony.

The story pleases while it teaches. So far I have illustrated its pleasing, entertaining aspect, but there is also its instructional dimension, for it has the potential for social criticism. The story examines the negative impact of poverty and the cruel effect of city life on low-income earners. The city breeds crooks. In some instances city life makes no distinction between house-wives and whores in the practice of the "oldest Profession". It is a measure of our contemporary city life that it can drive a poor man to desperation, forcing him to become a prisoner in his own house. For when a man is compelled to resort to ruses because he is assailed three times by three creditors in a single day, we must admit that for such a man life is far from being a bed of roses. A keynote sounded throughout the story is "hard times", difficult times.

This is even more so, especially now, in times like ours, times that try our souls. For are there not many of us here who are creditors to the state? If you are one paid by the state, go to CENADI in the Ministry of Finance and ask the computer what it has in its memory for you. And unless you're in an exceptional category, you'll surely come back to tell me something. You may well ask when will Ngong Tashi pay back your dues?

Professor Bole Butake, ladies and gentlemen, thank you.

End Note
The Way of The City is taken from Balafon: *An anthology of Cameroon Literature in English*, (1986) edited by G. De La Taille; K. Warner; and V. Tarkang, Published by Longman. (55-62).

13
THE ORALITY OF THE WORKS OF FOUR ANGLOPHONE WRITERS: LINUS ASONG, BOLE BUTAKE, BONGASU KISHANI, FALE WACHE

In their well-researched but very provocative and controversial book entitled *Toward The Decolonization of African Literature*, the Nigerian triumvirate of Chinweizu, Onwuchekwa Jemie and Ikechukwu Madubuike uphold the view that contemporary African Literature has been dominated by creative writers and critics brought up on the 'disorienting Euromodernist sensibility' involving imported imagery and attitude; that for this literature to be truly decolonized African writers and critics should sever ties with those espousing not only pseudo-universalism but also individualist obscurantism and "Hopkinsian syntactic jogglery"[1] and draw instead from, and be inspired by, the rich technical resources of African oral tradition from which a veritable Afro-centric sensibility can be nurtured. There are many African writers already doing what Chinweizu and his colleagues have recommended, drawing on the rich African heritage encompassing African thought, experience, folklore and myth, custom and religion to give their work a flavour and coloration that is essentially African.[2] Some of these writers are Chinua Achebe, Kofi Awoonor, Mazisi Kunene, Gabriel Okara, Pepper Clark, Wole Soyinka, Okot p'Bitek; and, in Anglophone Cameroon, Linus Asong, Bole Butake, Bongasu Kishani, Fale Wache, among others. This paper will be concerned with the examination of elements of oral literature in some of the works of the last four of the above-mentioned writers. Its aim is to demonstrate not only the presence and effective use of these oral features but also the relevance of the works in which they feature.

According to Tala Kashim, orature can "be defined as a work of art expressed in carefully selected language, irrespective of whether it is spoken, sung or chanted, and which deals with the thoughts, concepts, and ideas of an individual or a people. Thus whenever an individual expresses his joys and sorrows through language effectively, orature can be said to be in the making".[3] Orature is used for such functions as praising, mourning, moral instruction and entertainment, and is characterised by creativity, beauty and emotion.

Scholars and researchers collecting, transcribing, translating or analysing African orature have established elements integral to it. Among many of the features are proverbs, invocations or prayers, parallel phrasing, repetition, onomatopoeia, alliteration, songs, chants, praise names, and choral responses. A proverb is generally defined as a brief epigrammatic saying that has become a popular aphorism or an axiom. However, not all axioms, maxims or aphorisms are pure proverbs. The test for the true proverb is its generalizeability, that is, a real proverb can be, and usually is, applied to situations other than the apparent context of its coinage. The authentic proverbs are more figurative than factual, more metaphorical than matter-of-fact.

Two examples of epigrams from Chinua Achebe's *Things Fall Apart* will serve to illustrate the point.
1. He who brings kola brings life.
2. ... if a child washed his hands he could eat with kings.[4]

The first statement is not a proverb. It is literal and factual because it makes more sense only when uttered during an actual kola-nut-eating occasion than when there is no kola nut eating at all. On the other hand, the second statement is a proverb. It contains a metaphor and the proverb's full meaning usually lies beyond the actual context of eating; it makes more sense only when applied in a context where there is no actual washing of hands and eating going on. For example, it could mean, as it certainly does in the context of *Things Fall Apart*, that if a young person works hard he or she can attain a position of respectability, just as Okonkwo has done.

Depending on the degree of its distinctiveness or environmental coloration, a proverb can be said to be either traditional or universal.[5] The more environmentally colourful it is, the more traditional; the more colourless it is, the more universal. Of the four Anglophone writers, the works of Bole Butake and Linus Asong reveal the presence of this important feature of orature. From Asong's *The Crown of Thorns*[6], there are the following proverbs:
1. ... When a hen leaves the incubator, it must be chased far out of the house if the house-keeper does not want to step on warm excrement (p. 98).

2. ... A calabash should never have anything to do with a stone, because whether it is the calabash which hits the stone or it is the stone that hits the calabash, it is the calabash that breaks (p. 112).
3. When a man goes to the latrine without something with which to clean his anus he can do many wrong things (p. 118).
4. ... the tree which falls and touches the ground is the tree that grows alone (p. 137).
5. It was not our fault that he left so many dried leaves lying so close to the fire of Nkokonoko Small Monje (p. 194).

These are only a few of the proverbs found in that novel. They highlight in their various ways some of the issues raised in the novel. And the context here shows the conflict between the administration and the people of Small Monje, which eventually leads to a breakdown of communication. Proverbs 1 to 4 thus relate to the strained relationship between Chief Nchindia and his people, while proverb five points to that between the irrational D.O. and the very people. The proverbs then serve a thematic function within the context of the novel.

At another level they serve to delineate character, for all the proverbs are uttered by members of the Council of Elders in Small Monje, indicating their wisdom, age and maturity. The proverbs carry some environmental coloration, serving as a defining parametre of a unique cultural milieu. They are therefore not just "mere relics of a primitive culture"[7]. If we grant this supposition, then many other things fall in place; then the speech styles and linguistic peculiarities of the Nweh-Mundani that the novel deals with (though not explicitly referred to as such) fall in place; then their behaviour is normal and defensible. Herein lie both the proverbs' artistic function and the novel's artistic truthfulness.

From Bole Butake's *And Palm Wine Will Flow*, we have the following proverbs[8]:
1. The cockroach does not call a fowl to a wrestling match (p. 10).
2. The gorilla can do nothing to an iroko tree (p. 10).
3. The stream never flows uphill. The Leopard and the goat have never been bed-fellows (p. 14).
4. The louse and the jigger have no need for brains (p. 18).
5. The Leopard does not wrestle with a goat (p. 19).
6. The rat does not play with a cat (p. 10).

7. The lion announces its presence with roaring (p. 38).
8. The leopard prowls among the goats, and they scatter into the dark night! (p. 38).
9. The lion spreads terror among the cattle and the sheep! (p. 38).
10. When the elephant flaps his ears and sounds his trumpet, the forest is in disarray for he has gone berserk! (p. 38).
11. The eagle flies and flies but always returns home! (p. 42).
12. The prowling lion comes back to its den for rest! (p. 42).
13. After devastating the forest the elephant goes down to the river for a drink! (p. 42)
14. The farmer spent all day in the fields but returned home at dusk and went to sleep! (p. 42).

Most of the proverbs are full of animal metaphors with all that is implied in the animal's brute force, intelligence, smartness, or parasitism. In proverb 1 the voice warns Shey Ngong of his foolhardiness in attempting to argue with the great ruler of Ewawa. But in proverb 2, it is Shey Ngong who asserts his superiority vis-a-vis the Fon, and in proverb 3, the Chief Priest affirms the impossibility of his ever bowing down to the traditional ruler. Shey Ngong is a spiritual leader, the Chief Priest of Nyombom. He is therefore spiritually and morally superior to the corrupt Fon of Ewawa, and can justifiably claim to be the Leopard and the cat. In contrast, the parasitic stooges and bootlickers who surround the Fon are no more than jiggers and lice who have not much need for brains.

In a general way, proverbs 1 to 6 underscore the basic conflict between the Chief Priest and the Fon. They point to the moral superiority of the former over the latter. They are therefore thematically functional. On the one hand, the string of proverbs from 7 to 10 comprises multiple metaphors chanted by Shey Ngong as a prelude to Kibaranko's outing and activities, giving the audience a hint of the violent nature of such activities. For, in the words of Nalova Lyonga, Kibaranko is "the spiritual force that wipes out tyranny."[9] On the other hand, the other string of proverbs, 11-14, also comprising multiple metaphors, are equally chanted by Shey Ngong. This time they are chanted in preparation for the return of Kibaranko after his hectic activities. They point to peace after violence, calm after turbulence, rest after a hard day's work.

As in Asong's *The Crown Of Thorns*, the proverbs in *And Palm-Wine Will Flow* are uttered by elderly responsible people. Shey

Ngong is a man of high spiritual status in the society. It is fitting that he should speak in proverbs which, with the metaphors they embody, help to underscore the second and more important level of meaning of this play. They help to highlight its allegorical nature, for in the Cameroonian context, the play is a political allegory, a literary form in which objects, persons, and actions have meanings that lie outside the story itself. That is, the play dramatizes a political reality in the guise of another. And as such much of its "deep structure" meaning resides in these metaphors, hence their effective use.

With regard to invocations, Bongasu Kishani's *Konglanjo*, and Bole Butake's *And Palm Wine Will Flow* and *Lake God* will serve as examples. The world they depict is essentially traditional, one wherein the old spiritual order is still very much in place, for the ancestors, the living and the unborn are part of the cyclic trinity, with the revered ancestors and the deities still exerting tremendous force on the living, acting as their guardians and protectors. The living worship them and perform rituals for them; sacrifices and libations become a communication link that keeps the living, the dead and the unborn in communion.

With reference to *Konglanjo*,[10] there is Ngaa-Mbom, Owner of Creation, the Maker of All, placed unapproachably far up there, not to be bothered by petty details of daily existence. Ngaa-Mbom's worshippers constantly pray to Him and occasionally catalogue a list of blessings and favours that they want Him to bestow on them. They ask Him to ward off evil omen from their midst, to provide them peace, to enlighten their traditional doctors. They want Him to provide them with good and abundant harvests, to give them strength, long life and prosperity, and to make their children perpetuate their culture. Examples of invocation in *Konglanjo* are many. Indeed, the whole poem is essentially invocatory. The people not only invoke Ngaa-Mbom, but also their ancestors and their heralds.

>Ngaa-Mbom!
>May we espy and cry shame on whoever mocks you!
>May our foes be ignorant of our woes!
>May we sow and reap in folds of eight hundreds;
>May we grow strong - May we prosper.
>May the good-hearted live long
>Within the rhythms of the seasons
>May the evil-doer and the warrior miss their way!

May we build on the epitaphs of ancestral feats!
May the realms of our households never dwindle under our feet!
May our offspring hunt for game of therapeutic inspirations
From the upper stream forests to the lower
    stream forests;
From the hillside forests on our left
To the hillside forests on our right!
May echoes of our lineage name toll and spread
beyond years issuing from the echoes and rhythms
of these festal Manjong gongs! (ku-ngu-ngung!)!
(pp. 14-15)

In Butake's *And Palm Wine Will Flow* invocation and libation are performed by Shey Ngong, the Chief Priest of Nyombom, Nyombom a deity similar to Kishani's Ngaa-Mbom, while in *Lake God*[11] these rituals are carried out by Shey Tanto, leader of the Kwifon:

Shey Tanto: From *And Palm-Wine Will Flow*, Shey Ngong:
Hii-i-i Wong! Hii-i-i Bo-Nyo! Hii-i-i Kwifon!
Here present are the seven pillars of Kwifon.
Here present are the seven corners of the land.
We cannot give food and drink to our illustrious ancestors.
We cannot even gain access to the sanctuary of Kwifon.
Hii-i-i Wong! Hii-i-i Bo-Nyo! Hii-i-i Kwifon!
Here present are the seven pillars of Kwifon.
Here present are the seven corners of the land.
We cannot grease the sacred pot of the land.
It is now six years since we last saw the pot.
And Kwifon has been exiled from the land.
Hii-i-i Wong! Hh-i-illo-Nyo! Hii-i-i Kwifon!
We are met in this sacred grove of the Lake God
Because the land is no longer the land
You illustrious ancestors handed over to us.
Kwifon is in exile; and the women of this land
Are waging war against their men-folk

> Because the Fon, our Fon, the Fon you gave us;
> The Fon we thought you gave us, has sold the land.
> The Fon has banished Kwifon and given the land
> To strangers and rearers of cattle.
> And now the women starve their men.
> Hii-i-i Wong! Hii-i-i Bo-Nyo! Hii-i-i Kwifon!
> Here is drink for you gods!
> Here is drink for you ancestors!
> Give us patience.
> Give us peace of mind.
> Show us the right path.
> That we may bring peace again
> To this land which you gave us (pp. 56.57).
> From *And Palm Wine Will Flow,* we have:
> Shey Ngong: Oh! Nyombom!
> Creator and guardian of the land,
> And you our illustrious forebears,
> Grant me strength and wisdom
> To weather the surging storm.
> The Fon has lost vision.
> The noble men and elders of this land
> Now listen only to the inner voice
> Of greed and fear of a man who has
> Surrounded himself with listeners
> And watch-dogs to do his bidding.
> Nyombom, and you, ancestors,
> Grant me strength and wisdom;
> Grant me patience and love ... (pp. 11-12).

In these extracts of invocation some of the central issues of the works are raised. In the case of Butake's dramas the central issues generating the dramatic tension are almost literally stated in the invocation, indicating thus the obvious dramatic function of the invocatory appeal.

Other utterances of different rhythmic patterns are also features of orature. They are embodied in devices like parallel phrasing, repetition, alliteration, onomatopoeia and apostrophe, contributing to the overall lyricism of the poem. They are found mostly in Kishani's title poem and Fale Wache's *Lament of a Mother*.[12] The device of parallel phrasing consists of the repetition of certain words while the rest of the structure slightly varies; that is, it embodies variable and invariable components as in the following examples from *Lament of A Mother:*

> Thirty long years since you left us
> Thirty long years you've been away from us. (p. 1)
> Ten years since you left us
> Ten years since you've been away (p. 3)
> My eyes itch to see
> My ears yearn
> My hands long
> My back hungers ... (p.4).

In the first of these three extracts the repeated parts of the sentences are "Thirty long years', while the remaining portions are variable ones; in the second extract the invariable units are 'Ten years since ...", while the rest are the variable ones; and in the last excerpt the repetition is the possessive pronoun 'My", while the variable but parallel phrases are preceded by parts of the body: eyes, ears, hands and back. Sometimes the repetition of the name Ndikochong takes on the added quality of a refrain or, at times, an apostrophe:

> 'Ndikochong, my son, my husband'
> ...
> 'Ndikochong my son is it you?'
> ...
> "Ndikochong come back (pp. 1-2).

- all of this brought in at reasonable intervals. The immediate effect is emphasis, persuasion, conviction, for they help to lend force to Bokwi's appeal to her son to return home after thirty years of absence.

With regard to onomatopoeia, Fale Wache accurately captures the natural sounds produced by various weapons, as revealed by the quoted speech of the fiery freedom fighter, Nyamsai:

> "The pointed-end of the spear: F-i-a-p.
> The poisoned arrow: z-i-i-m
> The honed matchet: K-o-u-p
> The barrel of the gun: BOUM' (p.30)

The overall effect of these devices, of onomatopoeia, repetition, parallel phrasing and apostrophe, including the use of words intrinsically musical, is enchanting lyricism, alluring music. And this contributes greatly to our interest in the poem, enhancing its readability.

The poem is more than a literal lament of a mother over the absence of her son. The purported lament, incorporating as it does some qualities of orature, is actually only a vehicle employed by the poet to make scathing comments on the quality of life experienced by Africans in general and Cameroonians in particular during the colonial and neocolonial periods. In the process of developing his subject matter Wache reveals an attitude, a temperament and images emerging from an essentially African matrix of values. The worth of this poem rests not only on what the poet has said but also on how he has said it; in other words, the poem's strength resides in both its matter and manner.

With reference to Kishani's *Konglanjo*, the whole poem bristles with influences of African orature. As Siga Asanga rightly comments, the poem explores Nso mythology, legend, and ritual to bring out an Afro-centric perspective.[13] When people pray seriously and earnestly, they exploit techniques of eloquence for the purpose of persuasion; they pray with intensity of feeling, as demonstrated in *Konglanjo*. He has made use of devices of African oral poetic eloquence to compose a poem that is strongly rhythmical, readable and euphonious. These poetic devices lend force and conviction to the community's appeal to the supernatural forces.

As for parallel phrasing, examples abound. Two examples suffice, and the first comes from the section dealing with an address to the youth, Wa'bin:

Wa'bin!
Youth of every land! Youth of every time!
As if with the trappings of our royal wine-calabashes
We cease not to harness and oil your pumpkin-jaws!
As if invited by a drummer's voice
We dance our dance of age to the sway of time's tunes
To open the footpath of your dance
And spellbind you to rattle the cymbals of your fashion
And live the way our fuzzy forerunners live!
Not in vain do we keep unfolding these secret rites
Of the first spider-legged weeks we store still
With seasons of sunshines and rainfalls on those ledges of years
Whence we stem like a stream from its source!
Whence we stem like corn-grains from corn-cobs!

> Whence we stem like forests from the soil!
> Whence we stem like a knife from its handle!
> Whence we stem like rain from the sky!
> Whence we stem like a road from a homestead!
> Whence we breathe forth like life from our veins!
> Not in vain do we bequeen
> and name our daughter, Ntang
> *In commemoration -*
> *Yes in commemoration*
> of the first hammock-bridge
> of our first crossing away from parent homesteads! (p. 20)

It is easy to spot in this extract the fixed and the invariable components. The parallel phrases and anaphora emphasize, through the accumulated similes and the marked regular rhythm, the natural coming, the spread and the movement of the people from their places of origin.

The second example comes from the appeal to the youth to name, write down and praise things, lands, times and peoples:

> The first to have carved
> The first wooden doors and hearthposts!
> The first to have boiled
> The first medicine-plants in the first medicine-pots
> The first to have translated
> The first biddings of an earth-spider!
> The first to have sent and deciphered
> The first to have harkened to the first voice of kola nut parings!
> The first message with porcupine-quills! (p. 22)

Again, the anaphoric repetitions are the phrase 'The first to have' and 'The first", while the main verbs and most of the longer utterances differ from line to line.

Each complete thought consists of two lines, the short and the long, with the thought- units having more or less the same rhythm. A basic principle of parrallelism is at work here. It holds that similarity in form leads to easy identification of similarity in content and function, that is, the main verbs and their objects, in the quoted lines carry equal weight and are of equal importance. In essence this means that the events and activities referred to are of equal historical significance.

The poet equally makes use of alliteration as seen in the appeal to the elders in section seven:
> Taanto' take!
> Let this wine strengthen you to guide every incomer!
> Ngaywir take!
> Let this bloodstained feather bear testimony to our sacrifice!
> Taamfu' take!
> Let the sound of your drums
> and tusks assemble the Fon's people!
> Taangwa' take!
> Let our Mbokam game yield
> To the wishes of your spears and dogs!
> Taamanjong take!
> May you continue to lead our manjong standard-bearers!
> Taawonle take!
> May you open the ears of young folks to new things
> Yeewonle take!
> May you blow life into the children you name! (pp. 23-24)

There is the recurrent consonant /t/ present in initial positions. There is the alternation of short, stout lines with long cadenced ones, reinforcing one another and stressing what the celebrants want to put across. This powerful rhythm lends energy and urgency to their appeal, an alluring lyricism which gives the poem the mellifluous quality I spoke of earlier.

Apart from this particular music that emerges from the peculiar ordering and arrangement of the lines just quoted, there is more obvious music, italicised and worked into the poem. This is found most often in section 4, at the end of section 6, in the middle and at the end of section 7, at the beginning and at the end of section 8. It is music played in conjunction with such instruments as flutes, drums, and gongs. Here the poet also makes use of onomatopoeia as he successfully captures on paper the natural sounds made by these musical instruments. For the flute it is *fee fee*! for the drum, *ti-nding! ti-nding!*; for the gong, *ki-nging! ki-nging* and *ku-nging, ku-nging*

Thus the whole invocation, the supplicatory utterance, is recited in conjunction with musical instruments, giving the poem a powerful emotional unity, which is often an integral aspect of an effective oral performance.

Incantations are often made use of in oral literature. According to Tala Kashim, "An incantation is a curse or spell recited as part of a ritual and addressed to supernatural forces".[14] One can add that an incantation is also an utterance sung, chanted or recited as if it were a formula, a relatively fixed utterance that takes on a monotonous, mechanical aspect. An example of incantation of the type that relates to a curse is Earth-Goddess' pronouncement in *And Palm-Wine Will Flow*:

> The ground trembles in the valleys.
> The ground trembles where the streams flow.
> The ground trembles where the palms grow.
> The ground trembles! (p. 30)
> The curse remains;
> The plague remains;
> The pot is whole;
> The calabash is whole.
> The plague remains. (p. 33)

From Kishani's *Konglanjo*, there is another example of incantation contained in the prayer to the heralds in which the celebrants mechanically chant out:

> Let our children's children's children's children—
> Let our mother's mother's mother's mother
> Let our father's father's father's father—
> Let our parents' children's children's children—
> Let our ancestral parents' parents' parents—
> Let Le' and Jing, nay, the last born of this second—
> Re-echo our feats and failures up and down
> Time's sun and rain within the planets
> Be ye gods or humans! (p. 30)

The whole quotation is a periodic sentence wherein the celebrants' complete thought is delayed until the end of the utterance, until the arrival of the main verb 're-echo". In this parallel structure one notices the regular rhythm - the flow of lines of more or less equal rhythmic value - that betrays some monotony and repetitiveness typical of utterances churned out by rote.

Another device of oral literature is apostrophe, addressing or calling on someone absent or a supernatural authority as though he or she were present. The technique is evident throughout *Konglanjo*, especially in the sections addressed to Ngaa-Mbom, Wa'bin, the heralds and the ancestors. Often the names precede the appeals, but at times, the appeals are punctuated with the names. The effect conveyed is that of intimacy, drama and urgency.

Other features of orature like songs and chants, choral responses and praise names are also worked into Butake's plays (*And Palm-Wine Will Flow*, 2 1-22; *Lake God*, 30, 32 etc.) With regard to praise names the women in *Lake God* refer to Fon Joseph as the lion, the leopard, and the elephant; in *And Palm-Wine Will Flow* the ruler of Ewawa is also metaphorically called the sun, the elephant, and the lion. However, these praise names are used ironically. In the context of the plays and in the view of those calling these names, the two rulers have not given any positive account of the attributes incarnated in these animal metaphors. Thus Fon Joseph is the lion whose hunger must be assuaged at the expense of the people. He is the leopard "who pounces on his kind just to prove he is a leopard'. He is the elephant "that will trample on the shrubs in the forest while pretending to pull down the baobab" (*Lake God*, 18). In *And Palm-Wine Will Flow*, Kwengong uses praise names to refer to the ruler of Ewawa only to announce his death. He is the sun that has set, the elephant that has fallen, and the lion that is no more (45).

Conclusion

How relevant to our contemporary history are the issues treated in the works of these writers?

Asong's *The Crown of Thorns* treats the theme of the lack of genuine dialogue between the administration and the ruled. The two camps are at loggerheads, and they talk at cross-purposes. The local people have serious complaints to lay before the government regarding issues crucial to their material and spiritual life, but the government, through the Divisional Officer, adopts a rather contemptuous attitude towards them. The D.O. behaves as if the people's views and feelings do not count at all, engendering thus an impasse, a break-down of communication with the disastrous consequences registered at the end of the novel. Can we learn anything from there?

Wache's *Lament of A Mother* is an artistic review of Africa's unflattering social, political and historical experiences from the colonial period through political independence to the present-day. It is a litany of woes, tribulations, frustrations, disappointments and disillusionment. The poem deals with the bamboozling of the masses, not only by foreigners but, more tragically, by their own brothers. Can any issue be more topical?

In a similar vein Butake's *And Palm-Wine Will Flow* deals with dictatorial rule in a local Fondom, with wreckless leadership, the encouragement of mediocrity and hedonism, squandermania, etc. Thanks to its allegorical nature, the play is just as current as some headlines in our local dailies. One need only effect the necessary shift from one level of meaning to the other for a fuller appreciation. Can any play be more relevant?

All of this points to the commitment of the authors as 'writers in politics",[15] and in their politics they show great concern for the welfare of their society; they are on the side of the downtrodden. In this regard Bongasu Kishani would seem to be in a category all alone. Bate Besong once said that Kishani in *Konglanlo* does not treat contemporary concerns in the manner of a committed artist to give his readers a sense of moral direction.[16]

While agreeing with Bate Besong, it is necessary to point out that the concerns in Kishani's *Konglanjo* will remain a source of inspiration for the youth on whom the society depends for cultural continuity. Let the kite perch and let the eagle perch too ...[17] Let there be room for everybody in this triangle of ours. By thus drinking deeply from the Cameroonian pool of oral tradition for inspiration these Anglophone writers are undoubtedly making an essential contribution to African and World literature.

End Notes
1. Chinweizu et. als., *Toward The Decolonizalion of African Literature*, p. 175.
2. Adrian Roscoe, *Mother is Gold*, p. 249.
3. Ibrahim Kashim Tala, Orature: *A Research Guide*, p. 3.
4. For the two statements, see Chinua Achebe's *Things Fall Apart*, pp. 5 and 6 respectively.
5. See Nancy Schmidt, "Nigerian Fiction and the African Oral Tradition", p. 13.
6. Asong Linus Tongwo, *The Crown of Thorns*. Limbe: Cosmos Educational Publishers, 1990.
7. Chidi Ikonne, Chaakpii: *A Study Of Igbo Folktales*, Preface p. iii.
8. Bole Butake, *And Palm-Wine Will Flow*. Yaounde: SOPECAM, 1990.
9. This quote is from Nalova Lyonga's review of *And Palm-Wine Will Flow*, in an undated document advertising the staging of the play by the Yaounde University Theatre.
10. Bongasu-Tanla Kishani, *Konglanjo*. Yaounde: University of Yaounde, 1988.

11. Bole Butake, *Lake God*. Yaounde: Bet & Co. (Pub) Ltd., 1986.
12. Fale Wache, *Lament of A Mother*. 1990.
13. Siga Asanga, "Konglanjo - Spears Of Love Without Ill-Fortune: Poems - Bongasu Tanla Kishani". *Abbia* 38-39-40(1982), p. 406.
14. Ibrahim Kashim Tala, *An Introduction to Cameroon Oral Literature*. 1984, p. 20.
15. The phrase is the title of Ngugi wa Thiong'o's *Writers in Politics*.
16. Bate Besong, Bongasu Tanla Kishani As Cantor and Mystagogue' in *Cameroon Life* 1, 5 (Oct. 1990).
17. 'Let the Kite perch ... is part of a proverb from *Things Fall Apart*, p. 14.

Works Cited

Asanga, Siga. Konglanjo Spears of Love Without Ill-Fortune: Poems - Bongasu Tanla Kishani", *Abbia* 38-39-40. Yaounde: University of Cameroon, 1982.

Asong, L.T. *The Crown of Thorns*. Limbe: Cosmos Educational Publishers, 1990.

Besong, Bate. "Bongasu Tanla-Kishani as Cantor and Mystagogue", in *Cameroon Life 1*, 5 (October 1990).

Butake, Bole. *Lake God*. Yaounde: Bet & Co. (Pub.) Ltd., 1986.

_____. And Palm-Wine Will Flow. Yaounde: SOPECAM, 1990.

Chinweizu, Jemie O. and Madubuike, I. *Toward The Decolonization of African Literature*. Washington, D.C: Howard University Press, 1983.

Ikonne, C. Chaakpii. *A Study of Igbo Folktales*. Owerri: Pen Paper Publications, 1992.

Kishani, B.T. *Konglanjo*. Yaounde: The University of Yaounde, 1988.

Roscoe, A. *Mother is Gold*. London: Cambridge University Press, 1971, 1981.

Schmidt, N. 'Nigerian Fiction and the African Oral Tradition" J.N.A.L.A. (Spring & Fall 1968):5 & 6

Tala, K. I. *An Introduction to Cameroon Oral Literature*. Yaounde: The University of Yaounde, 1984.

_____. *Orature: A Research Guide*. Yaounde: A.B.E.T. Publication, 1987.

Wache, F. *Lament of A Mother*, 1990.

14
THE MODERNIST CHARACTER OF BATE BESONG'S POETRY

According to Bate Besong, the Cameroonian creative writer's art should 'become a fighting literature; he can write works which are artistically profound and politically correct: he can write works of indictment and works that show how his world is and could be' (1993:18). This quoted expression is an apt description of the distinctive combative spirit of most of Bate Besong's own poetry, or imaginative writing in general, for that matter; for it is impossible to understand the bulk of his poetic output outside this militant commitment. In his selected poems with the cryptic title of *Just above Cameroon* (1998), Bate Besong reveals himself as a firebrand poet irrevocably committed to the fierce denunciation of economic exploitation, political mismanagement, squardermania and dictatorial gangsterism. Like his drama, Bate Besong's poetry is manifestly concerned with public misdeeds and the practice of bad governance. These are the major public themes that dominate his poetry in addition to such private concerns as love and death.

Like any motivated satirist, Bate Besong is ridiculing, flagellating, and anathematizing those in authority with the moral intention of making them change their bad habits for the better. His severe criticism of public officers is an indirect advocacy of good governance, of economic and political transparency in the management of public affairs. Bate Besong's social vision then begins to crystallize. His ideal society would be one marked by moral decency, and rid of economic and political abuse, a society where there is social justice and fairness in the distribution of the wealth of the nation and not one in which this sharing is skewed in favour of the rich and the powerful, a society devoid of electoral chicanery, gerrymandering, corruption and the violation of the human rights of defenceless citizens. Ultimately then, by implication, Bate Besong is advocating authentic rigour and moralization in the conduct of 'la chose publique'; his poetry is aimed at the social deconstruction of Cameroon. But to articulate these objective realities Bate Besong employs a mordant, muscular style of verbal pugilism, and adopts a modernist or even a post-modernist approach, placing his poetic practice within the tradition of modern poetry, with some of its characteristic obscurantism.

As a mode of writing modernism is marked by a distinctive imagination and a clear, deliberate and strong break with traditional forms and techniques of expression. It is a collection of characteristics although not all of them are exhibited by any single writer considered as modernist. In this regard Besong is a self-conscious writer, determined to sever ties with the conventional past. A militant poet with an obvious innovatory poetic technique, he is continually experimenting and searching for new ways of expressing himself on issues that bother him. His imagery is conditioned by this peculiar pre-occupation. The subject matter of his poetry, the satirical butts of his verbal punches, are irresponsible political leaders and neo-patrimonialists pictured as buffoons, clowns, fools and dunces, people reduced to the level of animals, a cartel that, to satisfy its greed, seeks to grab all for itself, leaving little or nothing to the rest of the nation:

> For sure Jewry stood for an exploiting race, but our own middlemen manage to amaze them for all that. Indeed, they have sworn fealty to their Masonic lodges & to each other to bankrupt our national coffers.
> The curse on the heads of the corrupt
> banditti. 'Their Champagne Party Will
> End' (220).

No wonder the poet equally employs violent animal images evoked by such creatures as 'jackal', 'hyaena', 'mongrel', 'crocodile' and 'iguana' and powerful verbs of action like 'despoil', 'loot', 'plunder', 'bankrupt', 'ruin', 'butcher', and 'squander,' to depict the very destructive effect of these cruel, unpatriotic and unconscionable rulers. Conventional versification is not his inclination. Not for him the regular poetic lines, rhymes or fixed stanzaic forms. Like most modern poets, Bate Besong prefers free verse. He eschews 'poetical' expressions like 'dewy wine', 'bonny lass', 'verdurous pastures', 'pastoral eglantine' or some other adumbrations of romanticism. His poetic expressions are hard and stern:

'Prison blues (ii)'

...

> Only from such deranged insomniacs
> such precurors of the hydraulics
> of terror, dyspeptic,
> ghouls

>   whose thong-glued
>   calendars register
>   gaudier golgothas
>   for sanctuaries, breed
>
>   tombstones
>   from a crevasse
>   of communal lore
>
>   only such demented precursors
>   who, rejoicing, puke
>   prodigal lacerations
>   behind prison bars
>   ('Prison blues (ii)' (5)

At the level of diction, Bate Besong sometimes goes rather for the rare word, one that looks strange and seemingly unpronounceable and unAnglo-Saxon. Yet more often than not it is an English word e.g. 'djinns', 'thong', 'thaumaturge', and 'simurgh'. These words of less frequency often are not found in the average dictionaries. Even in the most advanced dictionaries a few of Bate Besong's words cannot be located, in which case they may simply be words of his own coinage, or borrowings from his local vernacular e.g 'Mfam' or 'Obasinjom'. Occasionally, Bate Besong boldly brings into his poetry words from such diverse languages as Arabic, German, French or Kenyang in an attempt to express an idea precisely. He is a poet with an elliptical poetic imagination; his poetry is often erratic in its movement. There is no rigid respect for chronology in the expression of his thought and ideas, nor an attempt to stick to syntactic logic in the structure of his sentences:

>   *At Auschwitz thro' treblinka*
>   A clan of minotaurs of Chaim
>   Hertzog
>   (*time again & again*) had,
>   doused.
>
>   the pogrom charters
>   with the yiddish

>   bitumen
>   of jew wiesenthal-
>
>   in whorls, suited
>   in whorls of quisling
>   carnations, he
>
>   nation-wrecker
>   buoyed
>
>   by the crack units
>   of cannibal hussars, indeed,
>   of a humpback
>   torah
>   who was to know
>   that—he—;
>   mandarin-thagi; and sophomoric
>   thaumaturge, had
>   promised
>   obasinjom assuagement
>   of the gravaments
>   of a humbugged
>   diaspora?
>   'The Kaiser Lied' (14)

The result is that in some places we have, instead of complete sentences, fragments of sentences that apparently make little or no sense. In fact some lines are made up of three or two words, and some others of only one word. This great freedom with syntax and diction has the advantage of lending his poetic utterances greater force and resonance, hence the extra-ordinary energy of his poetic lines. In these and other stylistic characteristics, there is something Hopkinsian about Besong's poetry. Its modernist character, to some extent, recalls the eccentricities of the British Jesuit priest and poet, Gerard Manley Hopkins, noted for his word coinage, compounding of words, use of ellipsis and, above all, disruption of conventional syntax in his poetry (Abrams 2126).

Bate Besong equally possesses a heightened poetic imagination teeming with analogies and parallels. He is never content with simply talking about one thing only, but he must seek parallels, analogies or contrasts here and there, hence the highly allusive nature of his poetry. His images at times take the form of cinematographic shots. To enter Bate Besong's poetry is to encounter a mercurial mind, one that makes use of just about any material; indeed, the universe remains his source of inspiration. Like Hopkins, Besong's deployment of his unusual poetic style emblematizes the 'stress and action' (Abrams 2126) of the poet's brain during high tension moments of poetic inspiration or imaginative apprehension. To read Bate Besong one should be prepared for bewildering, mental acrobatic feats, to move swiftly in space and time, sometimes for an elusive mental trip from Africa to Europe to America to the Middle East and back to Africa ('The Kaiser Lied'); one should be ready for an allusive excursion into history, literature and the Bible, and for scientific references from Biology, Physics and Medicine, etc. Indeed the following statement by T.S. Eliot is as enlightening with regard to Eliot's method in *The Waste Land* and the early poems as it roughly defines Bate Besong's approach in *Just above Cameroon:*

> Our civilization comprehends great variety and complexity, and this variety and complexity, playing upon a refined sensibility, must produce various and complex results. The poet must become more and more comprehensive, more allusive, more indirect, in order to force, to dislocate if necessary, language into his meaning (289).

These characteristics point to the erudition of the man Bate Besong, for he invariably brings his recondite knowledge to bear on his poetry. Obviously this is intimidating to the average reader. All of these stylistic quirks and idiosyncrasies have the net effect of rendering Bate Besong's poetry difficult, obscure and partly impenetrable. They account for the obscurantism of which he is often accused and guilty ('Just above Cameroon'). In this particular poem the poet-persona admits that his poetry is obscure and he betrays feelings of guilt as he wonders whether he had done a wrong thing to have adopted this abstruse style that has rendered his poetry inaccessible, 'was it a wrong turning I had taken?' ('Just above Cameroon').

Guilt:

> (Was it a wrong turning I had taken?)
> for, I too have crushed into silence
> the daylight robbery of hands soiled
> with heroes' blood & ill-gotten gains (&
> chewed the curd of complacency...)
> to lose sight from pain
> from the obsequies over the wall
> of state torture, friend;
> *come on and see come on and see...*
> for I too have exhumed the cadaverous
> past long
> worn its glorified ostrich mask,
> and poured
> the rubble
> of its narcissistic muse
> on my masquerader head...
> have built: poetries' Canaans
> in obscurities which led
> to the labyrinth of my own inertia
> (all that gone with the wind now)
> I too have
> imprinted a century's dark decade
> (this, to the best of my ability)
> hidden, in a curfewed song!
> 'Just above Cameroon' (19).

In this regard the title poem 'Just above Cameroon' must be interpreted not in terms of geographical location but in connection with the difficult nature of his poetry vis-à-vis the mental ability of the average Cameroonian to apprehend it. If our line of reasoning is correct, then what Bate Besong is saying through the intriguing title of his selected poems, *Just above Cameroon,* is that because of its obscurity his poetry is a little beyond the understanding of Cameroonians. It therefore stands to reason that to spare himself any more regret and free himself from further feelings of guilt it behoves Bate Besong to consider discarding his present arcane style in favour of one more accessible to his many fans and admirers, the masses on whose behalf he is waging a ferocious battle against the ruling elite. He should lay aside his poetic opacity, forsake his metallic words and thunderous sentences, and come down to earth and address his people in an idiom they can understand. Now, when he is widely read by the masses like the object of his admiration, Mongo Beti, he too can then be proud of having made a 'refulgent contribution' in the history of the flagellation of vice in the Cameroonian society.

Bate Besong's poems are not purely cerebral abstractions. Objectively looked at, the poems are not rarefied intellectual exercises but deeply felt emotional utterances. The nefarious comportment of the ruling class is the main-spring of Bate Besong's anger. If he did not feel strongly about the harm politicians were doing to the nation in both material and human terms, he would simply remain mute like the rest of the silent majority. But as seen from the poems, Bate Besong is an angry individual, a man with an intellectual passion for truth and social justice, and he possesses the moral courage to back up his insight. This explains his passionate dissatisfaction with the misconduct of those in authority and the fierceness with which he flays them ('Facsimile of a Jackal', 'The Party's Over!', 'Prison blues (ii)', 'The Kaiser Lied', 'You must come to our rally', 'For Osagyefo Thomas Sankara', 'Their Champagne Party Will End'). From this perspective, therefore, his poetry is both cerebral and emotional; it appeals to both the head and the heart.

True, Bate Besong's obscurantism is only too obvious, but the reader can still enjoy some of his poetry even when he does not understand it. This may sound contradictory but it is true. When one reads Bate Besong aloud, and does not enjoy his grandiloquent and often cacophonous poetic utterances, one will, at least, appreciate the fact that, from the harshness of the sounds, here is a passionate person who has lost his temper. After all when a person loses his temper, he does not usually speak smoothly and steadily. He shocks us, jolting us out of our complacency. That is what Bate Besong often does. Besides, the discordant note in his poetry reflects the moral ugliness of the depraved individuals he is castigating. 'His haughty use of humour and hyperbole does not water down his rage against the society, for when a society is deaf one must shout for it to listen' (Ngwane 24). The cacophony is therefore functional and effective.

The conscientious readers will reap more from Bate Besong. The sentiment of anger, that basic quality that runs through much of his poetry, is a boon to the readers. Guided by it, the meticulous readers can reasonably get into the core of many of the poems because the anger reveals Bate Besong's attitude towards his subject matter. One can always tell, especially in poems dealing with a public theme, that Bate Besong is bitter or angry about something or with somebody. This guiding sentiment is invariably couched in emotion-laden words, words with negative connotations: adjectives, nouns and verbs that reveal his subjective feelings. Some of these words and images we have already cited above. Here are some others: 'greedy brain', 'lame-brained', 'blood-suckers', 'zombie clamour', 'jokers' 'nation-wrecker', 'idiot-soaked demagoguery' 'numbskull establishment', 'dunce-stable', 'mongrelized-iscariots', 'The curse on the heads of the corrupt banditi', and 'A plague on the heads of the corrupt banditi...'

These words and expressions can be spotted by the assiduous readers. This done, the targets of Bate Besong's anger can then be more easily identified, and they are likely to be unconscionable, unpatriotic politicians, dictators, looters of state coffers, torturers, or stooges in the hands of some well-placed tyrants, some of them pictured in terms of wild animals. Once the butts of Bate Besong's satire have been spotted, it is not too difficult to discover what they have done that has provoked his anger. At this point the painstaking readers can be sure that they can talk reasonably about some of the major themes of Bate Besong's poetry, his attitude to his subject matter, and his style.

Given the many complaints, time and again, (Tabianyor 8) about the opacity of his poetry, Bate Besong would seem to be the most difficult Cameroonian poet today. The unpredictable movement and complexity of his poetry bespeak the capriciousness and complexity of modern man that it deals with. The perplexing title: *Just above Cameroon*, to me is a subtle challenge to Cameroonian literary scholars, and one that ought to be faced by critics. However, only an immodest literary student would claim to have mastered all of Bate Besong's poetry. The best a sober critic should do is offer to the literary community the benefit of his insight into aspects of the complex work of this avant-garde poet, Cameroon's enfant terrible, in the hope that other scholars will pick up the gauntlet and, with time, Bate Besong's poetry will be put in proper perspective. Only then will it cease to puzzle. Only then will the poetry have been demystified so that it will no longer be beyond Cameroon.

Works Cited

Abrams, M.H. Gen. ed. *The Norton Anthology of English Literature.* 6th Ed. New York. London: Norton, 1996.

Asong, Linus T. "BB's *The Grain of Bobe Ngom Jua*: An Artistic Milestone in the Development of Cameroon Poetry (Part II)" in *Cameroon Post.* N⁰ 0212 April 6-13, 1994.

Besong, Bate. "Literature in the Season of the Diaspora: Notes to the Anglophone Cameroonian Writer". Keynote Address in Lyonga, Breitinger and Butake (eds). *Anglophone Cameroonian Writing,* Bayreuth: Bayreuth University, 1993, 15-18.

_____. *Just above Cameroon.* n.p. 1998:

Eliot, T.S. *Selected Essays.* London: Faber and Faber Limited, 1932.

Ngwane, George. *Bate Besong (Or the Symbol of Anglophone Hope).* Limbe: Nooremac Press, 1993.

Tabianyor, T.M. 'Who is Afraid of Bate Besong?' in *The Post* No 0153 Monday January 10, 2000, 8.

15
THE QUINTESSENCE OF BERNARD FONLON

If Africa were to be destroyed by a flood today, and if some African books, on the strength of their intrinsic worth and beauty, were to float like Noah's Ark and remain to tell to the rest of the world the story of literary excellence from Africa, Bernard Fonlon's *The Genuine Intellectual* would certainly be numbered among the few to be so salvaged. And this would be due largely to the sound ideas contained in the book, and also to the way in which the ideas are conveyed to the reader. In other words, the strength of Fonlon's *The Genuine Intellectual* resides in its matter and manner.[1]

What is the book about? It is on the Nature, the End and the Purpose of University Studies. There is at the beginning of the book an interesting and absorbing history of the origin and growth of the university in the ancient and medieval worlds prior to modern times. Fonlon believes "that the university is not for a mindless mob but for the Talented Tenth" (8-9). According to him, "to create an authentic university and not a glorified secondary school" (9), we must create with it the following trinity: the University Library, the University Bookshop and the University Printing Press. It is about the university, with respect to Africa's needs and aspirations. At a time when Africa is still the fertile ground for imperialism and neo-colonialism, contends Fonlon, the university is the sure place to produce the genuine intellectuals who will be able to combat these "isms". The University is the nurturing ground for the people that will bring pride and dignity to the Africa that has been degraded, disgraced, demoralized and despoiled.

At the centre of University studies are the African youth, the genuine intellectuals in the making: Africa's hope for the future. An intellectual, by popular definition, is one who is educated, learned and clever, one, most probably, with a University education, and the higher his qualification, the better. Fonlon would say that if your intellectual was all this and nothing else, he would not qualify as a genuine intellectual.

Here then are the hallmarks of the authentic intellectual as conceived by Fonlon: the person must not only be clever, learned and broadly educated; he must be a tireless pursuer of knowledge and truth; he must be ready to delve deeply beyond the surface facts into the heart of things, the ultimate truth; he must be a constant researcher the results of whose findings, he must put into use, first for the benefit of his society, the commonwealth, before thinking of himself; he must be the conscience of his society, the eternal defender of truth and justice; he must shun all vice: he must be above petty jealousies, corruption, and meanness; he must avoid the love of wealth, or power and of fame. The genuine intellectual should be a lover of mankind; he is one whose breast is full of the milk of human kindness.

The genuine intellectual is one imbued with a questioning attitude; he must be one ready to question things fearlessly, instead of just accepting them facilely. In everything he does, the genuine intellectual evinces a scientific and philosophical spirit; he is one who, by virtue of his education, is ready to adapt to any situation, ready to apply his essentially scientific and philosophical approach to issues to analyse and solve problems, even outside his area of specialization.

Above all, the genuine intellectual must be humble, ready to acknowledge and correct any mistakes made; he must be prepared to do this because he obviously cannot know everything, not even in his own area of specialization. Knowledge is just too much for one person to carry in his small head. In brief, such are the attributes of a genuine intellectual by Fonlon's definition. Certainly my summary statements have left out so much. I am far from doing Fonlon full justice. Generally, however, these are the salient qualities of his genuine intellectual. Some of Fonlon's models of genuine intellectuals from history are Socrates, Mahatma Gandhi and Abraham Lincoln. Let us now quote him with regard to what he considers to be the function of university education:

> What then should be the lofty, large and selfless purpose that educators should have ever in mind in imparting university learning?
>
> Obviously, the End of University Studies, of which I have spoken so much above, that is, the formation of men armed with deep systematised knowledge in a specific field, men equipped, consequently, with a scientific and philosophical bent of mind, that is, the production of the genuine thinker-scholar, the scientist-philosopher, in short, the

production of the authentic intellectual, should constitute, in itself, and at once, a primary purpose of university education.

Yet the intellectual, thus conceived and fashioned, however brilliant, however skilful, however profound in science and scholarship, does not constitute an end in himself; you do not produce him merely for the pleasure of producing him, to set him up (for popular worship) like a golden calf in the wilderness of ignorance and mediocrity. The pertinent question is: what should he do with his learning and skill and mind; to what use should he put his specialised knowledge, his scientific and philosophical training? In other words, what should be the ultimate purpose for providing a given community, or society at large, with the university trained man - the scientist, the technologist, the thinker-scholar, the genuine intellectual?

I have pondered this question over and over again, and, ever I have come to one and the same conclusion, namely, that the purpose of university education should be, not merely to equip the rising youth with scientific and philosophical knowledge and skill and mind, but most especially to instil into them, over and above, a deep, keen and lofty sense of dedication to the service of the commonwealth, the immediate community to which they are members, and thereby, to the service of the world as a whole, of humanity at large.

But how should this sense of dedication and service be manifested, how should it be put into effect in the concrete; or, to put it more generally, what roles, what services, should a genuine intellectual perform among men?

The most obvious and immediate one is that he should put his special knowledge or skill (as an agronomist, an engineer, an economist, a social scientist, an educationist, a philosopher) at the disposal of the community. But this is not enough. To whom much has been given, from him much shall be required. And the university man out of academy and among ordinary men would be a woeful failure if he did no more than ply his special skill. What then is required of him over and above?

Needless to say that Fonlon's conceptualization of a genuine intellectual is heavily skewed in favour of the University-educated. Impressive or even intimidating as this definition of an intellectual is, some might still consider it a bit too exclusive in some respects; they might say intellectuals, even "genuine" ones, do not necessarily have to be University products, nor, for that matter, the products of formal education in the Western sense. These critics may say that intellectuals may also be those who, besides possessing some of the qualities listed by Fonlon, also possess these others: people with exceptional leadership qualities, thinkers with a drive to lead others, opinion moulders rather than opinion followers. Of course, this must exclude your demagogue, your populist, or your run-off-the-mill rabble rouser.

Some may say (and indeed have said) that Fonlon is a visionary, a dreamer. Where in this world of today, they would ask, can you find a single individual who fits your concept of a genuine intellectual? Nothing short of a miracle could bring this about. They may say M. le philosophe, your beautiful ones are not yet born.

By and large such an attitude is understandable; indeed, no less a personality than Fonlon himself acknowledges the near-angelic dimension of his conceptualization: An imperfect humanity is called upon to perform a perfect task. True, the task is all but impossible, yet we should try it. We may not get to the end of the task, but at least we can get somewhere. If we do not attempt it, we will surely fail; if we attempt it, we may fail. If we could strive to acquire some of the qualities enumerated by Fonlon, the lot of humanity could be improved. At least half a loaf of bread is better than no bread at all.

Yes, Fonlon may be called a dreamer. But life without a dream, without hope, would be intolerable. Thus, we should exercise the right to dream; we ought to dream, not only of the reality that is, but also of the reality that ought to be. And that, to me, is part of Fonlon's strength: the ability to inspire people to dream.

Before I proceed to examine Fonlon's technique, I would like to say one or two more things regarding the book's content. I said earlier that the book is about the University, the nursery garden for the intellectual on whose future Africa depends. One African university which Fonlon singles out for praise is the University of Ibadan, founded in 1948 and modelled on the University of London in England. And two of the intellectual products of Ibadan eulogized by Fonlon are Professor Victor Anomah Ngu, the great Cameroonian scientist, researcher and award winner, on the one hand, and Chinua Achebe, the renowned Nigerian novelist, on the other. In developing his overall subject, Fonlon does not propound any new philosophical system, it is more the scientific and philosophical spirit in which he conducts his inquiry and analysis that gives the book a philosophical dimension than the fact that he has constructed a new system of metaphysics.

In the process of developing his treatise, Fonlon makes insightful statements on many subjects under the sun, whether it be literature and language, or science and philosophy; whether it is education and psychology, or history and historiography. This fine book is replete with quotable axioms, only a few of which I will quote here:

1. "For, indeed the deeper genuine learning and scholarship penetrate, the more they should induce a profound and ever deepening humility." (117)
2. "Within even his special field, no scientist or philosopher or expert can lay claim to omniscience and infallibility." (117)
3. "In the rough and tumble of politics, the intellectual, dedicated to the Ideal, will have to learn to temper his Idealism with deep-sighted realism" (139)
4. "For once the intellectual ceases to think of himself as a humble seeker of the Truth in the vast unknown and assumes the airs of an omniscient demigod, the knell of his creative life begins to toll". (142)

Four factors are important as far as style is concerned: the subject matter, the audience, the language and the author. We have so far looked at Fonlon's subject matter. As far as his audience is concerned, it is the African freshmen, the University undergraduates. I agree with Professor Anomah Ngu that Fonlon's audience is more than this, that his book is "good enough for professors" themselves.

Now Fonlon's language, the manner in which he communicates with his audience, is partly influenced by the matter and the audience; above all, it is affected by the personality, the individuality of Fonlon himself. For Fonlon's intellectual background, his deep learning, his predisposition and his interests, etc. are brought to bear on his delivery method.

Fonlon's subject is a weighty one, and his audience, intellectual. Therefore, his language must not be childish. Indeed, it is not. On the contrary, and appropriately, the language is learned, and his style majestic. Some would say the book is difficult, and I would not blame them. Admittedly, it is not your arm-chair novel or some escapist stuff; nor is it a book that can be read in one sitting unless, of course, by the very committed and the most determined. Rather, this condensed work makes full demand on the reader. It demands, like any serious book, the full deployment of one's reading skills; it calls for full concentration and, above all, for the exercise of the reader's cognitive and aesthetic faculties.

Having said this, however, I hasten to add that the essay is not obscure. And this is because Fonlon always tries to make his point as simple as possible; he relentlessly strives after clarity and lucidity. Since he is dealing with abstract concepts, he endeavours, by the use of examples, illustrations and images, to make them concrete.

For example, his step-by-step conceptualization of philosophy, through what one would call the concentric-circles method, is clearer than an elusive dictionary-type definition:

> All the Sciences that we have seen can be considered as forming a series of concentric circles: the smallest of these circles delimits Biology, which deals with living organisms; the second is the sphere of chemistry, which concerns itself with the elements, the composition and decomposition of matter, whether living or non-living; the third circle is the scope of Physics, which is the science of the sources, the manifestations, the effects and uses of energy; the fourth is Mathematics, which has for its object quantity which is the ultimate property of the material world. The outermost circle, englobing all, is the science which treats of Beings, the property of the total universe.
>
> This final and all-embracing science which treats of the nature, the forms and the properties of

> Being is Metaphysics, the science of the universe, the science of the Universal. It is Metaphysics that is philosophy in the strictest sense of the term (100-101).

In this book Fonlon the learned man emerges, as evidenced by his enthusiastic quotations from, and references to, venerable classical authors, scholars and philosophers. He comes through to the reader as one steeped in the classics, in contemporary politics and history, and in science and literature. His many quotations are not simply a parade of his knowledge. They are not merely decorative, but functional and pertinent; they lend cogency and clarity to his argument. Throughout the book the reader has the over-whelming impression that he is in the company of one of the most lucid minds of our time.

Fonlon is matchless in his use of language. He exploits to the fullest the effects that words and phrases can produce. He is conscious of the referential meanings of words. But he is even more interested in words that combine meaning with music, words and expressions that when carefully strung together, evoke pleasant poetic effects. He constantly strives for "le mot juste": he is hardly satisfied until he finds the right word for the right slot in the sentence. In other words, Fonlon is not in a haste to state an idea. He usually takes his time to look for the most accurate word, the best expression, the truest phrase to string carefully in an unambiguous sentence, all for the purpose of perspicuity and felicity:

> If in this particular case, we see that Science and Technology and Research are the levers that lift the world of today, and that we cannot effectively master Science and Technology without mastering the language of Science and Technology, if English is this language so absolutely necessary; and, if we conclude, as a logical consequence, that the progress of no country should be sacrificed or jeopardized to save another country's face, and that English must, therefore, become the first foreign language of this country, within the Academy, without the Academy; then we must say so, and say so without pleasure, and say so without rancour, and say so without wincing, and say so without gloating, and say so without mincing, and say so remorselessly and say so

> unhesitatingly, and say so unrepentantly, and say so categorically (18).

This quotation exemplifies some aspects of Fonlon's style: the whole paragraph is a single sentence, Fonlon's typical periodic sentence. Here his ideas are set off by semi-colons. The semi-colons, together with the pattern of rhythm produce the effect of emphasis. Fonlon, exploits the device of alliteration: "lever ... lift," "say so:" "without wincing," "first foreign." When one adds to all this the modulated repetition of the sonorous "Science and Technology", and the symmetry and balance of "within the Academy, without the Academy," the overall effect is music. Indeed, as the reader gets towards the end of the sentence, the urge to accompany the reading with a nod of the head and a tap of the foot becomes compelling, irresistible.

But beautiful and mellifluous as the sentence is, it also contains a flaw: the fault of too much of a good thing. Towards the end of the sentence, the rhythm becomes a little too regular and insistent, calling attention to itself. One has the impression that Fonlon is just having a good time that he is clearly enjoying himself. The result of this is the weakening of the emphasis he intends to give to English as the world's number one language. This is obviously a stylistic weakness.

However, this is rare; Fonlon's style is usually effective. It may be, as Chinua Achebe would put it, this is but one of the pleasant "occasional departures into relieved competence."[2]

Just one more quotation and we will be done:

> Firstly, I have said earlier that the genuine intellectual should regard his university studies essentially as a springboard from which to plunge deeper still and deeper into the bottomless waters of knowledge; that he must remain a student, a researcher, a thinker all his days. The essential intention here is that these studies, this research, this thinking should result not merely in increased learning, on his part, for himself, but in the discovery of new knowledge for the humankind – a new fact, a new thought, a new principle, a new law. Thus, the foremost and never ending role of the intellectual is to be a seeker who finds, who discovers. As finder or discoverer he causes the horizons of

> knowledge to recede further back, he sets the bounds of learning wider still and wider, by adding something more, something new, to the existing store of human science and wisdom.
>
> Secondly, thanks to the finding of new facts, new thought, new laws, new principles, the scientist-philosopher builds up new solutions, concrete or abstract, for the problems that face his community or the world at large. In this way, like a man who fathers a son, he participates in the unending act by which God is ceaselessly creating and renewing the world. By such singular and original accomplishment, the scientist philosopher, the thinker scholar, the genuine intellectual, becomes a creator, a maker. To this category of makers obviously belong the greater benefactors of mankind who have invented sources of energy, new tools to make labour easier, speedier, more efficient, most prolific; and life more livable; who are creating or perfecting new means, new machines to make travel ever swifter, ever surer; to make communication more instant and clearer and, thereby, bring the farflung peoples of the world closer and closer, together (130-131).

The above passage shows how Fonlon thinks not only conceptually but also in images. It demonstrates a real blend of the informative and the creative language, a fusion of the conceptual and the experiential knowledge. By the power and beauty of the written word, Fonlon renders abstract ideas concrete and vivid by using similes: "as a springboard from which to plunge deeper...", "As a finder and discoverer..." "like a man who fathers a son ..." Fonlon makes us see a tireless researcher and producer of knowledge in terms of a relentless marine and geographical explorer. The entire passage is poetic prose; it pulsates with the characteristic rhythm of Fonlon's prose.

All this does not come about by accident; it is the end result of a meticulously worked out technique; it is conscious and painstaking art. For example, the last sentence of the above passage, in its complexity and elaborateness, is carefully written out to enact what it describes. The complex sentence, carrying its disparate components, moves gradually but inevitably towards its definite end, in the same manner as various aspects of complex and sophisticated technology gradually and inexorably bring the disparate peoples of the earth closer and closer to the emphatic finality – "together!"

"I always made sure my writing had a literary dimension" (Fonlon Interview 159). There you have the quintessence of Fonlon. From the purely literary point of view these are a few of the elements that raise Fonlon's formal essay to the level of literature; an essentially conceptual material is transmuted into art. Facts and ideas, otherwise bare and bald, are rendered juicy and palatable, making the whole book aesthetically and intellectually satisfying. Indeed, "A thing of beauty is a joy forever."[3]

Thus, the quintessential Fonlon emerges when he combines the ability to communicate an idea cogently and lucidly with the beauty of expression; the vintage Fonlon emerges when he conveys a noble idea in language above that which is normally beautiful, so that the language does not overwhelm the idea. That is, when there is a nice balance between matter and manner. So, when the manner pleasantly matches the matter, then there we have the essence of Fonlon, then there we have the Fonlon who appeals to both the head and the heart.

In his busy life Professor Fonlon proved beyond doubt that he was, to a large extent, the type of genuine intellectual he conceptualized in his book. A university-educated man, Fonlon put his university education to the service of the commonwealth: he headed several ministries, and did much in the area of politics. Among the projects he carried out, was one that took him five years to complete research on. And when he was completely satisfied with that research, he decided to put it to the benefit of his society and mankind. That research was none other than *The Genuine Intellectual*.

When, as a young man, I left the shores of Cameroon in 1981 for postgraduate studies in the US, *The Genuine Intellectual* was the only printed material I carried on my lap. Five years later, in 1986, when I returned home after bagging two master's degrees and a Ph.D., and carrying fourteen valises of books with me on the plane, Fonlon's *Genuine Intellectual* was the sole text I had on my lap. On both occasions that book was the only thing I valued after my life; it was the other thing next to my life that I was willing to escape from any possible air crash with. This slim but dense book is the quintessence of Fonlon. It is as full of sound wisdom as a boiled egg is full of meat; it is as beautifully written as a book can possibly be. It must be numbered among the most enduring documents of our time.

End Notes
1. Page References to this text are taken from Bernard Fonlon's *The Genuine Intellectual*. Yaoundé: Buma Kor, 1978.
2. Chinua Achebe, *Girls At War And Other Stories,* The 1972 Preface.
3. John Keats, *Endymion* Bk 1.

Works Cited
Achebe, Chinua. *Girls At War And Other Stories*. London: Heinemann, 1972.
De la Taille, G; K. Werner, and V. Tarkang (eds). *Balafon: An Anthology of Cameroon Literature in English*. Essex: Longman Group Limited, 1986.
Fonlon, Bernard. *The Genuine Intellectual*. Yaoundé: Buma Kor, 1978.
Keats, John. *Endymion* BK I. in M. H. Abrams (Gen. ed.). *The Norton Anthology of English Literature*. 6th ed. New York/London: Norton, 1996. 1774.

PART THREE:

BOOK REVIEWS

16
BOLE BUTAKE, *LAKE GOD AND OTHER PLAYS*,
Yaoundé: Editions CLE, 1999, 199pp

The publication of Bole Butake's *Lake God and Other* Plays by Editions CLE, Yaoundé, confirms him as one of the two giants of the Anglophone Cameroon literary theatre today. Whether drawing from a mythic imagination or from the contemporary social scene, Butake succeeds in making his plays scathing commentaries on contemporary social life in Cameroon, in particular, and Africa in general, especially where there is irresponsible political leadership, unconscionable dictatorial rule, rapacious greed, corruption, immorality and the misuse of power. This malpractice by the elite in control of the reins of power provokes the justified anger of the oppressed who advocate a change of the status quo, a protest in which women play a fundamental role. For in most of Butake's dramas women have moved from their traditional back-seat role of passive players to the foreground as a powerful force for significant social change.

The six plays in the collection handle various themes and social issues: the eternal conflict between traditionalism and modernity *(Lake God);* insatiable greed and the inhuman exploitation of a human situation *(The Survivors);* dictatorial rule in a local chiefdom, the use or misuse of power, as well as the powerful role of women in combating the forces of evil *(And Palm-Wine Will Flow)*; the negative effects, on the civilian population, of military dictatorship *(Shoes and Four Men in Arms)*; a classic illustration of the maxim that power corrupts and absolute power corrupts absolutely *(Dance of the Vampires);* and corruption and the travesty of justice *(The Rape of Michelle)*.

Owing to the caustic nature of his plays and the high political content of most of them, Bole Butake is regarded in Cameroon as a radical dramatist whose intention is to transform people's consciousness so that they can begin to explore ways of bringing about a new socio-political order. Working in close collaboration with the University of Yaoundé Theatre and the Flame Players, he has taken his plays to jammed theatre halls in the major towns of the Anglophone regions in Cameroon. But, above all, his plays have been staged in the capital city of Yaoundé, the seat of government and the socio-political nerve centre of Cameroon. Prior to their publication in

1999, one of the plays *(Shoes and Four Men in Arms)* was staged by the Flame Players in the three German cities of Leverkusen, Gelsenkirchen and Bayreuth.

That Butake is able to stage plays in Yaoundé that are critical of the political system in Cameroon in particular, and Africa in general, without provoking bitter reaction from political authorities, is a measure of both the playwright's ability to handle symbol, allegory and metaphor in which some of the plays are couched, and the relative freedom of the press under the 'New Deal' regime of President Paul Biya. During the rule of former President Ahmadou Ahidjo plays like Bole Butake's would certainly have been banned in Cameroon. Owing to his unique way of handling his subject matter, Butake has not suffered the fate of his contemporary and compatriot, the irrepressible Bate Besong, whose fiery play, *Beasts of No Nation*, when premiered in Yaoundé in 1991 got him into difficulties with government authorities.

The significance of Butake's dramaturgy in Cameroon lies in the fact that his plays are an important aspect of the on-going process of political sensitisation of Cameroonians in the wake of the wind of change from Eastern Europe in the late 1980s and the resurgence of multi-party politics in Africa, particularly in the last decade of the twentieth century. But above all, the successful production of Butake's plays in Cameroon is a pointer to the fact that in Cameroon today a skilful playwright or artist, that is to say, one with a good mastery of the English language, can be subtly critical of the political system without necessarily provoking a ban on his work. Butake's example is an encouraging reality which other Cameroonian creative writers are likely to emulate.

From the point of view of technique, Butake's craftsmanship manifests itself in his adroit manipulation of dramatic elements like passion and poetry, sound and sense, suspense and spectacle, tension and tone, creative lighting and imaginative decor. Some of the dramas are rich in African theatrical idioms injecting freshness into them and expanding their range of interpretation. The playwright skilfully incorporates such African theatrical elements as dance, song, ritual, mime, mask and spirit possession.

With the aid of high technology, theatrical effects like winds and storms can be effectively realised. Also effectively used is the flashback technique. The first instance is in *And Palm-Wine Will Flow* where Kwengong is shown carrying the horrible potion the chief was forced to drink; the second is in *The Rape of Michelle* where we see Michelle sexually importuning Mikindong, followed by her vain attempt to rape him. The effectiveness of the latter flashback lies in its persuasive corroboration of Mikindong's narrative. Butake endows his characters with language that is clean, clear and crisp, a factor that certainly endears him to the audience. So far these are some of Butake's dramatic strengths.

But the works betray a few artistic weaknesses too. The last scene of *The Survivors* has shown that, emboldened by the revolver in her keeping, Mboysi has successfully reduced the exploitative Officer to total submission. Threatening to kill the crawling Officer, she fires two shots off stage and then does a dance to celebrate her victory over him, inviting her companions to join her in the celebration. The audience then concludes that the man has been killed, only for the supposedly dead officer to make a ghostly re-appearance to kill Mboysi. There is no explanation from the playwright as to how the Officer has escaped death. This is artistically false.

With regard to the subject of rape treated in *The Rape of Michelle*, I find Mikindong idealised and Michelle lionised. It is not that Cameroonian society cannot boast of men of moral rectitude like Mikindong. But those men who make beer-houses and chicken-parlours their daily haunt and would still remain impervious to sexual solicitation and lewd advances from beautiful prostitutes are a rare species indeed. Our society abounds with their opposites.

Similarly, while sexual importunity and seduction on the part of a woman is a possibility, the reality in our larger social context is more likely to point to male sexual aggression as evident in the stories of seduction and rape attributed to men, and reported in our daily newspapers.

There are a few lapses in the italicisation of stage directions which in some places are neither in italics nor in parenthesis to differentiate them from normal lines, causing problems, however slight, to readers or producers. The most evident flaw is more technical than artistic - the absence of a table of contents, with the result that the reader is forced to constantly leaf through the book to locate the page where each of the six plays begins.

These flaws do not ruin the plays, nor do they amount to much when placed beside Butake's dramatic strengths. His ingenious deployment of dramatic technique, his searching exploration of a diversity of relevant themes, and his interesting projection of the Cameroonian woman on to an exciting theatrical foreground lend his dramaturgy a high social value, making him a major Anglophone Cameroonian literary dramatist. He and his compatriot Bate Besong are the two colossi who bestride the Anglophone Cameroon theatrical landscape.

17
LINUS T. ASONG, *THE AKROMA FILE*
Bamenda: Patron publishing House, 1997, 150pp

If a man deserves his fame, that man is L. T. Asong. With seven published novels to his credit, Asong who is already a household word in Anglophone Cameroon will inevitably push the limit of his fame beyond the national frontiers to impose himself on the international literary scene, making it impossible for readers and critics to ignore him.

One of the solid personal achievements on which his reputation will henceforth rest is the novel entitled *The Akroma File*, a rare fictional exploration of criminology with frightening implications and a high social significance value. Faced with debts at home and threatened by poverty, a brilliant and well-educated Ghanaian, Akroma, using unorthodox means, successfully gets into Cameroon where he is bent on making a fortune.

Akroma arrives in Cameroon virtually penniless but draws on his tremendous presence of mind to build up a great fortune, enough to wipe away all his debts back home in Ghana and still leave him a millionaire. This he does essentially by swindling a desperate land owner, Pa Sabbas, and by milking a wealthy but illiterate school proprietor, Anguissa-Anguissa Bertin.

How this illegal alien eludes the police or bribes his way through them is a mark of L.T. Asong's genius in character conception and a telling comment on the Cameroonian legal and security system, one that, for the most part, thrives on venality. Having landed in Cameroon it does not take long for Akroma to discover that in Cameroon money can buy just about anything. Accordingly, he sets his criminal mind at work and, within a short time, uses money to procure for himself two Cameroonian I.D. cards.

One bears Njonjo Fabian Mula, born in Tiko in the South West Region, and the other Bidias Polycarp Abessolo, besides his genuine Ghanaian passport. In addition, depending on the situation, Akroma assumes other aliases. Thus to his Cameroonian girlfriend he is Kojo Thompson Abreba, an oil merchant from Liberia; to Pa Sabbas, a land owner and a once prosperous businessman now in financial straits, he is Kojo Hanson, a Liberian investor traveling incognito to avoid taxes.

Therefore, with money Akroma buys for himself two Cameroonian I.D. cards, bribes his way through police checkpoints, and wins over a doctor to issue a false medical report when he murders a man in a hotel. With money Akroma transforms Cours du Soir Anguissa-Anguissa into a complete Grammar School (Lycée), shuts the mouth of the Director of Private Education about to expose his hanky-panky deals in Anguissa-Anguissa's school, buys over completely the immoral, criminal and unconscionable Divisional Boss of National Security, and gets himself into the good books of people who matter within his immediate environment.

Important as money is, Akroma knows only too well that people are even more so. Hence he makes friends with Cameroonians. He gets for himself partners and accomplices, characters without whose help he cannot make it in the Cameroonian society, characters who help him realize his financial dream. And for this he cultivates kindness and generosity for the service of wickedness. For he finally eliminates all these characters in the supreme interest of his personal security and financial empire.

Thus, without any qualms of the conscience he sets a hotel on fire which engulfs his girl friend Severina; he kills in cold blood his own host, Rev. Dieudonne Akwa in a hotel; he strangles to death his old time friend, Jean-Paul Mombangui (J-P); and he shoots point blank his closest accomplice and protector, Commissaire Essomba.

But corrupt as the Cameroonian Police force is, it is graced by an exceptional police officer, Kum Dangobert, out to track down the fugitive Ghanaian. The final squaring off between the Ghanaian evil genius and the best Cameroonian police superintendent is like the clash of giants that ends in a cataclysm.

In this novel Asong employs a narrative technique he has not used before: that of the journal or diary, the daily record of events, accounts and thoughts, etc. But the journal is that of the omniscient narrator rather than one kept by a character in the novel such as Toundi's, for example, in Ferdinand Oyono's *Houseboy*. Days, years and in some instances, historically verifiable events and personages, are recorded. Thus there is an occasional reference to the April 6th coup and its aftermath in Cameroon in 1984, the coming to power of President Jerry Rawlings of Ghana and his revolutionary economic policies, the emergence of Idi Amin of Uganda and his anti-Israel and anti-Christian policies, and the Jones Town massacre of 1979, etc.

To the uninitiated the narrative approach may pose a technical problem. The reader may feel that he is reading a mere historical chronicle and not a novel, that he is dealing with verifiable historical facts and dignitaries rather than a fictional account of substantial length concerned with imagined real people, in which case doubts about the effectiveness of technique will have been raised.

However, on closer examination, this will be discovered not to be so. Asong's psychological exploration of Akroma's character, detailed physical descriptions, dramatic evocation of events, arousing confrontation between characters; Asong's felicitous style and the compelling readability of the book – all of these features and more – lift *THE AKROMA FILE* to the realm of the novel par excellence.

Asong has used verifiable historical setting only as a pad for launching his fictional work, thereby placing it, within a social and historical context. Some personages and events with historical authentication are incidental to the bulk of his work whose main characters are imagined real people. As a character, Idi Amin is very minor in the novel, and so is Jerry Rawlings; as an event the Jones Town massacre is incidental in the novel, and so is the April attempted coup in Cameroon.

The real people who matter are Akroma, Jean-Paul Mombangui (J-P), Rev. Dieudonne Akwa, Inspector Kum Dangobert, Pa Sabbas, and Commissaire Essomba. They are essential to the novel because they are linked to Akroma's fate, his determination to outsmart the police and make his fortune in Cameroon. The only events that count are those set in motion by the psychologies and actions of two groups of characters: the intelligent Ghanaian crook and his Cameroonian accomplices versus the admirable Cameroonian police inspector, Kum Dangobert, alias Scotland Yard. All of these are imagined real people, fictional characters true-to-life and not true-to-history. For there is a difference between both. Imagined real people are fictional characters who, from the way they talk, behave, act and react, we can say, yes, under similar circumstances in real life this is how people could behave. And this satisfies the criterion of artistic truthfulness. There is another criterion that Asong's novel also satisfies and that is the criterion of social significance.

Several themes emerge from the novel, some of which include the willing contemplation and execution of evil, wickedness motivated by personal safety and greed, the ruthless exploration of a system that thrives on venality as the nadir of a social system, and the use of human beings as disposable tools in the service of personal ambition etc. All of these themes embody negative value statements with regard to the Cameroonian social system, pointing, therefore, to the social significance of *The Akroma File*.

Literature is not produced in a vacuum; it has a social base. That is, it is socially conditioned, a product of the social and historical experience of the people producing it. A realistic novel cannot be about nothing; it must be about something, about human beings doing certain things in certain ways. In other words it must be concerned with an aspect of human life, a dimension of the human condition. Therefore an examination of a realistic novel like *The Akroma File* must take into account its wider social context if we must arrive at its social relevance.

Some frightening implications would seem to emerge from Asong's novel. Akroma's criminal story shows that human lives and relationships count for little or nothing when personal ambition and safety are concerned, and that, ultimately, there is nothing like mutual trust and genuine love because all that matters is personal interest, a depressing extrapolation indeed. If such is the case, one may well wonder what type of world we are living in or of what use our love and friendly relationships. The world of the Akromas is one inhabited by dehumanized monsters.

By exposing to the reader's scorn the Cameroonian police system and mercilessly revealing the wicked, criminal methods of Ghanaians or foreigners in Cameroon, L.T. Asong helps to open the eyes of the general public to the type of havoc that can be wrought upon a people and a system no longer morally accountable. Asong helps to expose the limitless possibilities of evil orchestrated by foreigners who do not care a damn about their host country.

Any Cameroonian who reads Asong's novel will no longer look upon a Ghanaian or any alien, for that matter, as an innocent foreigner. For, in the words of Dangobert's uncle, "beware of a Ghanaian even if he is dead." Herein lies the social relevance of *The Akroma File*, a very filmable novel that deserves to be read by every Cameroonian, particularly the police force, for its eye-opening value, and implications.

Yet the conclusive force of the above moral message is tainted by what I consider a structural weakness in Asong's novel: Akroma's survival. It certainly jars on one's sense of poetic justice that this Ghanaian, who has so successfully exploited the Cameroonian system and killed half a dozen Cameroonians, including the only jewel within the Cameroonian police force, Kum Dangobert, should be left alive at the end of the novel. Is this not a glorification of criminality?

Shadrach Ambanasom

18
ALOBWED'EPIE, *THE DEATH CERTIFICATE*,
Yaounde: Editions CLE, 2004, 308pp

Alobwed'Epie's *The Death Certificate* (2004), is a national allegory of great resonance which, like Bole Butake's dramatic parable, *And Palm Wine Will Flow* (1999), is set in a fictional African country called Ewawa. The text's anti-hero is Mongo Meka who, dead or alive, remains the subject of interest for most of the narrative, and this because of his pivotal, if unpatriotic, function in the novel.

A native of the First Province and doubling as Treasurer General and Acting Director General of the Central Bank, Mongo Meka is the keeper of the keys to these financial institutions. He therefore enjoys unlimited access to cash at any time. Being an unconscionable individual, however, he embezzles the whopping sum of 550 billion francs, most of which he stashes away in a Parisian bank under the name of his French wife, and then fakes death in a road accident in a neigbouring country, in a bid to forestall a possible prosecution for denuding the national treasury.

His death is mourned, and he is duly buried, with a certificate of death established in his name. Taking Meka's death in earnest, his widow, Yvonne Antoinette, remarries, this time, a Frenchman, Roger Girard, a development that threatens Meka's machinations, forcing him to come back from the land of the dead to embarrass the living, with his ghostly reappearance. He initiates costly lawsuits against the French couple with the intention of putting them asunder. However, Meka is hoisted with his own petard, as his stratagem becomes a boomerang. His death certificate being genuine, Meka is legally considered dead, and the man now going by that name, an impostor! To compound Meka's discomfiture, his alienated wife dies in a storm at sea in Australia, leaving her French husband the inheritor of Meka's 350 billion francs in her account, legally putting the money far beyond Meka's reach, a dramatic turn of events that impels the now impoverished and fugitive Meka to commit suicide in France.

This plot synopsis emerges less from a monologic narrative than one of multiple perspective. For, from the point of view of focalization, the author has deployed an ingenious narrative technique wherein the story is told by a crew of narrators with their own techniques; that is, different perspectives are adopted to comment on the same or related event, a kind of polyphonic narrative in which no narrator alone owns the complete truth, although the sum total of their various accounts constitutes the whole truth: knowledge about Mongo Meka, his kins-men and the state of the national economy of Ewawa. Though to some extent isolated by the very uniqueness of their narrative vantage positions, the various narrators, each assuming a chapter or more of the text, are united in this, that they are drawn into the vortex of a common maelstrom called Mongo Meka and his misadventures.

The central theme, the judgmental statement, emerging from the text must be situated at the level of the behaviour of Meka and his consorts of the First Province in relation to financial management. For, if you cut any highly placed citizen of Ewawa who is in a position to manage finances, he will bleed embezzlement.

To have a rough idea of the administrative set-up of Ewawa, it is instructive to mathematically conceptualize it in terms of ten concentric circles, each representing a province, thus making a total of ten concentric provinces. The province in the centre, the seat of political power and economic influence, is known as The First Province. The closer one is to the centre of power and influence, the more satisfied, or less censorious, one is with regard to the system; and the reverse is true, discontent emanating from the periphery. Criticism is thus proportional to the distance from the centre, and the prerogative of the marginalized. No wonder, then, that the greatest critics of the government come from the marginal 9th and 10th Provinces. However, distance here is a kind of cultural-ideological entity, measurable not necessarily in spatial but in ideological terms.

There is the hegemony of citizens of the First Province in all spheres of influence. They head key ministries, major lucrative companies and organizations, key financial institutions, the army, gendarmerie, and the police, etc. Their identifying terms are 'sons and daughters of the soil,' or 'brothers and sisters of the First Province. With ethnicity thus exalted, nepotism, favourtism and tribalism are accentuated in the novel, as tribal Manichaeism is everywhere manifest. Perceiving themselves as the Superior Self, fellows of the First Province orientalize those of the peripheral provinces as the Inferior Other. Wildly extravagant, these sons and daughters of the soil squander money with impunity.

The other Anglophone texts that *The Death Certificate* appears to interrogate most are Bole Butake's *And Palm Wine Will Flow* (1999), Bate Besong's *Beasts of No Nation* ([1990] 2003), and Tah Asongwed's *Born To Rule* (1993). Their intertextual echoes are affirmatory of the recklessness and indiscipline with which some African political elite handle monetary matters. Propelled by runaway greed, the latter become unconscionable looters of public funds and initiators of capital flight, helping thus to place their own nations in a state of perpetual pauperism, with begging bowls ever stretched out to international donors.

Beside moral decadence, there is also the important theme of the power of investigative journalism in providing credible information, exemplified by the laudable job carried out by the linchpin and the most conscientised of the narrators, Mula. He plays a crucial, albeit indirect, formative role in the development of the critical consciousness of some of the other narrators, notably Nchinda, Musa and Ndjock. Without the exercise of their critical intelligence and the deployment of the skills of investigative reporting, particularly those of Mula, much of the narrative, as we have it, would not be as constructed; the facts, the comments, the truth, as they appear in the text, would not be so presented, either.

Towards the end of the novel the following idea is floated: the imminent purification of FramMki, Marie-Claire's bastard son, who has eaten the coagulated blood of Jacqueline Diwona, an abomination in itself. According to Marie-Claire's father, the cleansing ceremony will be a public act, involving 'an assembly of elders of our two communities' (303). Given the allegorical quality of the novel, the 'cleansing' or 'purification' is a metaphor for a possible forum of national consultation, an appropriate arena, some would say, that will allow the nation, after a moment of soul-searching, to arrive at a resolution which will help clean up the current mess created by financial mismanagement that has placed Ewawa precariously on the cliff of fiscal perdition.

However, any such gathering will not come easily, in view of the strong antipathy of some of those who matter. For, according to the Minister of Territorial Administration (M.T.A.), for instance, 'Only over our dead bodies can natives in the form of traditional doctors put us on trial. They can go to hell. Zero cleansing' (304). Though aversion like this poses an obstacle to an imaginative solution proffered by the novelist, it should not necessarily cancel the possibility of such an idea ever taking root within the text's larger social context.

Written generally in a critical tone, with a somber opening chapter and a gloomy concluding one, and punctuated with functional poetic patches that reinforce some of its themes, motifs and issues, *The Death Certificate,* eventhough it contains some editorial lapses, is an impressive first novel of high social relevance, and a major contribution to the growth of the Anglophone Cameroon novel.

Shadrach Ambanasom

19
JOHN N. NKENGASONG *ACROSS THE MONGOLO*, Ibadan: Spectrum Books Limited, 2004, 200pp

Coming on the heels of Alobwed'Epie's *The Death Certificate* (November, 2004), John N. Nkengasong's *Across The Mongolo* (December, 2004) is a welcome addition to our burgeoning imaginative writing, and, against a rich background of anterior Anglophone publications, proof of the vibrancy of Cameroon literature of English expression. Considering its subject matter and the manner in which it is constructed, *Across The Mongolo* (across the Mungo) is a novel which, in the Cameroonian context, is almost guaranteed, I dare say, to inspire critical commentary for some time to come.

After a sound secondary school education in the Anglophone state of Kama, the novel's central character, Ngwe Nkemasaah, proceeds to the Francophone state of Ngola in the bilingual, Federal Republic of Kamangola to acquire university education in Besaadi, the only university in Kamangola. But it is in Besaadi, within the hegemonic influence of the French language, that Ngwe meets his academic Waterloo.

Unlike in the Anglophone citadel of academic excellence of College of Arts where discipline, orderliness, hard work, and merit are the cardinal values for success, fraud, personal interest, gamble, injustice and disorder are the Besaadi order of the day. Despite the official bilingual status of the country with, English and French as official languages, Ngwe is compelled to write his examinations only in French, a language he does not master well. In the novel, Francophones ideologically "textualize" the Anglophone as the inferior Other. Their orientalising attitude consists in perceiving him as a kind of comic freak whose behaviour gives rise to debasing appellations like "Anglofou", "Anglobête", "esclave", "salaud", etc.

Ngwe goes through a great deal of humiliation, degradation and debilitating frustration which inflict on him traumatic stress disorders that, several times, bring him close to a nervous breakdown before he is finally done in. But he draws on his great presence of mind and is determined to make it in Besaadi. However, for all his tenacity on to his ethic of hard work and honesty, after six years in the university, and even changing faculties, his academic endeavours end in failure, leaving him with zero degree.

Gradually it dawns on him that his humiliation is not an isolated fact but one shared by other Anglophones; that the Francophone government in place has a hidden agenda to annihilate the Anglo-Saxon culture in the United Republic of Kamangola, with the university as the experimental nursery ground; and that the Anglophones co-opted into the government are there to destroy the Anglo-Saxon culture. It also becomes clear to Ngwe that the older generation of Anglophones have failed and that unless the young people do something to rescue the situation soon, the Anglo-Saxon swan-song may well soon be sung. Consequently, he forms the Young Anglophone Movement (YAM) to help keep alive the Anglo-Saxon heritage, to fight for the Anglophone rights to full citizenship and not just to be "some assistant somebody" (138). In short, YAM's goal is to uphold the Anglophone identity.

Though eventually hounded to madness by his woes and tribulations, his is a treatable mental disorder. It is thanks to his gradual recovery from his insanity that Ngwe now recollects and reconstructs his narrative from a cave in the forest of his rural Lebialem.

Across The Mongolo thematizes the struggle for the survival of the Anglophone identity within the Francophone dominance. It is significant that, at the end of the novel, Ngwe, though irremediably frustrated , is nevertheless alive. His survival emblematizes the existence of YAM, and thus symbolizes Anglophone hope.

The social relevance of the novel is high, indeed. It is the only Cameroonian novel of English expression, to date, to be a significant site for the dramatization of two antagonistic ideological hegemonies: the assimilationist authoritarianism epitomized by the formidable Babajoro (Ahidjo) pitted against the federalist cohabitation espoused by Ngwe's YAM. *Across The Mongolo's* uniqueness equally resides in the fact that it attempts to transcend merely deconstructing Anglophone victimhood to reconstructing some of the positive values that constitute the "Anglophoneness" that Anglophones are yearning to perpetuate.

Nkengasong's condition of coloniality is an interesting phenomenon evident in his text. He is a post-colonial subject whose text is written in an imperial language, English. But the intimate and immediate circumstances of his life that make up his subject matter are Cameroonian (African). He is a child of two worlds, the one by virtue of his British colonial educational upbringing, the other by his close attachment to his Nweh tradition. His characters speak in English but an English refashioned, in many cases, to reflect the speech patterns, thought, idioms, and rhythms of Nweh native speakers, a reality bespeaking Nkengasong's hybridity. Therefore, to go by the flavour of the language of its characters, any informed student of English literature reading *Across The Mongolo*, will instantly recognize it for what it is: a post-colonial text belonging not to English literature but to literatures in English.

Technically speaking, and despite a few editorial defects, the author handles plot, structure, characterization, language and the narrative perspective well. He shows ingenuity in conceiving the narrative point of view, focalized essentially from the text's central consciousness, with only occasional interpolations from the omniscient narrator. Even when, in characterization, Ngwe is made to utter what some may term barbarism committed on the French language "Je suit dit que" (61) etc, this, in the circumstances, is functional, realistic and in character. It defines the speaker as one who is not only bad at French but a character who has come to "loathe French" (66). This subverts the Francophone colonial "text" that set out to rewrite itself in the Anglophone Inferior Other, for there is a big gulf between the "pure text" and "performance".

Within the Cameroonian context *Across The Mongolo* is a serious indictment of Francophone hegemony, and a scathing attack on Anglophones who deny the existence of the Anglophone Problem. Ultimately, the text amounts to an unsettling interrogation of history, a people, in short, the Cameroonian society as a whole. A gripping human story beautifully conceived and constructed, it is a lyrical, soulful cry from a sensitive mind, and a significant contribution to the development of the Cameroon novel in English.

20
ALOBWED'EPIE *THE LADY WITH A BEARD*,
Yaoundé: Editions CLE, 2005, 118 pp

Barely under a year when he breezed his way onto the Anglophone Cameroon literary scene with his celebrated novel, *The Death Certificate* (November 2004), here struts Alobwed'Epie once more, and in no less a flourish, with another imaginative work bearing an even more catchy title, *The Lady with a Beard*, a novel that further enriches our literary landscape. The text portrays another side of the author, underscoring how it is sometimes risky to pass a definitive judgement on an artist based on a single imaginative work. If, ideologically speaking, Alobwed'Epie's previous novel projects visionary radicalism, the present one evinces liberal humanism, both of which tendencies, in my humble opinion, should be accommodated within our imaginative writing that cannot be confined to a monolithic matrix of values.

Set in the mid 1950s within the Bakossi cultural heartland in the South West Province, *The Lady with a Beard* is the intriguing story of Emade, the initially extraordinary and charismatic female character from whose name the novel derives its title. A widow for long at loggerheads with the men of her village because she has refused to 'become an elephant killed at the cross-roads' (116), Emade is, as a result, derogatorily nicknamed, 'The Lady with a Beard', an epithet that incidentally fits her temperament and which she accepts with equanimity.

At the centre of Alobwed'Epie's narrative, Emade is endowed with full subjectivity as well as an arrogant and contemptuous discourse, particularly towards the men and Inferior Others. Hers is a counter discourse confronting the hegemony of patriarchy. She defies the men and women of Atieg and Muabag. In many ways she comports herself like a 'malewoman' as she accomplishes several manly tasks even better than the men themselves. Through various rituals related to marriage, birth and death, involving song, recitation, invocation, narration and, above all drum communication, Emade proves herself an adept of her culture. However, her expert oral performances and other feats, which invariably put her on a collision course with the men whose prerogatives she arrogates to herself, are controversial, giving rise to rather mixed reactions: admiration as well as criticism.

The Lady with a beard holds men in great contempt and debunks time-honoured ideas of male chauvinism. She subverts the prevailing gender hierarchy, standing it more or less on its head; she thus reverses the familiar gender allegory of man/woman, into woman/man, thus "holding the world by the neck" (117). In her feminist challenge of patriarchal authority, Emade stands virtually alone in the whole of Mbuogmut Clan; even her dearest sister, Ahone, is opposed to Emade's extremist feminism that threatens to undo her.

Paradoxically, Emade's intimate attachment to her culture, in a way, becomes her bane; for it is her strong belief in superstition, as she seeks the help of diviner priests and 'protection' for herself and her lone daughter, Ntube, that proves, in the end, that Emade is only an ordinary woman, after all. Confronted with traditional situations that seriously threaten her life and that of her beloved child, Emade behaves in a way that shows she is, after everything, only a timorous and fearful mother, seeking protection like any other human being; she thus acts in a manner that betrays her as 'a cockroach with a mane seeking refuge elsewhere' (104).

Therefore, in Emade Alobwed'Epie first builds up an admirable female character and then cuts her down to size; he constructs a heroine who deconstructs patriarchy only to be deflated herself at the end of the novel. His text purportedly sets out to foreground the woman. It initially valorizes her but then discredits her at the end; it places her on the pedestal but then pulls the rug from under her feet, indicating the failure of a woman who once posed as a 'malewoman'. Towards the end of the novel, Emade discovers to her chagrin that even in the domain of divination certain powers and abilities are available only to priests and not to priestesses. Very much against her wish and when she cannot undo what has been done, it dawns on Emade that her puzzle has been solved by a mere male, palm-wine tapper as "she moved away in humiliation" (117). Ultimately, then, the author thematizes the limitation of the woman, despite her occasional knack for rising to certain occasions.

In this regard, it would be hard to completely refute the essentially feminist charge that the novel indicates its author's intention to spite the woman and advocates of gender politics who support the rights of the woman. In other words, *The Lady with a*

Beard amounts to an imaginative critique of one kind of feminism. One can then affirm, in the light of this insight, that the text's title has a cynical ring to it.

The whole novel is constructed around a few key incidents, particularly those related to Ntube's misfortunes and Mechane's illness, death and the celebration of death that follows thereafter. As these and other incidents are fully developed, Emade's fame steadily rises, reaching the climax at the end of the 'closing door' ceremony marking the demise of Mechane. But when she returns to Atieg, Emade's reputation begins to decline until, by the end of the text, she is reduced, in relative terms, to almost a despicable woman.

In depicting his Mbuogmut characters in situations, in action and living reaction to the pressure of events, Alobwed'Epie takes a satirical look at the antics of the group, mercilessly exposing eternal human foibles like meanness, selfishness, fawning and hypocrisy. In doing so, however, he has immortalized the culture of his people; for the projection of the rich oral tradition of the Bakossi people must be recognized as one of the major themes emerging from the novel.

The narrative texture of the text reveals a creative imagination that draws on a rich African (Cameroonian) oral tradition (proverbs, praise-names, song, invocation, recitation, ululation, narration, and, above all, drum communication). There is a judicious deployment of sociological material to serve as realistic background to the story, particularly to define character. The use of proverbs in this text will make even Chinua Achebe turn green with envy. The novel is a veritable treasure house of Bakossi proverbs. It contains at least 70 proverbs, the most rhetorically and thematically significant of which is 'A woman's urine does not cross a beam' (336, 66, 100, 104 etc).

There is, some would say, a surfeit of proverbs, and this incidentally constitutes the text's structural weakness. Sometimes the proverbs come in rapid succession, leaving the uninitiated little or no time for the digestion of each before the next. The overall effect is the slowing down of one's reading speed or, alternatively, reading without adequate comprehension. This, however, is a neglible flaw compared to the author's artistic strengths revealed in his competent handling of plot, characterization, language, point of view and overall structure.

Compared with *The Death Certificate, The Lady With A Beard*, is on the face of it, a slight and perhaps retrogressive work, in view of the impressive and progressive dimension of the previous novel. Put differently, *The Lady with a Beard*, with a bias for cultural documentation, is a different kind of book from the earlier substantial novel; in its own category it is an interesting text and one that explores issues of social relevance. One need not judge it solely on the criterion of radical commitment with reference to contemporary socio-political issues, by which I mean the "politician's politics". In a way, the new text is not devoid of politics, although its own kind of politics is gender politics. Flowing from the pen of the same author, however, both novels point to the realistic direction of the growth of the Anglophone Cameroon literature: towards a comprehensive social vision and not a limited perspective issuing from a homogeneous mould.

All in all, constructed in captivating proverbial language, *The Lady with a Beard*, dramatizes an ideological conflict. It is a loving and lasting tribute to the Bakossi cultural heritage and a welcome addition to the rapidly growing Anglophone Cameroon novel.

21
JOHN N. NKENGASONG, *THE WIDOW'S MIGHT*,
Yaounde, Editions CLE 2006, 152pp

With L.T. Asong, Margret Afuh and Alobwed'Epie about to make a forceful comeback onto the Anglophone Cameroon literary scene, each with a new novel, here enters John N. Nkengasong with *The Widow's Might*, his second novel in less than two years. One can imagine, with such a flurry of fictional creativity, that lovers of the Anglophone Cameroon novel should be having a field day. Indeed, from the look of things, the future of this genre in Anglophone Cameroon has never been brighter.

A post-colonial text that juxtaposes the conflicting discourses of modernity versus tradition, *The Widow's Might* opens with the death of the pivotal character and politician, a man with a resonant Zairois-kind of name: Hon Makata Mbutuku, husband of Akwenoh, the central consciousness of the narrative. Set in Bakomba Town and Ekaka Village within the contemporary Cameroon, most of the story takes place within the time Hon Mbutuku dies and when he is finally laid to rest. Initially told by the third person omniscient narrator, the bulk of the story is focalized, through the elaborate use of the flashback, from the consciousness of Akwenoh, the text's female subject. As she agonizingly waits for badly needed, but eventually non-existent, funds to give her spouse a befitting burial, Akwenoh goes through the traumatizing rites of widowhood.

It is during this time that the author, through his adopted narrative technique, takes us to the shadowy past of Hon Mbutuku, and the wanton behaviour of Akwenoh. Indeed, the novelist does even more; he critically but artistically passes in review the hard realities of the Cameroonian socio-political and religious scene, encompassing the overwhelming pressure of indigenous values on the Western-educated, modern Cameroonian.

The reader thus comes to discover that Hon Makata Mbutuku and the Popular Democratic Party in which he militated are neo-patrimonialists opposed to the imperial principles advocated by the opposition party the 'Socialist Democratic Party... forcefully launched in Bamankon... in the early nineties' (46). The narrative of multiparty democracy projected by the opposition is therefore read negatively by the ruling party. Mbutuku and his PDP emblematize political malpractice: election rigging, the stuffing of ballot boxes, the destruction of truth and even the elimination of political rivals like the unfortunate Barrister Same Same. Given the skeletons in his cupboard, Mbutuku's sudden and untimely death is a classic situation of nemesis catching up with him, and a lesson to those in powerful political positions who think they can perpetually play the God over the dregs of humanity.

Essentially a nymphomaniac, Akwenoh cannot be sexually satisfied by a single man like Mbutuku, so she seeks sexual gratification outside wedlock. Like Chaucer's Wife of Bath Akwenoh has a number of paramours, and the one she is most sexually obsessed with is a certain Ebbi. It is in this promiscuous context that she comes into contact with a post-imperial Catholic priest with the very suggestive name of Father Vaginus, who has made cuckolds of several husbands in his parish.

Father Vaginus is a post-colonial character and a neo-patrimonialist who has contaminated the imperial 'text'. From Nkengasong's text, therefore, Catholic theology as an imperial narrative is nowhere practised as pure 'text', but only an approximation.

Enter Ma Eseke and Chief Ekwe, respectively elder sister and brother of the deceased, and representatives of the conservative, indigenous values. They want to bury their late brother in a befitting traditional manner in their ancestral grove right in Ekaka Village. But the modern woman of the city, Akwenoh, will not yield, hence the drama over the corpse, the tussle between tradition and modernity. However, it seems to me that in this strife, through a series of coincidences all linked to Hon Mbutuku's murky past, the argument is weighted against Akwenoh. If tradition triumphs over modernity, if Akwenoh succumbs to the conservative forces at the end, it is not necessarily out of the force of their argument but rather because of the argument of destiny.

First, following the death of the powerful politician, the widow is shocked to find only a paltry FCFA 20.000 in his briefcase; secondly, the much-needed Parliamentary Group Support that would have covered all funeral expenses is not forth coming; worst of all the widow's already dire situation is further problematised by the fact that the deceased had defaulted on his loan with the National Bank of Credit and Commerce, in consequence of which the latter has impounded his compound as collateral, sending the proud widow packing, not only penniless but also homeless, with a bunch of brats to provide for. Thus crushed by fate, as it were, and eager to escape from the gloating smiles of her enemies and the mortification of the world, Akwenoh has no choice but to co-operate with the annoying relatives of her late husband.

Although it can be justified, the title of the text is a pun on the biblical 'the widow's mite'. Akwenoh, the widow, does empty her purse to enable the casket bearing the remains of her husband to be transported across an impassable patch of the road to Ekaka Village. 'Akwenoh took out the rest of the money she had in her life and gave' the driver (147).

Slightly slim and slight in comparison with *Across the Mongolo* (2004), *The Widow's Might* is, nevertheless, a work of high literary and social significance. If it lacks the lyricism and adumbrations of romanticism of the earlier novel, it gains in the concentrated, distilled nature of its narrative texture. However, in its psychological exploration of character and high readability, it is equal to the previous work. Above all, the socio-cultural and political themes including issues of moral decadence that it highlights will resonate well with many Cameroonians today.

22
JOHN NGONG KUM NGONG, *WALLS OF AGONY*,
Yaounde, Editions CLE 2006, 60pp

A Cameroonian educationist, John Ngong Kum Ngong, has graced our literary landscape with two new imaginative works. They are *Battle for Survival* (June 2006) a play, and *Walls of Agony* (June 2006) a collection of 40 poems. For now, I am concerned with the latter, putting on hold the former. *Walls of Agony* has as its general subject matter the post-colonial Cameroonian society which the poet criticizes and educates.

Cameroon emerges from the poems as a society composed of people of various cultural and ethnic backgrounds. But instead of this cultural multivalence becoming a source of strength and a potential for positive change, it translates into a narrative of national anomie, an occasion for the construction of walls of incomprehension and misery. The poet's anger is directed against all those who erect these polyvalent tribal walls of division and misunderstanding between the Superior *Self* and the Inferior *Other*. His ire is aimed at those who fan the flames of tribal Manichaeism ('The Battle continues', 'Powerless').

The Cameroon that the poems examine is a country blessed with many natural resources which are unfortunately mismanaged by a few privileged citizens to the detriment and misery of many. The poet pictures the country as having been ruined and destroyed by the profligate few but one that needs to be rebuilt by real patriots. It is in the dimension of reconstruction that the poet situates his role and that of genuine nationalists. On the whole the poet is pre-occupied with familiar themes like exploitation, deprivation, marginalisation, cruelty, insatiable greed, corruption, indecency, injustice and exclusion etc.

It is axiomatic that the essence of poetry is imagery, the use of figurative language. Ngong Kum's collection is highly figurative, particularly with regard to the use of metaphor. The human leeches, the parasites and destroyers of the country are metaphorically read as 'caterpillars on our grazing land' (43); 'greedy dogs' (24); 'grey-haired sharks' (24); 'human locusts' (41); 'fleas and rats' (32); 'worms' (54); 'maniacs' (24); 'cursed castrated curs' (29), etc. This use of emotive language shows the poet's anger and critical attitude towards his subject matter.

However, the author does not only deconstruct; he reveals his desire to reconstruct, to rebuild what has been destroyed. While he is critical, the poet eschews runaway radicalism or outright recourse to violence as a means of reconstructing a new Cameroonian society. He believes the law can be invoked for the redress of some of the social ills, ('Ridiculous Walls').

In places the poet's critical but patriotic tone of voice becomes combative. He sounds like a man of action, a fighter. But his weapon is neither the spear nor the gun, but rather the barrel of the 'pen' which he intends to use to 'fire' our 'brains' so that 'those who career with justice / Will for sure join the rescue team / That will give our country a new face' ('Ridiculous Walls').

He entreats his ancestral supreme deity, Kezeh, to give him artistic wisdom to reform his Cameroonian society, 'A brush and paint for reconstruction' with which 'to challenge corruption to combat and batter the heart of exploitation' ('Better than Flight'). He appeals to Kezeh to 'Mould me into a fine poet / That my songs may my people revive' ('Let me in').

It is logical that a man as committed as the poet is will not look kindly on those who refuse to speak out against societal ills. Indeed he criticises those who remain silent in the face of social injustice and misdemeanour; that is, 'those who still do not see / The folly of not speaking out' (53). He believes that he and his generation will be held accountable to history, to posterity ('Touch Down' and 'The Combatant'):

> Your children will be ashamed
> When the story will be told
> Of how you shamelessly backed down
> From the position you took
> To combat cutthroat exclusion
> ('The combatant')

The poet thus encourages those who matter to join him in condemning the moral wrongs of society in the hope of eventually reforming it. He urges citizens to play an active, positive role in constructing 'walls' of understanding while demolishing those of incomprehension.

The poet wishes he were thunder and lightning so that he could raze to the ground all symbols of retrogression and underdevelopment; he wishes he had the magic balm with which to sanitize his morally sick society; he wishes he could reinvent the Cameroonian society 'to trace a new path for us' ('Take Heart').

Written in free verse and accessible language, *Walls of Agony* is very readable. In it the poet effectively exploits sonal services, especially the use of alliteration. His poetic style is economical, his poetic line very tightly controlled, with no unnecessary words and expressions. The poet's sentiments are mature and sincere, and his moral intentions for his country, honourable. But the collection betrays a few editorial flaws.

The social relevance of this collection resides in the fact that it is a soulful, patriotic appeal for the rebuilding of a beloved and richly endowed country ruined by all kinds of petty-minded people who privilege mean projects and pursuits as well as divisive, egotistic tendencies above concern for the commonweal and love for the fatherland.

23
JOHN NGONG KUM NGONG, *BATTLE FOR SURVIVAL*, Yaoundé: Editions CLE 2006, 87pp

About a fortnight ago, in this column, we mentioned in passing *Battle for Survival,* with the intention of coming back to it. With an insightful foreword by Bole Butake, John Ngong Kum Ngong's play is set in an imaginary African country called Inayeh. It deals with the subject of satanic, blood-sucking practices as a means of achieving political and material prosperity. The play foregrounds the Scarlet Star Booster Club, a demonic cult which has as its exclusive members, the military, political and bureaucratic elite.

Once you access this club, you can consider all worldly sufferings over: promotion, wealth, power and material possessions come easily. Once in it, you may well say, 'suffer done finish' as the world knows it. It therefore takes a great deal of courage and moral rectitude on the part of an individual not to belong to such an attractive society, especially when he is an intellectual elite with two doctorate degrees bossed over by a mere chief clerk of thirty years' standing, and bossed around by an intellectual featherweight. It takes great guts and moral uprightness for a man to resist these material temptations, especially when he has a nagging wife with a materialistic, 'grong-cargo' mentality.

Is there such a man in a difficult, materialistic society where everybody is struggling to survive by all means? Yes, there is, and he has got the gumption. His name is Wujwab, the central character around whom the drama is constructed, the conscience and the last upright man in Inayeh.

He refuses to become a member of the demonic fraternity and be transformed into a political superstar on the back of innocent blood. He asks his wife:

'You want me to deny myself
And sacrifice innocent souls
For a place among monsters? No' (44).

The play makes it clear that the ruling class is ill at ease with such a man of unsullied integrity; his moral purity remains a threat to their diabolic practices in honour of mammon. He must be co-opted into their club so that their almighty 'messiah' may rule supreme with guaranteed longevity. In vain they attempt to break his will; they imprison, torture and starve him. The carrot and the stick approach is ineffectual to win Wujwab over.

Having failed to convert the man, General Nyamitauyi orders Captain Wokikoh to ensure the physical elimination of Wujwab:

> 'Clear this dirt from my office...
> I don't want to see the brat again
> Or hear his name mentioned anywhere' (74).

However, Wujwab gets off the hook thanks to the venality of Wokikoh the crook. He saves his neck from the captain and escapes to a foreign country, only after giving away all his life-savings and uncompleted house.

Hopefully, from the foreign nation, Wujwab and his now persuaded wife will launch a moral war 'To continue the combat from outside

> Until the sharks in this bleeding nation
> Are set in the stocks' (87).

So, despite its pessimistic atmosphere, the play ends on an upbeat note. This optimism hinges on the action of one upright man on whom will depend the salvation of Inayeh. Therefore, Inayeh is still waiting for its moral saviour. But who will that be? That is the question the play's construction elicits from the reader, and one on which we should all reflect in materialistic, satanic times like ours.

Written in verse which lends concreteness and seriousness to its subject matter, *Battle for Survival* is situated within conventional, realistic drama. It is structured in six scenes and essentially a drama of conscience wherein Wujwab is pestered by his former friend, Wazwoh who has since joined the ranks of the members of the Scarlet Star Booster Club. But at other times Wazwoh is simply Wujwab's alter ego, his own conscience tormenting him. Wujwab's struggles with Wazwoh, on the one hand, and Njwahkwam his wife, on the other, occasionally give rise to some interesting dramatic ironies. The venal Captain Wokikoh with his humorous brand of broken English provides a kind of comic relief in this grave drama.

However, I think the hero's buying of his life from the venal soldier is a structural weakness. This betrays the hero's life-at-all-cost stance. The author could have found a more dignifying way out for Wujwab.

Some major leitmotifs of *Walls of Agony* resurface in *Battle for Survival*. The moral intention of both works and their smooth, readable and refined language testify to the fact that they are imaginative treasures from the same pen. Indeed, a man of the moral fibre and calibre of Wujwab in *Battle for Survival* could only have been the construction of the poet deeply burdened by the moral sickness of his country in *Walls of Agony*. With these impressive artistic works Ngong Kum has imposed himself on the literary and intellectual community, making it impossible for critics to ignore him. The works deserve a place in public and private libraries, while their author must be numbered among Anglophone Cameroonian finest creative writers.

24
INTRODUCING L. T. ASONG: "THE MAJOR TALENT OF CAMEROON FICTION IN ENGLISH"

In their seminal article, "Cameroon Literature in English", in the now defunct ABBIA (1982), Nalova Lyonga and Bole Butake stated unequivocally that the Cameroonian novel of English expression, with only three published titles then, was the least developed genre in Cameroon. However, barely above twenty years after that pronouncement, more than twenty titles have since appeared to the credit of the Cameroon novel in English. And out of this lot seven have been written by Linus T. Asong, the major talent of Anglophone Cameroon fiction, and the most prolific Cameroonian novelist of English expression.

His seven published novels within the last decade of the twentieth century include *A Legend of the Dead* (1991), *The Crown of Thorns* (1993), *No Way to Die* (1993), *The Akroma File* (1996), *Stranger in His Homeland* (1997), *Salvation Colony* (1997), and *Chopchair* (1998). With such a wide range of titles covering a broad spectrum of imaginative experience, it is difficult to find a single theme that could neatly capture the spirit of all of Asong's creative works. However, one thing that is clear with Asong's fiction is that all his novels are constructed around anti-heroes, a deliberate rather than an arbitrary artistic decision, one involving the author in a careful selection, construction or distortion of his central male characters, meticulously building them up and then cutting some of them down to size, debunking, demystifying them in accordance with his aesthetic goal and authorial vision. In the hands of Asong, then, anti-heroism becomes a device of technique for effective artistic creation.

A possible thematic approach to Asong's novels would be to treat them in groups; and the most prominent category is the now-entitled *How a People Die,* the single volume comprising the three familiar texts of *Stranger in His Homeland, The Crown of Thorns* and *A legend of the Dead.* The trilogy tells the harrowing tale of rural folk fatefully brought into confrontation with an arrogant, heavy-handed and dictatorial governmental system. The outcome of the encounter is a communal catastrophe for the people. There is the desecration of their god, the destruction of their chieftaincy institution, and the debasement of their customs and traditions.

But the causes of the people's physical, moral and spiritual death are varied and complex, traceable in flaws inherent in human characters, in the governmental system, and in the king-makers' submission to the forceful, energetic external pressure from the District Officer to bypass the rightful heir to the throne of Small Monje against the wise will of the late Paramount Chief.

Written in clear, crisp and classical prose *How a People Die*, as a single volume in three parts, is a great, readable novel with a wide canvas of interesting characters and numerous instances of arousing, dramatic situations. Above all, it contains enough substance to occupy critics and scholars for a long time.

No Way To Die (1993) is the story of Dennis Nunquam, the central character and anti-hero of the text. Victim of fate and unique circumstances, Dennis is misunderstood and later rejected by friends and relatives. He lives below the poverty line and ekes out his livelihood as a small office messenger in a tiny co-operative. Because he has been crushed by fate, he withdraws into himself and becomes a baffling psychological case. Yet Dennis is not mad but simply a victim of a peculiar set of circumstances that cannot be fully apprehended by his acquaintances.

The novel's narrative technique is that of interior monologue. With complete authorial detachment, the technique consists of the individual characters telling the story from their own perspectives, as if they were speaking their thoughts aloud. The result is immediacy, casualness and freshness, producing prose different from a leisurely and discursive narrative guided by the omniscient narrator.

Asong's other novels like *The Akroma File* and *Salvation Colony* are works pre-occupied with societal crooks, the former with a swindler and the latter with a counterfeiter, both of whom are foreigners operating in Cameroon and taking advantage of some of the security loopholes in the Cameroonian security system.

The Akroma File is a rare fictional exploration of criminology with frightening implications. Faced with debts at home and threatened by poverty, a brilliant and well-educated Ghanaian, Akroma, using unorthodox means successfully gets into Cameroon where he is bent on making a fortune. He arrives in Cameroon virtually penniless but draws on his tremendous presence of mind to build up a fabulous fortune for himself. How this illegal alien eludes the police or bribes his way through them is a mark of L.T Asong's genius in character conception and a telling comment on the Cameroonian security system, one that, for the most part, thrives on venality.

Asong employs in this novel a narrative technique he has not used before: that of the journal or diary, the daily record of events, accounts and thoughts, etc. But the journal is that of the omniscient narrator rather than one kept by a character in the novel such as Toundi's in Ferdinand Oyono's *Houseboy*.

Salvation Colony, on its part, concerns itself with an exclusive community of members of a Cameroonian religious sect, founded by an American, Rev Pastor Shrapnell. It is made up of the scum of the Cameroonian society, the dregs of humanity that society has turned its back on. Rev Shrapnell gives them spiritual fulfillment and a sense of self-worth. However, inquisitive journalists expose Shrapnell for what he really is ... a rapist, a dismissed medical practitioner, a counterfeiter and a bogus pastor. A hardened criminal and a devil in disguise, Shrapnell poses as a devout spiritual leader. His Salvation Colony is built on a sleazy foundation, on counterfeited money secretly produced by him and smuggled into a local bank.

The thesis developed in the novel is that religious sects pose a grave danger to society; for a brilliant criminal like Pastor Shrapnell, the anti-hero of the text, can assume the innocent mien of a religious leader to wreak havoc on a gullible community. Virtually deified by his devotees, Pastor Shrapnell wields total control over his sheep. It is against such unconditional loyalty to influential but potentially dangerous religious leaders that Asong's text appears to be warning us. The horrendous example of the mass suicide of Jim Jones's faithful in Guyana in the late 1970s is still fresh in the minds of many readers.

As for *Chopchair* (1998), a novel on the subject of succession in a local kingdom, it is the only fictional work that, from conception to execution, is specifically written for a targeted school population: young adolescents or junior secondary school pupils. It has a simplified plot and a narrative thinness not found in Asong's major novels but possesses the familiar hallmarks of Asong's fiction: conflicts and suspense.

L. T. Asong has adopted the novelistic form and the English language to serve the Cameroonian vision. Although one of his novels can be faulted for editorial shoddiness or lesser artistic flaws, he has handled plot, characterisation, structure, point of view and language generally successfully. Within the critical realist mode in which he writes, his technical range is impressive, indeed. He has adopted a diversified narrative perspective and an inexhaustible list of effective devices of technique; explored themes of contemporary relevance as well as eternal verities; conceived a vast canvas of intriguing human characters, some of whom have become household names in Cameroon; and inspired many young Anglophone Cameroonian novelists. Herein lies the significance of his literary output in Cameroon. Asong's seven novels must, therefore, be recognised today by the literary establishment as a major contribution to the development of the Anglophone Cameroon novel.

Works Cited

Asong, L. T. *A Legend of the Dead*. Bamenda: Patron Publishing House, 1991.

___ ___ ___. *The Crown of Thorns*. Bamenda: Patron Publishing House, 1993.

___ ___ ___ *No Way To Die*. Bamenda: Patron Publishing House, 1993.

___ ___ ___. *The Akroma File*. Bamenda: Patron Publishing House, 1996.

___ ___ ___. *Stranger in His Homeland*: Bamenda: Patron Publishing House, 1997.

___ ___ ___. *Salvation Colony*. Bamenda: Patron Publishing House, 1997.

___ ___ ___. *Chopchair*. Bamenda: Patron Publishing House, 1998.

Lyonga, Nalova and Butake, Bole "Cameroon Literature in English: An Apraisal," in Bernard Fonlon (ed.) *ABBIA: Cameroon Cultural Review, 38-39-40* (1982): *123-174.*

25
FRANCIS B. NYAMNJOH, *A NOSE FOR MONEY*
East African Educational Publishers Ltd, 2006, 202pp

Francis B. Nyamnjoh is a prolific Anglophone Cameroonian writer whose publications in fiction, drama and scholarly essays have won him rave reviews. *A Nose for Money* (2006) is his third novel, coming after *Mind Searching* (1991) and *The Disillusioned African* (1995). With *A Nose for Money* Nyamnjoh identifies himself with the traditional, conventional novel, in marked contrast to his previous texts constructed within the modernist mode of discourse.

Set in a fictional African country called Mimboland and depicting the changing fortunes of its central male subject, Prospère, *A Nose for Money* is a classic tale of a man growing from rags to riches. A semi-illiterate and a struggling truck driver with the Mimboland Brewery Company (MBC), Prospère nurses the ambition to be a rich man one day, and, accordingly, begins to save towards that end. As luck would have it, a financial windfall comes his way one fortunate day, catapulting him onto greater financial heights, thanks to his timely connection with his tribesman and government Minister, Mr. Matiba.

Mimboland, particularly its capital city, Nyamandem, is a society in the grip of materialism and the crave for pleasures of the flesh; the text reveals the accentuated predominance of the quest for lucre and the pursuit of sex, the two related aspects of the overarching theme of moral decadence. Unlike in the previous novels, politics does not take centre stage here; however, it pulsates in the background, manifesting itself indirectly through the economic activities and the financial malpractices the text highlights. Since the government in power is 'the number one contractor and consumer in the entire country, what businessman or citizen could stand on his feet without the government's benediction?' (141) asks Matiba.

Therefore, those who carry out successful business activities in the society are individuals who have connection with government Ministers. Prospère is phenomenally rich because of his links with the Ministers whom he bribes and corrupts so as to be awarded juicy contracts and granted business licences to carry out his extensive chain of businesses. Thanks to his identification with the political party in power and accessibility to insider information, Prospère can very easily spot lucrative contracts. He 'oils the lips' and 'scratches the back' of the director of customs and the Minister of Finance to import expensive goods under subterfuge, paying virtually no taxes on them. As a consequence, it is the state that loses billions of FCFA in tax revenue which go into private pockets.

Owing to the infamous practices of oiling of lips, of scratching of backs and of goats eating where they are tethered (170) the reader discovers the sleazy processes that produce the wealthy Prospères and the government Ministers who ruin the country's economy for their own personal wealth. Prospère is now numbered among the five richest men in the country. It was this mad pursuit of Mammon, this crave for filthy lucre that twice placed Mimboland on top of the world corruption chart, 'a game that had made Mimboland a world leader for two consecutive years' (159).

Now what does a Minister, a director or a businessman with excess filthy money on his hands do? They consume it, and they do so in grand, arrogant style. They dress expensively and drive prestigious cars, imitating 'la fierté des Français' (139); they provide cars for their wives; they put up fabulous villas in the elitist Petit Paris neighbourhood, and send their children to study in France. But, above all, to slake their appetite for things of the flesh, they look for young girls, 'young juicy fruit[s]' (157) on whom they shower their wealth. Here emerges the text's second related theme of sexuality and marital unfaithfulness.

The types of girls these tycoons go in for are those of university and high school levels. These are the Marie-Claires, the Charlottes, the Chantals and the Moniques, pampered and spoilt with ill-gotten money, fripperies and trendy dresses. The sponsors and keepers of these young girls are mostly married men with wives at home. One thing is therefore clear: they are cheating on their wives, regardless of whether they eventually marry the younger women.

But the girls themselves are no fools. True, because of their insatiable appetite for money and material possessions peculiar to women, they stick to their sugar daddies, preying on their wealth as much as possible. However, for optimal sexual satisfaction, these young girls or wives, in turn, look elsewhere. They secretly keep and provide for young, virile lovers 'for the purposes of thorough libidinal servicing' (143). So, of the central married female characters in the novel – Rose, Marie-Claire, Charlotte, Chantal and Monique, only the latter can be credited with fidelity. The rest, like the men they are married to, are all guilty of infidelity.

From Prospère's bitter experience regarding the unfaithfulness of Rose, it dawns on him that women are impossible to live with; but, as his subsequent, bootless efforts to look for the alienated Rose and come to an understanding with her indicate, it is also impossible to live without women. The same paradox is at work in the lives of Charlotte and Chantal, Prospère's first and second wives who share a mutual sexual secret unknown to their husband until the last few pages of the narrative: that he is sterile, hence their secret love affairs outside wedlock. In their view, then, it is impossible, for the sake of procreation, to live with their husband; but it is equally impossible, because of his wealth, to live without him. Paradoxically then, the wives cannot live with their husband, but they cannot live without him.

A parallel infidelity is the relationship between the wealthy spinster, Lizette, a woman in her mid-forties, and her young virile lover, Théodore. Despite being showered with gifts and free sex from Lizette, Théodore proves his unfaithfulness to the woman by inviting a more 'succulent' girl friend to make love to him in Lizette's house!

Now, concerning Prospère and his wives, when the crucial truth from the other side of the sexual divide is revealed to the man at the end of the novel, it kills him. All along, Prospère had been knocking his chest of being the proud father of eight children. Alas, they have all been fathered by other men! All along Prospère has been the only 'fool'. The man commits suicide. Indeed 'La vérité blesse.'

However, fatal as their revelation is, the women's infidelity is not the sole cause of Propspère's demise. His is partly a self-inflicted tragedy; he is the author of his own downfall, given his track record of sexual recklessness. Prior to coming upon his windfall that propelled him onto greater financial heights, enabling him to access more attractive young women, Prospère had led a life of sexual wantonness. He had contracted veneral diseases and resorted to self-medication instead of seeking standard medical treatment. Part of the punishing revelation is that, unknown to him, Prospère has killed his own beloved wife through an incurable disease running in his blood and now in that of his remaining two wives. On the last page of the text, a police officer voices the moral of Prospère's tragedy: 'Don't they say as you make your bed so shall you lie on it?' (202), an axiom expressed earlier by the omniscient narrator when he said, 'the future never forgives the reckless past' (28). So, one need not be a great perceptive reader to realize that nemesis has finally caught up with Prospère: the wages of sexual recklessness is death, a dictum of great resonance in promiscuous times like ours.

From the point of view of technique, *A Nose for Money* is quite a different text from Nyamnjoh's two previous novels, *Mind Searching* and *The Disillusioned African*. Written in a modernist mode, the earlier novels are texts wherein the author, like the modernist novelists, has thrown overboard much that is commonly considered indispensable to the novel, making elaborate use of the stream-of-consciousness technique and the lack of chronology in his narration. In contrast, *A Nose for Money* bears the hallmarks of the traditional novel. There is a discernible plot, a conflict and a description of people and places; there are arousing dramatic scenes, climaxes and conclusions; unlike the pale and vague ciphers of *Mind Searching,* we have in the latest novel solid, identifiable and realistic human characters.

The high readability of this novel resides in its suspenseful story, its crisp prose, the surprising twists in its plot, its interesting instances of irony of situation, the lively characters and their mutual infidelities, the paradoxicality of the sexes, and the colourful rumours surrounding the phenomenal wealth of Prospère, etc. In constructing the character of Prospère, in particular, and the young women, in general, Nyamnjoh reveals himself as an adept in psychological exploration of human characters, particularly with reference to sexual relationships. In depicting these and other characters, and making judicious use of sociological material, the author beautifully and effectively captures the psyche of city dwellers in modern materialistic times like ours when men worship in the temple of Mammon, and relationships are evaluated in terms of cash rather than in love.

With regard to the artistic relevance of the lurid tales that rationalize Prospère's impressive wealth (183-190), this is what we can say: True, these rumours are not founded on facts. Of course they are only the figments of the fertile imagination of their creators. But in our view, they constitute part of the sociological realities underpinning Prospère's story; similarly, such are the sociological realities of the text's larger social context as any Mimbolander (Cameroonian) would affirm today.

The presence of morsels of dialogues and expressions in French sprinkled all over the narrative testifies to an artistic reality occasionally noticed in Anglophone Cameroonian fiction. The fact is that, like Mbella Sonne Dipoko's *A Few Nights and Days*, *A Nose for Money* is dealing essentially with Francophone characters whose ideas, thoughts, feelings and emotions are rendered, almost completely, in English instead of in French by the Anglophone, but bilingual, omniscient narrator. Occasionally, however, for the sake of realistic characterization, the author is obliged to bring in bits of their utterances in the original French language.

By the same token, when, in the last chapter of the book, the story moves to West Mimboland, i.e. in the English-speaking part of the country, we have the illiterate diviner priest, Ngek, addressing his clients in an English-based pidgin language. Given the sociolinguistic realities of Mimboland (English-French bilingualism) and the author's cultural background, the interplay of English, French and Pidgin English in his narration, far from being a linguistic weakness, constitutes, for Nyamnjoh, a mark of his linguistic sensitivity and stylistic competence. **From the point of view of the conventional, realistic novel,** *A Nose for Money*, **because it does not carry the distracting modernist features of Nyamnjoh's earlier novels, and because it is a work of interest and one likely to resonate with many readers, is, I will submit, his best novel, and a welcome addition to Anglophone Cameroon fiction.**

CONCLUSION

A great deal has happened in the development of Anglophone Cameroon literature ever since the first essay in this book was presented as a keynote address in 2008. Dr Joyce Ashuntantang's EduArt Inc, a motivational organization to reward literary excellence has taken off with its first laureates in 2008, while Ashuntantang herself has since published her critical text: *Landscaping Anglophone Postcoloniality* (2009); Emma Dawson, the General Editor of World Englishes Literature (Fiction) has edited and published *The Spirit Machine and Other New Short Stories* from Cameroon (2009); Professor Edward O. Ako has edited and published *Cameroon Literature in English: Critical Essays on Fiction and Drama* (2009); Professor L. T. Asong launched three new novels in Bamenda by the end of 2010, while a few more Anglophone imaginative works have been published.

But by and large the most significant single literary event that has occurred within the Anglophone literary community in the first decade of the 21st century is inextricably linked to the name of Professor Francis Nyamnjoh, a prolific creative writer in his own right. That event is the coming into existence of Langaa Research & Publishing CIG, Mankon, Bamenda, an international publishing house with distribution centres in North America and Europe. In less than ten years Langaa RP CIG alone has published more Anglophone Cameroonian works than all the other publishing houses of the last ten years put together. Langaa alone has distributed Anglophone Cameroonian literary works to virtually all corners of the modern world. And thanks to Langaa and with the help of Internet connectivity Anglophone Cameroonian writing is now available to anyone with just the touch of a button.

The main blemish on this otherwise rosy story is the prohibitive prices of Langaa's publications, especially to readers in Cameroon who can ill-afford the high prices of Langaa's print runs. We look forward to the day when Langaa's prices will be within the reach of the average Cameroonian readers. While to err is human, editorial blemishes can still be spotted in Langaa published works, albeit in less frustrating bulk than other Cameroonian publishing houses.

Nevertheless, Professor Nyamnjoh's service to his people is laudable and immeasurable indeed. The day is coming, we believe, when this son of the Anglophone Cameroon native soil will be honoured with a worthy red feather. I would like to think that our forefathers smiled in their graves on that day when Langaa RP CIG, not without their ancestral blessing, came into being.

With the coming of Langaa, Anglophone Cameroon writing has received its much-needed tonic and is now irreversibly set on a promising path to great things; with the coming of Langaa, the story of Anglophone creative and critical writing will no longer be the same; with the coming of Langaa, Anglophone culture in Cameroon has received a great boost; but, above all, with the creation, by the Head of State of Cameroon, of the second Anglo-Saxon University in Cameroon, the University of Bamenda, the promotion of the Anglo-Saxon tradition in Cameroon has been further strengthened, and the growth of the Anglophone Cameroon creative writing, a crucial aspect of the potential rise to greatness of the Anglophone Cameroonians is guaranteed. A famous African American poet[1] once said:

> A people may become great through many means, but there is only one measure by which its greatness is recognised and acknowledged. The final measure of the greatness of all peoples is the amount and standard of the literature and art they have produced. The world does not know that a people is great until that people produces great literature and art. No people that has produced great literature and art has ever been looked upon by the world as distinctly inferior (qtd in Gates Jr Gen. ed. xxxv).

Anglophone Cameroon literary critics and creators should borrow a leaf from the above quotation, particularly from its last sentence.

However, the way to literary and artistic greatness is not smooth but one fraught with obstacles and difficulties. It entails diligence, assiduity, self-criticism and hard work. As one of the essays in the volume asserts, to ascend to literary excellence, we have to move our creative and critical writing from its present common ground level to a superior higher ground, an endeavour that will demand overcoming a number of challenges spelt out in that essay, one of which is the mastery of our medium of imaginative expression.

Perspectives on Written Cameroon Literature in English

Criticism being a handmaiden for creativity, our literary critics are called upon to maintain objectivity in the exercise of their critical activity: neither to be complacent with mediocre works, nor to be grudging in the recognition of excellence wherever it is found. But above every other consideration, our quest for literary excellence calls for the exercise of intellectual honesty. For, we must admit, there is a leech in the Anglophone Cameroon literary pond sucking the blood from Anglophone imaginative effort: plagiarism, misrepresentation and piracy. These ignoble acts of intellectual theft or robbery threaten to reduce our creative and critical effort to the level of mediocrity. Our critical culture is not yet high and therefore needs great improvement. As custodians of our fledgling literary culture, we need a whistle blower to rescue our creative and critical efforts from degenerating into mediocrity, disgrace and dishonour, a misdemeanour even more unacceptable when committed by a literary icon.

In the keynote address referred to above, I mentioned there that I was working on a collection of my critical essays. Here they are then, humbly submitted first to my immediate Anglophone Cameroonian community and then to the larger reading public. And I do so in the true spirit and in the essential sense in which Bernard Fonlon understands the term a genuine researcher, as conveyed by essay number fifteen. There he holds that a conscientious researcher must toil and moil relentlessly in his quest of the truth. And when he is completely satisfied with the findings of his project, he then submits them first to the service of humanity before thinking of himself.

In His mysterious and generous ways, the Almighty God has endowed the Anglophone Cameroonian writers, just as He has done with writers in all climes and times, with various talents: To this person He gives the ability to write a novel or novels; to that one the talent to write a play or plays; to this person He provides the gift to craft a short story or stories; to that one the skill to pen an essay or essays; to this person He gives the genius to produce a poem or poems; to that one the aptitude to criticize or chronicle all of the above. As for me, He has blessed me, so far, with the gift to write a novel, a collection of poems and, above all, a handful of critical books, to make a modest contribution to the development of the

Anglophone Cameroon literature, a project I embarked upon, long ago, as stated earlier.

When I elected to accentuate literary criticism over literary creativity, I did so for specific reasons. While there was evidence of increasing Anglophone Cameroon imaginative writing, there was a clear absence of a corresponding criticism to match the burgeoning literature; while there were signs that sooner or later Anglophone Cameroon might produce novelists close or equal to the calibre of Chinua Achebe, Ayi Kwei Armah, or Ngugi wa Thiong'o, or playwrights and poets in the tradition of Wole Soyinka, Christopher Okigbo, John Pepper Clark, Gabriel Okara or Okot p'Bitek, it was not yet clear to me that there were determined Anglophone Cameroonian literary critics in the making. With the notable exceptions of Professor John N. Nkengasong with his *Stylistic Approach to Literary Criticism*, (2007) and Professor Peter Abety with his *An Approach to Poetry Appreciation (2006),* it was not yet evident, until these recent exceptions, that Anglophone Cameroon could boast of devoted literary critics.

Of course there were, and still are, many flashes of critical talents here and there, as pointed out in essay number one. But it was obvious to me that Anglophone Cameroon was yet to boast of a tribe of critics of the stature of Eustace Palmer, Eldred Jones, Abiola Irele, Chinua Achebe, Ngugi wa Thiong'o, Emmanuel Ngara, or Chinweizu, Onwochekwa Jemie, and Ihechukwu Madubuike, to cite but these few. These are literary critics with significant critical works to their credit. And, although Alexander Pope in his famous "Essay On Criticism" dismisses critics as failed imaginative writers, I would argue that many of those cited above are equally successful creative writers who, I believe, therefore know what they are talking about in their critical works.

I hope it is in this vein that I submit to the reading public these critical essays. I am not misty-eyed in believing that they are perfect pieces, but to say so is to make no point at all, for nothing made by human hands can be perfect: "Whoever thinks a faultless piece to see/Thinks what ne'er was, nor is, nor e'er shall be"[2]. Therefore, I have not been afraid of failure resulting from imperfection. A critic of vision should never be afraid of failure. Failure is but an occasional suspension of success; with hard work success is bound to come sooner rather than later. Should the Anglophone Cameroonian or

African reader derive some satisfaction or insight from reading the essays, then I would like to believe that the season of literary labour and the long difficult years that went into the realisation of the critical project would have been worthwhile; then I would like to think that I have made a contribution to the development of the Anglophone Cameroonian literature. In fact these sustained critical efforts have culminated in the development of my literary critical approach: the Socio-Artistic Approach, elaborated in my earlier critical work, *The Cameroonian Novel of English Expression* (2009/2007).

End Note
1. That poet was James Weldon Johnson whose famous quotation appears in Henry Louis Gates Jr., General Editor, *The Norton Anthology of African American Literature*. New York. London: W.W. Norton & Company, 1997 (xxxv).
2. Alexander Pope. "An Essay On Criticism." in M. H. Abrams (Gen. ed.) *The Norton Anthology of English Literature*. 5th ed. Vol 1. New York/London: Norton, 1986. pp. 2214 – 2232.

APENDIX: SOURCES

General Essays

1. "Half a Century of Written Anglophone Cameroon Literature." Paper presented first at the fifth ACWA Conference in the British Council in Yaoundé (2008), and then later as a keynote address on the occasion of the EduArt Literary Awards Night at Capitol Hotel Buea July 18, 2008. Posted at EduArt Website.
2. "Critical Approaches in the Criticism of Cameroon Literature of English Expression." Paper presented at a language and literature seminar organised by the English Department of the University of Buea in January 2001. Published in Chia, Tala and Jick (eds.) *Globalisation and the African Experience: Implications for Language, Literature and Education.* Anucam 2005.
3. "Cameroon Creative Writers and the Language Problem." Paper published in *South-South Journal of Culture and Development.* Special Edition, Volume 3 No. 2 December 2001.
4. "The African Writer and the Preservation of Cultural Values." Paper first published in my monograph: *Matter and Manner* Bamenda: Unique Printers, 1990. Still in the early 1990s the very version of the paper was published by *Cameroon Tribune*.
5. "The Cameroonian Novel of English Expression." Paper published in *South-South Journal of Culture and Development* Volume 8 No. 1 June 2006.

Specific Literary Studies

6. "Ideology in Three Dramatic Works: Victor Epie Ngome's *What God Has Put Asunder*, and Bate Besong's *Beasts of No Nation* and *Requiem for the Last Kaiser."* Paper initially programmed to be published by the English Department of the University of Buea as Perspectives on Anglophone Cameroon Drama.
7. "The Educational Significance of the Cameroon Novel of English Expression: Focus on Four Texts." Paper presented at International Conference on Language, Literature and Education, University of Yaoundé I. 11 – 14 May 2006. Proceedings published in Kenneth Harrow and Kizitus Mpoche (eds.) *Language, Literature and Education in Multicultural Societies*, Newcastle: Cambridge Scholars Publishing, 2008.

8. "Deconstructing Gender Hierarchy: A Study of Margaret Afuh's *Born Before Her Time.*" Paper presented at ACWA first Annual Conference in Bamenda 2003. Presented again in its present form at 1st International Conference on Language, Literature and Identity, University of Yaoundé I 31 March – 3 April 2005. Proceedings published in Paul Mbangwana, Kizitus Mpoche, Tennu Mbuh (eds.) *Language, Literature and Identity.* Göttigen: Cuvillier Verlag, 2006.
9. "The Anti-Heroes of L. T. Asong's Fiction: Focus on Four Texts." Paper published in Edward O. Ako (ed.) *Cameroon Literature in English: Critical Essays on Fiction and Drama.* Berlin: LIT. Verlag, 2009.
10. "Two Opposing Trends in Mongo Beti's Fiction: A Study of *Remember Ruben* and *Perpetua.*" Paper published in *Epasa Moto*. Volume 2 No. 1 March 2004.
11. "Pedagogy of the Deprived: A Study of the Plays of Victor Epie Ngome, Bole Butake, and Bate Besong." Paper presented at Conference on Cameroon Literature, University of Buea in 1994, whose proceedings were published in a special edition of *Epasa Moto* 1996.
12. "Anatomy of a Short Story: An Analysis of Bole Butake's *The Way of the City.*" Paper presented in Yaoundé on the occasion of Professor Bole Butake's 50th anniversary, 1997.
13. "The Orality of the Works of Four Anglophone Writers: Linus Asong, Bole Butake, Bongasu Kishani, Fale Wache." Paper presented at Workshop on Anglophone Writing in Cameroon held at the Goethe Institute, Yaoundé 1993. Proceedings were published that very year by Bayreuth African Studies 30 (WEKA No 1).
14. "The Modernist Character of Bate Besong's Poetry." Paper published in *Epasa Moto* Volume 4 No 1 March, 2009.
15. "The Quintessence of Bernard Fonlon." Paper published in my monograph: *Matter and Manner*, Bamenda: Unique Printers, 1990.

Book Reviews

16. Bole Butake, *Lake God and Other Plays.* Yaoundé: Editions CLE, 1999. Review published in M. Banham, J. Gibbs, F. Osofisan

(eds.) *African Theatre: Playwrights & Politics.* Oxford: James Currey, 2001.
17. L. T. Asong, *The Akroma File.* Bamenda: Patron Publishing House, 1997. Review published in *Voices: The Wisconsin Review of African Literatures.* (Fall 1999) Issue 2.
18. Alobwed'Epie, *The Death Certificate.* Yaoundé: Editions CLE, 2004. Review published in *The Post* No. 0639 (Monday February 7, 2005):8.
19. John Nkemngong Nkengasong, *Across The Mongolo.* Ibadan: Spectrum Books Limited, 2004. Review published in *The Post* No. 0635 (Monday 24 January 2005): 4.
20. Alobwed'Epie, *The Lady With A Beard.* Yaoundé: Editions CLE, 2005. Review published in *The Post* 0707 (Monday 10 October 2005):8.
21. John Nkemngong Nkengasong, *The Widow's Might.* Yaoundé: Editions CLE, 2006. Review published in *The Post* No. 0745. (Monday 6 March, 2006): 5.
22. John Ngong Kum, *Walls of Agony.* Yaoundé: Editions CLE, 2006. Review published in *The Post.* No. 0777 (Friday June 30 2006):9.
23. John Ngong Kum, *Battle for Survival.* Yaoundé: Editions CLE, 2006. Review published in *The Post.* No. 0788 (Monday August 7, 2006):8.
24. "Introducing L. T. Asong: The Major Talent of Cameroon Fiction in English." Review published in *African Literature Association ALA BULLETIN 29.3* (Fall 2003/Winter 2004):185 – 188.
25. Francis B. Nyamnjoh, *A Nose for Money.* East African Educational Publishers Ltd, 2006. Review published in *The Post* No. 0762 (Monday, May 8, 2006):8.

www.ingramcontent.com/pod-product-compliance
Lightning Source LLC
Chambersburg PA
CBHW072128290426
44111CB00012B/1818